Memories and Musings of a Post-Postmodern Nomadic Mystic Madman

By Jeffrey Charles Archer

Prologue

I am a dead man walking—er, actually I am currently sitting and sipping a highly honey-sweetened cup of Wyoming-roasted coffee with cream on the back patio of a coffee house in downtown Laramie. The pale-brown liquid within my cup has grown quite cold over several hours sitting and exposed to the elements of a high-country afternoon, though ice has yet to form around the rim. I sometimes gaze into the swirls of milk fat floating on the surface and the patterns of variously mixed solutions of bean juice and water and honey and half-and-half to scry with what shapes might emerge to tell of things present, past or possible.

I don't mean that someone has me as their mark, necessarily, or that I am keeping a wide-eye open for fear of potential assassins, necessarily. My point with these words is in fact rather more stark. What I actually mean by this opening statement, these first words in print after flyleaf and front matter, is that I have *already* been murdered, and perhaps on as many as five occasions. The most poignant and certain instance of experiencing my own homicide occurred one ordinary summer's day at dusk in Golden Gate Park, when two bullets were rather randomly and I dare say undeservedly introduced to the inside of my skull after an otherwise pleasant and uneventful day on Hippie Hill.

In addition to such homicidal intrigues, I have encountered sasquatch, a skinwalker, apparent holes in space-time, and a shape-shifter who did her turn whilst astride my lap. In pursuit of romance and the hidden secrets to life and history, guided by instinct, intuition, chance, and sometimes helpful deities, I have been granted many such glimpses behind the veils of normalcy—at moments to my delight, and at others to my terror.

At a certain point in life I decided I had a desire to unabashedly seek the truths that seemed unavailable in academia or conventional religion, and to discover what hidden magic and beauty and adventure this world really has to offer. I concluded at some moment of disillusionment or discontent that merely reading books of fiction or supposed scriptures to find inspiration and truth, else vicariously viewing others' explorations and adventures on TV or on the big screen proved insufficient means to satisfy my yearnings to experience or to satiate a want to know, and thus I decided that I had a need to endeavor the quest, and by the most quixotic and heroic means I might have need that I might find what abides behind life's curtains.

And so I began to live as a wandering renunciate before I truly knew what this meant or might imply, hitchhiking and train-hopping and back-country rambling on a simple and more or less innocent search for answers and quest for love both transcendent and terrestrial. Thus began the ride of my life. Visions and experiences that answered to my curiosity and were revealed to my searchings surpassed extraordinary, and indeed met with the sublime, and even Divine.

I have been tailed by a tornado in the badlands that bore the certain imprint of God made manifest, and have pursued an apparent apparition or Avatar of the Goddess across the breadth of the continent. I have crossed the threshold between life and death more than once, though still I breath, drink, eat, piss, shit, think, and even occasionally fuck, and thus by all appearance and common indicators I am quite alive. In the most recent third of thirty-six or so years lived I have experienced things most would assume the stuff of fairy tales or fantasy, mythology or merely a wild imagination.

Yet here I sit, just where I sat some twelve years ago, and with little if anything overt to show for my years of questing, labors of love, challenges to the system and changes to myself. I now have a PC upon which I type these words, whereas then I had a Mac. This evening I pen (er, type) my early memoirs, whereas then it was my Master's thesis I labored to complete. Little else overt has changed, save that I am now long since estranged from then-wife and son, church and institution, I have lived over a dozen years more, and these days don a beret and wool overcoat instead of a thin cotton trench coat and ski cap. Three fat dreadlocks also now dangle amidst the otherwise unknotted past-shoulder-length hairs on the back of my head.

The sun is setting behind the Snowy Range Mountains, and the oft-ferocious high plains wind is only a gentle breeze this evening. I'm watching this rather dull spectacle (compared to the best or even average of Laramie sunsets) from the back patio at Coal Creek Coffee Company's downtown coffeehouse and roastery. A freight train is roaring past beneath the steel footbridge that spans the railroad tracks which reside between my vantage and the sunset. This bridge links the downtown to the Near West Side, and purportedly is or at least was longest of its kind in the country. Random pedestrians in wool coats and down parkas pass by both near my seat and strolling over the human viaduct in the background, faces only glimpsed between snuggly wrapped scarves and hats pulled low, and fewer I know now than I knew in days past in this small city on the high plains.

 Said painted black steel and concrete span, occasional trains rumbling beneath, the derelict smokestack tower that stands ten stories tall behind, and people passing by in warm winter gear provide an excellent foil for the now dark gray clouds and fading light and subdued colors of this evening's sunset show—or would it be the other way around? Regardless, it seems to me at this moment, this picture painted in words might offer a poignant backdrop for you to bear in mind as you read on, dear reader, providing a scene that appropriately sets the tone for the tales to come in this text.

 Before the beginnings of my wild and weird cross-country adventures, before I tried to make a break from the system's sometimes subtle and subliminal hold, I would often sit at this very table laboriously researching and writing my Master's thesis, "Non-Essentially Occidental: Heteroglossia in the European Discourses on Islam." Back then I still held on to some semblance of the assumption that there was a comfortable place for me within "polite society" and inside the bounds of the popular consensual reality of Anytown, USA, and its various venerated institutions.

 Never quite finished this thesis, and thus abandoned hopes of becoming a certified PhD professor-type. Instead I decided to seek the truths of self and other (and "Self" and "Other") outside of familiar text and tradition and institution, to take to the open road to search for evidences of heteroglossia (many tongues) telling different versions than the officially-sanctioned and academy-approved, and to find a more personally valid and abiding title or state of being than "Doctor" or "Professor."

In this loosed condition, wonderful and weird magic and mystery unfolded before my sight and other senses. Wisdoms both beautiful and terrible were bestowed as the wide world opened doors to mysteries archaic as well as immediate, from revelations regarding obscured secrets of ancient myths and migrations of ancient Gods and their peoples to the manifestation of divine plays presented first-hand in my own life-lived. Such accounts are the substance of this bound book, dear reader, presented for your entertainment, and perhaps for the enrichment of your own life-lived in this everyday world, where truth proves more than meets a mere two eyes . . .

Introduction

There exists within the minds of many in the modern world a rather compromising division between what has been officially deemed rational truth, i.e., that which has been "scientifically proven" of the natural world, taxonomized and isolated in a laboratory setting under artificially controlled circumstances, and that which has been deemed "superstition," or at best "supernatural" or "spiritual." This dichotomy, emblematic of relatively recent ways of knowing in the philosophies of Europe and America, has created a stark separation between, say, religion and politics (though perhaps not so complete in practice as in theory), between physical sciences and the social sciences and humanities, and especially between practical living and mysticism. This is surely a symptom of the broader and indeed rampant compartmentalization of life in this modern (or postmodern/post-postmodern?) age, where once was arguably a more holistic way of being.

A farmer or blacksmith or scholar or merchant of times past did not divorce occupation from home, and finding some semblance of satisfaction in life did not assume an escape from the office or other place of employment. Similarly, religious or ritual practice did not take place solely on Sunday (or whatever given day, per whatever religion), but was in fact integrated into the everyday. Myth and the mundane, science and the spiritual, magic and material reality were similarly inseparable facets of life, the rhythms and rhyme of the day and night yet succinctly attuned to the natural world.

Though one can argue that there are benefits to current modes of dividing the day or week, or even to current conventions of separating ways of knowing, certain disparities and psychological conflicts unquestionably arise from these arrangements. Indeed, I might go so far as to argue that a selective blindness has o'ertaken the masses, something not unlike a tunnel vision that prevents most from seeing much of the beauty and wonder of life, an institutionalized myopia that shrouds a natural, magical, divine and eternal aesthetic that underlies and pervades all that is.

It was with something like a half-baked awareness of these notions that I set out to discover secrets hidden by the official institutions and popular paradigms, to reach for truth and beauty and divine love, to endeavor to discover a more complete aesthetic, and to seek to find myself—or better phrased from the perspective I now maintain, to find Self. *Atman, brahman*, the true and good Divine Self seeded within each and every and all as well as Universally present and pervasive, most succinctly and distinctly (in my humble but fairly well-informed opinion) expressed in said Sanskrit words. "God[1]" already present, rather than requiring an invitation and a bath. With some subtle awareness of this existence of something better and more valid, I wandered away from convention and conformity, parting with programmed presumptions and the purported truths presented me during years of education and social and religious training, and hit the open road.

What I discovered upon opening myself to the freedom of wandering the highways and wild places and sacred spaces of this land, by loosing my mind from the fetters of so called "common sense," and upon learning to see with more than two eyes blew away the paradigms of church and university training and shattered the shallow assumptions and officially sanctioned presumptions generally made of experiential reality. On these journeys and intermittent sojourns I encountered shape-shifters and sasquatch, faeries and freakish, anomalous, serendipitous and synchronistic incidents that far surpassed expectations of what I'd imagined I'd discover upon disembarking from the programmed path and setting aside unnecessary societal expectations. The following short story accounts are a few of the more salient and readily recountable happenings from my journeys through time and space and mind.

To tell the truth of what's to come in these forthcoming pages, these tales told in print are intertwined in time such that a clear chronology is not necessarily to be read in the progression

---

1   An oft invoked sacrosanct intonation derived via the Germanic *Gott* from the Sanskrit *go*, which translates directly to English as "cow," as in the Divine creatures say "moooo . . ."

from each account writ to the next. Some events are visited more than once within separately titled tales, to some extent tying these only somewhat temporally arranged narratives together in the midst of potentially confusing webs of causation and sequence. In other words, though each chapter does build upon or is built upon the others to some degree or other, this temporal progression is not without loops and reveries—indeed, as life experiences in a general sense are not necessarily granted meaning by strictly linear arrangements of memory, time and travel. Hopefully, then, the repetitions of certain accounts will serve to clarify or elucidate preceding or succeeding events which might otherwise have only minimal sequential grounding in the text, rather than proving redundant.

These things said, each chapter might nonetheless be read either as a separate and self-contained and fully satisfying story, as well as indeed part of an interwoven narrative which spans the expanse of the text, from page one to the end. The reader is therefore free to peruse any given chapter without feeling as if she or he has missed some vital element of a particular passage's emplotment in pages skipped or in one story passed over to favor another, else she or he might choose to endeavor a more traditional linear reading. I might also note that these accounts were not necessarily penned in the sequence in which they appear in the text, and thus the tone, style and content included in each differ according to the inspiration, mood and memories that came to mind as I separately typed each tale.

The stories herein writ are mostly telling of time spent to some degree or other *in-transit*, of wanderings across the North American continent with in mind to discover evidences of magic and beauty and mystical truth still surviving somewhere underneath a sheen of American Dreamish normalcy. And as is the nature of a transit state—time and space being relative and so forth and certain bends and distortions, if not outright instances of "time-travel" as potentials whilst in such a state (again, by the principles of relativity and so forth)—a traveler in transit might not only find quite altered the linear appearance of an ordinary time line, but might even find the certainty of spatial continuity in question, if he or she looks closely enough to denote discrepancies. Home found at the end of a journey may indeed *not* be the same place left behind, once one has traveled afar. Or to offer another illustrative metaphor for the sort of time-space displacement possible to a truly open traveler, imagine jetlag-squared or cubed or times a thousand.

And these tales, though truly true-life accounts, are also journeys of and in *Mind*. Visions manifest from dream or imaginings directly onto the screen of "reality," déjà vu, and extrasensory awakenings were indeed as much a part of the *trip* of these travels recorded as were simple reckonings of point "a" to "b" and "what happened" in-between. Indeed, whatever interconnectedness or "synchronicity" of time and space exists or what road magic is manifest to the wonderment of a traveler is conceived and wrought in and through Mind, thought, imagination and intentioned "manifestation," and not merely via "rational" or "common sense" modes of causation. Thus, when you are told of unusual experiences or anomalies you encounter, "Oh, it's all just in your mind," you might justifiably and aptly reply, "Perhaps, but that doesn't mean it isn't real."

To travel any distance in time through space conveys a very different consciousness than is active in a more routine state of life, especially when wandering to places unknown, as one peripatetically preoccupied is freed from psychological and psychic ties to everyday habitual practices, and his or her mind naturally opens to experiences and possibilities not normally granted attention in the midst of life lived nine-to-five. The traveler notices things otherwise overlooked—the shape of a cloud hanging over an unknown mountain peak, the scents traveling on the air at a market, the shapes of faces or a sparkle in the eyes of a stranger. A willing traveler is tuned-in to encounter alterity, difference, the possibility of novelty, and despite the seeming contradiction is also opened to an heretofore unknown unity with others and experiential reality. Travel thins the veils, and reveals the unity as well as relativity of time, space, mind and life-lived.

I will apologize in advance for a lack of engaging dialogues, with quote-bound conversations only sparsely interspersed within long stretches of narrative. I have done so to avoid potential misquotes, to prevent even the least misrepresentation, and to forgo inaccurate improvisation due to a lack of concise memories of specific exchanges. I fully intend to relate these events with as much verity and precision as I might, and thus must admit I have left out many interesting conversations for lack of perfect or even paraphrased accuracy. I shall surely include more dialogue when or if I try my hand at writing and publishing works of fiction.

As I recognize that much of the content of these accounts will be hard to swallow, and even more difficult to digest, I have gone to great lengths to be certain to avoid any distortion of events and to refrain from even slight embellishment. Indeed, everything I have written is accurate according to my perceptions and recollections and in many cases with other reliable witnesses present, though given the fantastic nature of much of what I have to tell I shall not hold it against the reader who questions what I represent in these accounts, and in fact would hope for a thoughtful and indeed critical response.

Simultaneously, however, I would hope these narratives (which, again, I stand by as true) will cause you, dear reader, to question the constructions of reality by which you have been trained to formulate your own perceptions of experience, and to open your eyes and other senses to the beauty and magic that exists only a short distance from the everyday consensual reality you've been so subtly (and sometimes surreptitiously) conditioned to believe.

A Pilgrimage to Nowhere in Particular

I was back in Laramie after an intense year of studies, still not quite finished with my Master's thesis, and far from any semblance of a mastery of life. I was restless, and not at all content with the conditions in which I found myself. No, that's not quite the right way to phrase things, for I was far from finding myself at said juncture in life—a journey of about a thousand miles, and perhaps then some.

I was married and had a wonderful young son, and had nearly completed a Master's from one of the most tauted schools in my field. I had received excellent marks in all my courses, and some of the top names in the relevant academic disciplines were quite impressed with my work. I was unsatisfied, however, both with the progress of my thesis and with the teachings I had received at the University of Chicago, in spite of the relative excellence of the education offered at said institution of higher learning and the tutelage of inspiring professors.

At a gut level I felt as if the underlying truths I had a desire to discover were scarcely given a nod, even at one of the most renowned universities in the world. I instinctively sensed that what I sought was still veiled beneath comparatively inconsequential discourses, if not intentional fictions, indeed as I had felt previously whilst an ordained Southern Baptist minister and student of religion and history at Oklahoma Baptist University.

I believed (or have come to believe, and knew at my core) that there might be something not unlike a consensual agreement among academics, as amongst the more perceptive ministers of the conservative denomination to which I once belonged and in like institutions, to skirt else categorically deny the deeper issues that might be controversial, unpalatable or even paradigm shattering. Somehow I discerned and have since determined definitively that there is indeed some twisted and deep-seated conspiracy to intentionally dissimulate regarding certain known truths that might unsettle the integrity of those institutions and disprove those sacrosanct myths which hold up their prestige—and keep their pocketbooks filled.

Either this, or these supposed learned men and women might merely be blind to the subtler truths of reality and history, unable to see beyond disputations about angels dancing on pinheads or what tactic was decisive in a particular battle, the cadence of Shakespeare's sonnets or how the chili pepper had arrived in India. Not that there is no value whatsoever in these sorts of exercises and inquiries, mind you, nor to a fair amount of what learning I acquired from lectures and assigned readings both as an undergrad and in graduate school. Rather, I was not satisfied with these as the gateway to those subtler truths I sought, which were certainly not readily to be realized within institutional confines and even if thus realized, not likely to be accepted within the discourse of the academe.

Whilst in Laramie, I attempted to find work lecturing at the regional junior college, or anything remotely related to my field of study. I ended up working on a highway construction safety crew. My evenings were mostly spent at what was Laramie's only full service coffeehouse at the time, Coal Creek Coffee Company, working away at my thesis and unwittingly beginning to show signs of being *sadhu*, though I shall leave unwritten the specifics of those beginnings of my tantric practice. After Coal Creek Coffee closed for the evening, I'd most often wander on to the Buckhorn Bar.

I readily became quite smitten with one of the baristas at the coffeehouse, but hadn't the self-confidence to engage her in even the most casual of conversations beyond ordering coffee or tea and a scone. Rather introverted after a grueling year at graduate school during which my wife (pregnant at the time) and I had first separated, and my mother, grandfather and family dog of seventeen years had died within a period of about three weeks. It was only once I was at the bars, a belly full of booze, that I had the wherewithal to be at all socially adept, and there a bit much so considering my presumed marital status.

So besides this sober reticence regarding the prospect of approaching said beautiful barista beyond the most casual of exchanges, I was married, and she also happened to have a boyfriend with whom she seemed quite enamored. Still, something about her moved me, inspired me towards a deeper search, a quest for the essence of what is beautiful, true and transcendent.

It was somewhere before Thanksgiving of that year, 1996, that I decided to go on what I deemed a "pilgrimage," though I had no particular place in mind as a specific sacred destination. I had concluded that my life was at a standstill. My marriage was failing, my spirit stifled, and within me was a deep-seated desire for some sort of change the which I could not quite yet put my finger on, an angst issued from some seed not yet given the room to grow. I had lost faith in the claims of Christianity, seeing too many holes in their theology and claims regarding history, and similarly found academia wanting, as it seemed it had likewise grown too attached to the assumed verity of its dogmas and tradition. I wanted some semblance of answers unalloyed by a fear of questioning bygone authorities and institutional walls, unfettered by hollow convention and shallow tradition.

I recognized it was also trying on Holly, my wife at that time, to deal with my malaise and still overtly concealed carousing ways, and so we agreed she and our son would return to Oklahoma to stay with her parents while I attempted to get things together, to find steady employment and finish my thesis. I drove with her and our son Kieran Drew as far as Shawnee, where Holly and I had both attended college. From there, I set off on my first attempt at hitchhiking, intending only a short stop in Santa Fe before returning to Laramie to find work commensurate to my education and career aspirations and which would properly support our family. I felt like this "leap of faith" sort of experience might help me to clear my mind and figure some things out (I had grown quite fond of Kierkegaard's writings as an undergraduate).

I said goodbye to Holly and Kieran, watched the black Honda Civic drive away, shed a few tears, and walked on. I was hoping to find one of a few of my more open-minded college friends still abiding in Shawnee—i.e., the *truly* liberal arts majors and not the theology and religion folks. I went to Deem's Bean Scene for a coffee, Shawnee's only coffee house at the time, hoping to run into someone I knew. No luck there, so I strapped on my frame-pack and headed towards the highway, less than forty-dollars in my wallet.

I spent a couple of hours at the Denny's by the interstate, hoping I might meet someone there who was driving west. A friendly waitress gave me a few tips from her somewhat limited knowledge of hitchhiking. I finished my coffee and whatever I had to eat (I think it was either an omelet or a cinnamon roll), then started down the on-ramp and proceeded to hike along the shoulder, extending my thumb every time a vehicle would approach. It was somewhere after 1 a.m., Thanksgiving Day, 1996.

The night air was a bit chilly, though not so cold as in the high country where I'd been less than a day previous. I said or thought a semblance of a prayer somewhere along the way, an invocation that was something like, "God, Goddess, Universe or whatever you are, if you are there and you hear me, show me your providence, and love . . ."

After less than fifty cars and trucks and tractor-trailers had gone zooming by and less than an hour after I had started walking down Interstate 40, a pickup pulling a load of glass pulled over to the shoulder. A couple of dime-store meth-cowboys invited me into their ride and told me they were headed to Las Vegas after a brief stop to unload their trailer. I rode with them as far as Albuquerque, rolled my last two joints of Mexican brick-weed to smoke with them on the way, and fell in and out of a half-sleep state over the course of the ride (the driver didn't seem to have any trouble staying awake).

Less than five minutes after hopping out of the pickup, a low-rider with fading and scratched paint screeched to a halt on the ramp between I-40 and I-25. I scurried to catch up and climbed into this second ride. The driver was a longtime local, and he offered a few tips about regional etiquette. He said his family had lived in the area for hundreds of years, and that I should be careful to refrain from calling the longtime non-indigenous (i.e., descended from early colonial) inhabitants of the area "Mexicans." He informed me these people were properly categorized as "Spanish" or at least "Hispanics," and that anyone with roots going back to the Conquistadors and first European colonists of New Mexico would take great offense if referred to as "Mexican."

Though I can understand this man's pride in his heritage, said kind low-rider cruisin' "Spaniard's" lecture gave me cause to consider how people sometimes grasp for categorical differentiations to distinguish themselves from whatever perceived "others," to question why folks so often seek to elevate themselves by depreciating others, or at least to separate their own group from whatever other group they (or the wider society) may have deemed lesser. I had most succinctly encountered this unfortunate social phenomenon whilst attending high school in Oklahoma, where many of my pale-skinned peers derogatorily referred to our peers of African descent by the well-known epithet—if also often noting that those of our African American classmates they happened to like were not to be fitted in said category. Trying to fit in, I admittedly joined in on an occasion or two, though quickly recognized such words didn't belong in my mouth.

Of course being in Oklahoma, most of these "whites" were to some degree or other of Native American descent (as am I), yet memories of the Trail of Tears and other such abuses of their ancestors, which should have taught them (or perhaps more accurately, their parents) compassion for minority others, had seemingly given way to the frustrations of being born into a particular socio-economic "caste," so to speak, and to a want to find some other group in relation to which they might imagine their own status superior.

Not to do this very thing to those thus pressed to the periphery of the prosperity and social elevation of this nation by means of this analytical assessment, mind you. I do not desire to judge herein. Rather, I would merely wish to point out a cycle of social dysfunction that has maintained separations amongst oppressed peoples that ought to instead recognize a common cause. Members of such disenfranchised groups should well realize they have reason to unify, to break down these barriers that do little more than continue to maintain socio-economic disparities and to divide those who might rise together to overcome the injustices that have for too long held far too much sway in our world.

The CIA and other such organizations have subversively employed "divide-and-conquer" techniques in their covert actions, as has nigh every ruling class and empire throughout history in order to prevent a unification of potential foes. A few years later I would encounter the divide-and-conquer tactic first-hand whilst living at Big Mountain on disputed land in Arizona, where the Hopi and Diné were supposedly squabbling over the desert scrub they'd been forced to share since subjugated to the rez. There was no significant overt dispute between these tribes regarding this land, in fact, until a mineral extraction company decided they wanted access to this land, and thus the Department of the Interior, the BIA and purportedly even the FBI got involved, and the human rights abuses began (er, continued).

I would like to point out from another perspective that there is clearly great good in maintaining the integrity of cultural identities, so long as these don't divide the oppressed where they ought to unite, nor cause strife where they should cause celebration. What a boring world if it were all of one culture and if we all looked the same!

This proposal is indeed a tenuous balance, to maintain pride in one's people and traditions, and yet uphold respect for those who maintain other identities and cultures and lifeways, and still to determine and defend those basic and universal standards of justice and human rights that ought to transcend whatever traditions. And as should be apparent by these assertions, I'd also help incite, if I might, this world's yet oppressed peoples to find what common ground they might to fight the still threatening swells of commercialism, neocolonialism and economic exploitation, to stay the destruction of native homelands and prevent the erosion of healthy and beautiful indigenous lifeways, languages, tribes and families.

Pardon the digression. Where was I? Oh yeah, on my way to Santa Fe. In truth, said descendant of New Mexico's early Spanish colonials was doing me a favor by offering advice regarding the socio-cultural lay-of-the-land, regardless of whatever personal prejudices or pride may or may not have justifiably or otherwise motivated his monologue.

After this kind gentleman let me out at the southern edge of New Mexico's capital, I started towards the center of town. I had called in advance to find out what arrangements for lodging I'd need to make at the Santa Fe International Hostel. Though I had left on this journey with only forty dollars, I was still want to ensure a comfortable and safe bed awaited me at what was intended to be a half-way point between Shawnee and my return to Laramie.

I was quite green to the ways of wandering, and completely unaware of the traveling hippie culture that was still going strong just after the end of the Grateful Dead's long strange trip. My assumption upon extending my thumb was that this hitchhiking endeavor was relatively unique in a decade I believed had long left those aspects of the hippie movement behind. I had not, by the way, read any Kerouac at this point in my life, and was familiar with the Grateful Dead scene only by having attended a few cover band shows in Oklahoma City and Norman, OK, and thus by interacting with the eclectic audiences these performances attracted (yes, there were and are Deadheads and the likes even in Oklahoma . . . really). Oh, and I was also made privy to Head-lore by befriending Suzanne, my smokin' hot upstairs neighbor and fellow MAPSS student at the U of C who had done the Dead scene when Jerry was still on stage.

Upon checking into the hostel, I was pleasantly surprised to find that the residents and staff were preparing a mostly vegetarian feast for Thanksgiving dinner. I enjoyed this unexpected delight, then sat out in the courtyard sipping some wine and smoking a joint being passed between some of the other residents. A light snow was beginning to fall as I endeavored to engage these other hostel-goers in conversation. I thus made the acquaintance of Natalie and Louisa, who were amongst the party puffing on the patio, and my first acquaintances to become friends in Santa Fe.

Natalie was a Canadian, and Louisa was from Amsterdam. Natalie was exceedingly effervescent and amicable, and Louisa rather reserved if not reticent. Natalie had red to brown hair, and Louisa was a blond. Both were rosy cheeked from wine and the chill of the snowy evening. Also present was a rather pretentious Latino in a poncho who was telling tales (however tall) of his father's associations with Che Guevara. He didn't much seem to appreciate my presence.

Natalie informed me that her boyfriend Arvo had need of help in constructing, as she described it, "a straw-bale, environmentally friendly, chemical-free as much as possible" home in the wilds north of Santa Fe. I decided this was likely another act of the "providence," for lack of a better term, which I was seeking, and the likes of which had appeared amply displayed in my journey thus far, to my heartfelt satisfaction.

    On a later excursion with these first two friends in Santa Fe, plus my employer at the time, Arvo, a mail order pot-pipe producer who lived in Tesuque named Dan, many *Negra Modelo* and swills of cheap tequila and spliffs smoked in a hot springs on a snowy hillside . . . I received a mild concussion after walking off the rock ledge above the upper pool (I think the Tequila softened the blow a bit, though was also the probable cause I fell off the precipice and got concussed in the first place), virtually carried Louisa (who was suffering from some apparently dismal revelations that had come to her on a Psilocybin induced vision quest) up, and then after my concussion, back down the slippery snow-covered pathway. I later discovered that a hippie mama named April from the Laramie crew died in these particular springs sometime thereafter, and that Native American Indian lore tells that hot springs on the sides of mountains are potential bad medicine. I don't go there anymore.

    Of course the heater didn't work in the station wagon as we piled back in to head down the mountain into Los Alamos. Then whilst huddling under a blanket with the two ladies in the back seat as the wagon proceeded down the icy road, a rather disconcerting proclamation with a German accent proceeded from the driver's seat: "Shit! Elk! Shit! Shit!" I felt the car swerve and then a thud, as apparently we had struck the tail end of a cow elk crossing the road. A few moments later, our driver informed us that the brakes had failed.

    After many tenuous curves on our way down, we made it to the bottom of the incline seemingly alive. In order to fix the brakes we made an unscheduled stop at the home of Dan's dad, who was of course one of those X-Files type Los Alamos scientists who couldn't even tell his own family what he did for a living. At least we weren't abducted by aliens on some deserted stretch of highway between Los Alamos and Santa Fe (so far as I can recall).

    I sat for a while enjoying the buzz of good food and wine and weed in the hostel's courtyard, unaware of many such odd adventures which awaited. Indeed, I was quite blissfully and obliviously observing and absorbing my surroundings, endowed with a lightness of spirit I had not known for many years, if ever before—save perhaps in the solitude of the wilderness. The air was charged with a magical quality as symmetrically fractaled snowflakes lazily fell in the subtle light of my first Santa Fe night.

The chill did not seem the least uncomfortable, but in fact quite exhilarating. I breathed in the rarefied air of freedom and exhaled contentment and peace as I contemplated the steam of my breath and shimmering snowflakes falling under the floodlights. I felt liberated from an oppression that had weighed upon my true self since childhood, as if I had outrun death or slavery. I had discovered a renewed innocence in this state of detachment from society's tracked and plotted place for me, and felt unfettered from a guilt and subjugation to which I had seemingly been yoked and which in fact didn't belong to me in the first place. Indeed, by sticking out a thumb whilst standing next to the open road, one is inviting more than free conveyance from one place to another, and certain adventure if not outright conveyance to another world or paradigm, the likely consequences.

Please do not mistake, this liberation I felt was not about being loosed from the responsibilities of being a husband and a father. Rather, I was glad to leave behind the subtle factors of unnatural institutional influences and unnecessary social and psychological control, and to at least temporarily ditch the direct sway of those lies that uphold the assumptions of authority used to justify manipulations of the masses and unwarranted intrusions into our lives. Somehow I seemed to have evaded "the system's" tracking system, and had broken some of so many strings tying me to the stultifying expectations of religious and social tradition and karmic ties to others' pasts, "sins of the father," and myths of some taint of original sin we're all supposedly obliged to carry. It was these unhealthy and oppressive ties I was grateful to sense were severed, and not those more endearing and important bonds.

In departing from householder role, I was seeking to attune a soul not yet well or properly adjusted to this world. Indeed, in my mind were intentions to find somewhere within myself that self who'd best serve as husband and father and whole human being in whatever context, and indeed I did much lament separations from those beloved persons I had to leave to find what it seemed I lacked. I might also recall one particular instance of prescience (at the time only available to my gut) that told me Holly and I were not meant to last, and which in fact occurred very soon after we started to date in high school. We were standing in the hallway at her family's home, and after sharing a kiss, she told me that as a girl she had believed or wished she would marry a man with the last name "Wood" so that her married name would become "Holly Wood." As she spoke these words, I experienced the proverbial "gut sensation," a literal if slight ache in my innards that should have told me then that our relationship was not to last. Within approximately one year of officially divorcing me, Holly married a man named Jeff Wood. Even things like divorce do happen with rhyme and reason, at least some of the time.

    Next morning after snagging a couple of complimentary pastries and performing my requisite chore at the hostel by scrubbing a tub, I wandered towards the plaza and made my first of many visits to the infamous Aztec Café to spend my last five-dollars, received as the return of my deposit upon completion of the aforementioned assigned chore.

    I was amazed at the colorful clientèle of this officially state-designated "Cutting-Edge Art-Space." More mohawks and dreadlocks and non-traditional piercings were displayed than I had seen in all my life. Hippies and punks and artist sorts, Deadheads and florescent-dyed and dreaded hair dominated the scene. Hippie mommas were braiding hemp, and various freaks had their handcrafted pipes and wire-wrapped semi-precious stones and crystals out for display on tables next to lattes and maté gourds and croissants and bagels.

    This was a wonderland I had only dreamed existed, and these were the natives of the polymorphic-postmodern-nomad culture to which I had always an instinctual knowledge I belonged, despite being quite oblivious that such was yet thriving. Or at least I felt I belonged here more than in the midst of the bourgeois conformity I had known heretofore, that sanitized and assimilated culture to which I had become never quite comfortably habituated previous to taking this assumedly unconventional leap of faith.

I soon made the acquaintance of a number of interesting wandering and local freaks, some who'd grown up in communes and some from the suburbs, some who'd followed the Grateful Dead and some who'd come to Santa Fe to study art or the classics, and some who had just hopped aboard some brightly painted bus and didn't know where they were going. There were white kids who wanted to be Rastafarians, a few with knotted hair who legitimately fit said category, and more than a handful of trustafarians. There were blacks and whites and browns and yellows and reds and any number of beautiful hues in between, and each with something outside and in they bore to endeavor a free-expression of self and to differentiate from the dysfunction of mainstream culture, else perhaps to display his or her chosen mystic path. At least this was how my rather innocent eyes perceived what I encountered here in the wonderland of "cutting-edge" Santa Fe and the Aztec Café, the hippie caravan scene still lively as Deadheads had not yet let go of their gypsy ways, the Rainbow Tribe's Gathering at a peak in the number of eclectic and ragtag pilgrims converging.

Hope for peace and a transformation of society by love, compassion, and transcendence was strong amongst these seeming free spirits, and as more than a mere echo of the sixties. I was in awe at finding what I had longed for consciously since a lecture in a sociology class at OBU when a professor had given a rather inspiring speech about the hippie/protest movement of the sixties and early seventies, and for what my spirit had wanted unconsciously at least since my elementary school days, if not from past lifetimes immemorial.

In retrospect, having been made privy to other perspectives and at times forcefully pressed to see a less beautiful view of these and other events in my life, I realize I was somewhat naive, for better or worse (likely for the better). I had chosen to be emptied of all prejudices and to let go of the conditioning I had received by so many years in and influenced by institutions, from school to church to media-fostered consumer-training and so many other modes of propaganda designed to assimilate inhabitants of this land to the so-called "American Dream."

Though at the time I felt very much a novice amongst these veterans of the road, as I held no presumptions that I was wiser, cooler, or more hip than any of these, I have come to realize in some ways I already held a consciousness and spiritual freedom many of these seemingly superior in the ways of counterculture lacked. Not to judge any in particular from whence I sit and type these words, but it has become clear to me that even amongst many of these seeming free spirits there were yet vestiges of competitive intentions, oneupmanship, schemings and connivings, etc., or at least the sometimes apparition thereof.

Not that there was not also and indeed more prominently true camaraderie, expanded awareness and good intention, and indeed likely some who were ascended souls. Yet to wear tie-dyes and dreadlocks or black-eyeliner and purple hair or an eight-inch mohawk does not necessarily mean one has a true grasp of the principles of legitimate protest or genuine and unalloyed intentions of free-expression, a solid desire for solidarity or even a half-assed, half-way integrated aesthetic or philosophy. I have come to realize heart and mind do not necessarily always accompany overt signs of affiliation with various counter-cultures, modes of dissent which indeed most often maintain compelling and substantive messages, well thought-out symbolic expressions of protest and legitimate individuation, and very much valid ideas and ideals for social transformation.

From yet another perspective, it might be noted that if one wears a mask often or for long enough, one might well become what is represented thereupon. Or to put it in another context, this is not unlike the often held understanding that devotion to whatever given deity is designed to bring devotee into union with said expression of divinity—i.e., Yoga ("yoke" or "union"), "be one with the father, as I am one . . .," theophanies and theogonies, apotheoses and the self-realization of avatars, etc. To meditate upon or imitate a form is to receive or become the essence of that form to whatever degree. Bow to an image of Krishna and you may find yourself drawn to dairy farms. Wear hippie or punk clothes, or those of a businessman or woman, and you are not unlikely to find yourself to whatever degree conforming to the spirit and essence of those subcultural paradigms, just the same.

There is thus a certain level of truth to the perception that you are what you wear, and indeed, sometimes clothes do make the man. Essentially, signs matter.

I did not make even these critical assessments at the time, however, though well-enough trained in semiotic analysis and cultural criticism, as I was determined to be open to whatever expression of guru (though not quite yet a term I would have used) might manifest through these new and exciting experiences, these doors opened into the world of wanderers, renunciates and mystics. And indeed, lessons and would be teachers and even veritable gurus appeared in many guises during this first pilgrimage on the road and similarly throughout the course of my journeys thereafter.

I called Natalie's boyfriend Arvo to inquire about employment. The terms were six bucks-an-hour, lodging in a camper parked behind his house in town, and all the homegrown I could smoke whilst on the job at his homestead north of Abique. My employment entailed stuccoing straw-bale walls with a mixture of mud and sand and portland cement, chopping wood and carrying water.

Like most I met in Santa Fe and thereabouts, Arvo was a rather odd (or perhaps better, "interesting") character. A well traveled German of Latvian descent, he had run away from home at the age of seventeen and somehow ended up in Indonesia, where he met a Dutch journalist who he then accompanied to Afghanistan in order to tote sound equipment whilst said journalist covered the Mujahedeen insurgency against the Soviet occupiers. His graying-blond hair was constantly disheveled (when not covered with a ski cap or other hat), and he generally had automobile grease on his outerwear, as he was a freelance mechanic by trade. Given to the stereotypical emotional outbursts often touted a trait of Eastern European sensibilities and simultaneously to the typical German work ethic and sense of efficiency, Arvo was not an easy man to work for, if nonetheless a good-hearted and genuine fellow. I was certainly grateful for this "manifestation" (hippie/Rainbow/road parlance for a seeming spontaneous and helpful something somewhere between providence and magic) of employment and shelter, and in my state of intentioned humility took whatever personality conflicts in stride for a few months until I was hired at the Natural Foods Co-op in Santa Fe and took lodging with a long-haired guitarist named Miguel.

    Among the more intriguing people I met in Santa Fe was a woman named Coreena (or was it "Careena"?). She was a tall and thin and beautiful artist with short brown hair, and on one occasion we had one of the best conversations I experienced during this stay in Santa Fe as we smoked a joint one night in De Vargas Park. I had been introduced to the work of an anthropologist by the name of Gregory Bateson by one of a few professors I had as an undergrad who overtly sought to expose his students to freethinking and who unabashedly encouraged a questioning of the Southern Baptist dogma and the policies of thought and action that issued there-from. I mentioned some of Bateson's ideas regarding the formation and emplotment of binaries and their implications in the construction of consciousness, and Coreena grew exceedingly excited as she proposed the idea that if a spacecraft such as Voyager landed on a lifeless planet, playing the well-known recordings sent along into the atmosphere, the sound vibrations would over time bring order to the soil and rocks and whatever elements present, eventually creating life according to the frequencies and rhythms transmitted into the atmosphere. As she grew intense in her elocution and at least intellectually aroused, I almost kissed her, but for some reason was restrained from this boldness.

    Coreena's roommate Mila, whom I scarcely got to know, had grown up on one of the area hippie communes. She was tall and blond, and was rather quiet if not aloof on the few occasions we were in each other's company. This pair and their peers were given to wearing feather boas and displaying various similar carnivalesque or burlesque expressions of fashion, as well as to those sorts of artistic and other modes of alternative expression somewhat expected of hip young Santa Feans, and were of course mostly bisexual. As I recall, one or the other worked at the Cowgirl.

    The Cowgirl is around the corner from the Aztec and attracted some of the same eclectic clientèle. The waitresses and lady barkeepers I've encountered over the years at this iconic bar-and-grill are generally quite hot, clad in cowboy hats and tight jeans or short skirts, and often present demeanors as they take an order that indicate they are of the sort who fancy nose-candy—to enhance their service, of course. Not my poison, by any means and for a number of reasons: "Hey, can I offer you a line, fortified with sodium carbonate-dissolved peasant flesh? C'mon, you'll like it!" . . . but definitely a favorite of more than a few waitresses and cocktailers and strippers from the LA to NYC, Seattle to Miami. Not to judge, mind you.

Arvo once related a story he had been told by Mila about her years on the commune which I found rather emblematic of the communal movement during the seventies. It was near Christmas (or Solstice, depending on which hippie you ask), and the mostly vegetarian communitarians were having a rather lean holiday season. One evening one of the community's inhabitants stepped out of the house and startled a passing deer, which promptly ran into a wall and expired on the spot due to a cleanly broken-neck. The communal crew dined heartily that holiday—even, according to the version of the tale I was told, some of the otherwise vegetarians, who viewed this seeming self-sacrifice as a sign.

This is how a generation of wild and free people learned to live, freed from the fetters of false, churchy spirituality in order to relearn and redefine the meaning of words like love, blessings, liberty and divine providence. Cut loose from the chains of supposed civilized society, these "rebels" sought to learn how to return to a closer relationship with divine Mother Earth and Her gracious bounty, and thus to a more abiding means of earthly existence in the here and now, and how to conform to a state closer to nature and to reform life lived into a reflection and remembrance and recognition of the unity, harmony, peace, purity and magic more natural to human beings than suburban box houses, concrete and steel, and living around a schedule of 9-to-5.

Some eventually dropped-out of dropping-out, though many of these have tried to remain tuned-in. Others still carry on these traditions manifest from meetings of modern and ancient, tribal and multicultural, wild celebration and sincere meditation, conscientious living without puritanical misgivings. And many of these wild and freed spirits of this first grand wave of elevated, altered, and expanded consciousness called the hippie movement continue to convey what they have learned to those who have turned-on or tuned-in sometime since the sixties and seventies.

Regarding other romantic or nigh romantic exchanges, my experiences in Santa Fe were less than fulfilling. After a night at the bars playing pool with Natalie, having consumed much tequila and beer and both made-up with eyeliner and rouge for our playful excursion, we returned to the house and I ended up having sex with my temporary roommate Kristina, an attractive eighteen-year-old local. Nothing ensued from this one night stand, nor from the odd tryst with a somewhat neurotic rich girl who decided to scoop me up whilst passing by in a taxi and take me home to her bed. The most "substantive" (nigh) romantic experience I had during this period of introduction to the wild and whimsical world of hippies, artists and gypsies generally was with an older woman named Pilar.

I met Pilar at a reggae show at a bar up Canyon Drive. She was a New Yorker in her upper-thirties, and was from South America originally. I was twenty-four and from southeast Wyoming. Upon leaving the show together, we walked beside the Santa Fe River—a rather meager excuse for a waterway bearing that designation, and she told me of her failed relationship with a Rasta musician who had numerous other paramours as well as offspring. We later took a trip together to stay at a monastery next to the Rio Grande as retreat from the everyday and sometimes warped "metaphysical" milieu of this old New Age city at the foot of the Sangre de Cristo Mountains.

Our mutual friend Tom conveyed us in his seventies vintage Pontiac (if I recall correctly the make of this behemoth of a ride) north from Santa Fe and towards consequential encounters with sacred sites of three religions. Tom was a thick-framed on-again off-again junkie from New York City I met at the Aztec Café and with whom I smoked much hashish and learned a great deal about heroin (not from any personal experience, mind you, as this is yet another poison I want nothing to do with), about the drug-courier scene in New York City, and about Buddhism.

Among other tales, Tom told me several somewhat scandalous stories about Chogyam Trumpa, the famous/infamous renegade monk who mingled Tibetan traditions and hippie culture in the sixties and seventies, including an account of a dildo named Mr. Happy. Oddly enough, Laramie had an analogous heavy-set Buddhist storyteller named Tom (much older and recently deceased), who would sit at one or another of the local coffee houses and offer tales about Trumpa, touted Buddhist philosophy, and similarly claimed a strong liking for heroin.

On the way to the monastery, we stopped for a brief visit at a mosque in Abique, site of a sizable "white-Muslim" community. We met the imam, and I discovered from ensuing conversation that one of my professors from the University of Chicago (who was in fact at one point my thesis advisor) had preceded us for a visit to this mosque by only a week or two. A notable synchronicity, I suppose.

We reverently or at least respectfully entered the adobe mosque under rounded domes rising towards the deep-blue desert sky. As I recall, we removed shoes and washed our feet in the tiled foot bath (or at least I remember intimately examining the tile-work of this basin, if I didn't get my feet wet) before passing through the arched earthen doorway into the *sajadah* (prayer room). I pondered the idiosyncrasies of this center of worship as I examined the Arabic script and mosaic on the *mihrab*,[2] considering this desert setting with in mind analogous scenes surrounding mosques from North Africa to Arabia, and wondering of the lives and motives of the mostly converted members of this Muslim community in northeastern New Mexico. I opened my senses to assess my surroundings, or perhaps "endeavored to feel the 'vibrations'" of the worship which transpired in this place, and indeed found some things in the atmosphere there in fact more comfortable than what I'd known in most Christian houses of worship, though still not by any means something perfectly fitted to my spirit.

I had written my Master's thesis (which I never quite completed) on European discourses on Islam, basically with a view to exploring European writings which did not characterize Islamic people with the usual stereotypical essentializations. I was

---

2   Area of a wall facing *Qibla*, i.e., decorated area giving indication of the direction to Mecca.

interested in dichotomies of "self and other," and why conflicts arise as well as how resolutions and harmonies are manifest between "us" and "them," however deployed in any given context. This visit thus fit well with themes I had already given much thought, providing an interesting example of the evolving relationship between "the West" and Islam.

After a night's stay with a friend of Pilar's who lived on a hilltop just outside Abique, we continued on to our intended destination, the Christ of the Desert Monastery. This Benedictine monastery sits next to a particularly picturesque section of the Rio Grande. The buildings are all earth-tone adobe, though stained glass and frescoes embellish some spaces. Of the several earth-built buildings, a prominent bell tower rises highest above the lush valley.

I could almost imagine this scene the same, three-hundred-plus-years in the past—minus the cars and trucks in the parking lot and electrical lines dangling overhead, that is. Despite the antique appearance, however, the monastery was actually founded less than fifty years previous. In the midst of the construction of an addition, however, adobe bricks stacked and ready to be molded into new earthen walls with worn wooden scaffolding erected for the task, this place elicited sensations reminiscent of the early colonial missions established in the region, centuries before—or at least Hollywood renderings thereof. Vintage Clint Eastwood films came to mind.

Thomas Merton, a Trappist monk who had spent time in Asia studying meditation and the philosophies of China and Tibet and India with Buddhist monks and other renunciates and who consequently became well known as a proponent of the ecumenical movement had apparently spent a span of time at this monastery previous to his death in 1968. The gift shop offered a wide selection of his books, for sale at retail prices.

This monastery had a policy of offering retreat to world-weary strangers in exchange for a little work and worship—a worthy expression of saintly duty and charity. We ended up staying for only a couple of days, however, as Pilar was unhappy with some of the expectations the monks held for visitors. As we had started to form something of a romantic connection I decided to accompany her to Taos, where she intended to attend a festival which was to occur at a Hindu temple coinciding with the night before the new moon during the month of Maaga—that is, sometime in February or early March.

We hitched a ride down the long dirt road and into Espanola, then happened to meet an acquaintance of Pilar's named Casey, who just happened to be going to the same festival with his girlfriend, and who thus just happened to offer rather cozy conveyance in his VW bug up the Rio Grande Gorge and into Taos.

Pilar showed me around town, and introduced me to some of the odd and interesting characters of Taos proper and others who lived out on "the Mesa." The Mesa, which consists of two primary settlements, Two Peaks and Three Peaks, is a hodge-podge gathering of hippie homesteaders both young and old who took advantage of the bankruptcy of a land development company whose holdings on the west side of the Rio Grande Gorge were regularly offered at back-taxes auction for less than a couple of hundred bucks per-acre. I have heard the Mesa affectionately described as "the largest free-range insane asylum in North America."

Among the more memorable Mesa inhabitants Pilar introduced me to was Two-Raven (or as I have heard him called, "Too Ravin' Crazy"). This character had grey dreads to somewhere near his waist or knees with blown glass beads and bones and any number of other odd objects woven in, and wore two or more tattered layers of robes. Two-Raven gave me a "medicine card" reading that told me I was a good man to bring women water whilst they are in "the moon-lodge," and that I have "dragonfly-vision" (i.e., can deal with cantankerous women and can't see straight?). There are quite a number of other characters nigh as eccentric out at Two and Three Peaks—"wing-nuts," as these are designated in turn of the millennium Hippie-speak, a mostly endearing term often used to describe the craziest amongst the tribe.

These two communities consist of a chaotic conglomerations of asymmetrical earth-ships and other unique adobe and straw-bale structures, recycled wood chalets and permanently parked VW and school buses which have been home to many a wildman and woman, freaks and heads and punks and anarchists and various uncategorizable others who have sought retreat from the *real* madness of the consumer-driven, spiritless mess manifest destiny, capitalism and the conventional take on the American Dream have made of a once wild and free land. Indeed, if these are insane for their discontent with the dysfunction of a society that has poisoned the rivers and cut down the forests and placed cookie-cutter houses and box-shaped chain-stores where once was habitat shared by many tribes of free people and animal and plant life alike, then count me amongst the insane.

Pilar and I spent a night or two at the Laughing Horse Inn, a rather unique place of lodging with eclectic themes for each domicile. Our room had bunk-bed style accommodations with a television built into the slanted ceilings above the upper bunk, and Navajo blankets and rugs embellished the rustic Southwestern ambiance. We also stayed at another of her friend's homes, where we came as close to having sex as we would during this time spent together, though she halted the act just as our respective genitalia had become only slightly acquainted. Likely for the better, as she and I had definite personality conflicts.

Though I spent a bit of time with her upon the occasion of later visits to Taos, little more developed of our friendship. I must say I am at the very least grateful for Pilar having encouraged me to attend this Sivaratri celebration, an experience that indeed conveyed me to a remembrance of myself—or rather of *Self*—that I had begun to experience unwittingly via odd signs and indications of being *sadhu* that had already surfaced in behavior and thought, karma and dharma.

We arrived at the temple a bit early, and were thus enlisted to help with preparations by stringing garlands of flowers and prepping food for the coming night's celebration. I took a little time to read some of the literature lying around, as some inhibitions instilled from my days as a church goer and Christian minister still held some sway in my mind, and I thus had a wish to be better informed regarding the nature of the coming celebration and rituals. As I read about the intentions in creating representations of the Divine in *murtis* (statues and other depictions), I came to the realization that visual portrayals of the sacred were indeed no less adept nor less acceptable as modes to inspire devotion and right[3] action than the written word I had been taught to believe and revere in the Christian tradition. In contemplation I concluded that in consideration of so many wars and other contentions over the "correct" interpretations of writ dogma, and in light of Inquisitions and a variety of other abuses of human rights done due to slight divergences of belief, that in fact such universally accessible depictions as *murtis* (icons/"idols") might be understood as less likely to be subject to manipulation than even the most concisely written sacred script, and perhaps that much more likely to elicit or evoke sincere and unalloyed devotion and positive transformation. Indeed, especially when such speak so eloquently and archetypally and psychologically if not scientifically validly as doth a well portrayed *murti*. One example which not so subtly portrays this: the Ten Avatars of Vishnu quite clearly portray human physical and social evolution, a religio-scientific construction dating back thousands of years and certainly long before Darwin and Marx.

As the long night of *kirtan* (call and response chants) began, I at first stood in the foyer outside the temple room, still hesitant to step inside to where linga (sacred phalluses) that sat in a yoni (sacred vulva) chalice were being anointed with offerings. As these ancient songs accompanied by *sitar* and *mrudungam, tablas* and *harmonium* (if I recall right) played into the cold night, however, I began to feel a warmth and resonance in my soul that far exceeded the relatively shallow responses elicited in revivals and youth conferences and church camp meetings I had experienced during my days amongst Baptists and other evangelicals.

My body began to sway in ways heretofore unknown or forgotten, as if these vibrations were awakening something had lain dormant, an energy awaiting a cue to animate a dance in time with

---

3   *Rta* action, mind you, and not "right" as opposed to "left." *Rta* is the Sanskrit origin of the word "right" which does not maintain the later, skewed additional meaning of the derived English word. Indeed, the latter rather twisted denotation of the word "right" has notably been utilized in recent times by spin-doctors of a particular political persuasion to benefit their decidedly *ARta* ("not right") platform (at least according to my personal opinion, that is).

my true spirit, if only immaturely and shyly expressed as yet in *nATa* (dance). I observed with a combination of curiosity and instinctual remembrance as rhythm and rhyme were performed in the ancient tongue that is parent (or at least great-aunt or uncle) to even modern English, as *pujaris* (priests and priestesses) dressed in ochre robes poured yogurt and rice over the sacred grey and red linga stones gathered from India's Narmada River, reverently rubbing the mixture over said phallic figurations and carefully caressing the thick concoction through and out of the yoni shaped stone chalice, rinsing and repeating with different colored ingredients mixed into the thick edible ointment, later the *prasad* partaken of by devotees as well as food for Deity.

This ancient recognition of the Divinity in even the supposed base union of penis and vagina, and thus affirmation of life's abundance, nature's pathways as pure, spirit's (or better, *prana*) flow in physically manifest form felt more akin to the spirituality I had known laying upon a mountainside as a child, wandering amongst pines and tundra and next to snow-fed streams and rivers and alpine lakes high above my hometown and above the understandable confusion I felt as I was being socialized and institutionalized, even at the relatively open and liberal elementary school I attended during my early years of this lifetime. This worship resonated with my wildman's soul. This was closer to nature, to naturally being-human, and was indeed something at least a step or two beyond a liberal education and churchy indoctrination.

From my perspective of the proceedings from the plant filled atrium that surrounds two sides of the inner room, I decided to venture deeper into the temple to sit amidst devotees and *murtis* in two and three dimensions placed 'round the sanctuary according to ceremony. Ancient memories and primal energies rose up and 'round my spine as I sat, *kundalini* awakened. The vibrations of the Sanskrit intonations and tabla beats, sitar and harmonium, melodies and harmonies and rhythms untied knots I didn't know were tied, and opened channels I had only the least awareness existed. I again consciously compared these sensations to what I had experienced in the highest points of devotion I had known in the Christian tradition, and quite succinctly concluded this more ancient and primal devotion was more genuine, more true to myself and to the truth of the Divine, life and nature and all that is than anything I had encountered at dozens of youth rallies and revivals, retreats and tent meetings.

Through the course of the night, I would alternate between sitting and chanting in the temple and hanging out by the fire and chatting with devotees, sipping chai and smoking cannabis (mostly) in the shadows. *Charas* (hashish) is a sacrament traditionally consumed during this festival in India, Nepal, and other nations with long established Hindu populations, and as such is more than tolerated in those places. This aspect of the festival is not officially endorsed at this particular temple in Taos, however, as the sacred use of marijuana products has not yet received the same acceptance as even its medicinal use, nor the legal recognition granted peyote for use by Native American Church members. This despite the true status of *charas* (hashish) as the most anciently and continuously utilized sacramental plant, or perhaps sacrament generally for that matter, of any religion in the world.

As the sun rose shortly after the last watch of the ceremonies I made the decision to return to Oklahoma to endeavor to patch things up with Holly and to see my son. I had discovered much of what I had set out to find at the inception of this unconventional pilgrimage, and a change of heart I had much need to experience—though as it turned out my hopes to salvage said marriage were already doomed to failure.

I could continue on to tell details of my brief but blissful stay at the Lama Foundation (an interfaith retreat center in the mountains above Taos)—a pleasant transition before departing from the Land of Enchantment to travel to the Sooner state. I could also take a page or two to describe the rather epic scene set alongside a state highway on the way to OK, wherein a Kansas deputy dipped his pinky finger into what I am rather certain was a bag of crystal LSD—though a cop prepared for the trip by having attended Grateful Dead shows, at least by his telling told me whilst the ride was being searched by another deputy and before he *accidentally* sent himself into a reality of heavy-duty fractals and spirals and seemingly good vibrations and thus grew suddenly mostly silent, but I'll leave those stories and details for another time or medium.

I believe even to this day, and after having been given cause to reconsider nigh everything I ever once, and then later understood as "true," that through these experiences I had become reintroduced to Self, to *Atman,* to *brahman,* the good and true nature and source of Being, compassion and purity that had in fact always inhabited my vessel, and which pervades throughout this good earth and her inhabitants and throughout the universe, if scarcely noticed or noticeable in places.

Though I do now maintain the conviction that certain traditions of practice as best maintained and taught in India and known generally as *sanAtana dharma* are nearer a root, primal and well considered understanding of the nature of humanity and existence and God/Goddess, and I believe offer a more valid historical and philosophical purview of humanity's recent spiritual and literal pathways and pilgrimages than do those religions which proceed from the "Abrahamic traditions,"[4] I would not claim to be "Hindu" (actually a rather recent term for the most ancient continuously practiced religious traditions in the world), though I might accept the designation, "tantric practitioner." Nor would I reject those good teachings which do exist within Judaism, Christianity and Islam, various indigenous traditions, nor those offered by the philosophies of secular humanism, etc. I learned on this journey that there is a more substantive strand of righteousness, spirituality, compassion and celebration of life and the eternal that exists in so many places and lifeways, and which cannot be narrowed to any single dogmatic system of belief I have yet encountered.

This "pilgrimage" had no particular intended destination, no specific sacred shrine in mind nor revered location as a motivation to wander. The holy place I sought and was led to was instead a sacred understanding within my heart and mind and whatever other *chakra,* a beatific recognition that there is much more to this world than is generally noticed by the dulled

---

4 Which are in fact (in my humble but easily verifiable opinion) quite clearly derivative of the religious traditions of ancient Bharat—i.e., the lands of India. For more insight on these assertions, see footnote 21.

awarenesses we have inherited from an industrialized, urbanized and suburbanized society, which has become too nearly divorced from the natural world and from those spiritual connections instinct and primal memory would have us enjoy.

    I came to realize over the course of this first quest that it is not in creed nor in dogma that truth is contained, though written traditions may offer a certain degree of elevation to human beings. And though I have found myself quite convinced of the verity of what's expressed in and by the term *sanAtana dharma*, "eternal teachings"—the most ancient and abiding religio-philosophic-scientific tradition in the world, I came to understand a less rigid religion than some o'er proscriptive brahmanical code, i.e., the wisdom of the consummate Wildman, who just happens to be none other than Great God, Mahadeva, a wisdom conveyed by naked forest dwellers, *sadhu* and *nagababa* and postmodern post-Grateful Dead tour Rainbow gypsy wandering tribespeople, among others, who remember and recognize this primal spirituality, linga-yoni *good*, pure yet not puritanical, playful and fecund, abundant and free.

    Indeed in this more earthy and potent, even pungent spirituality, divine truth is writ elsewhere and everywhere, if one only has the willingness to allow its revelation through the course of a life lived with openness to good guidance and the inherent beauty and truth of Nature, to an honest questioning of institution and the status quo, a willingness to let loose attachment to popular versions of reality and to endure whatever potential hardships as one endeavors this sacred pilgrimage offered to any and every life lived.

A True Account of a Murder: From Another Side

  I suppose I have told this true tale enough times, I ought to find it an easy task to commit said narrative to writing. Nonetheless, I shall approach this written record of actual occurrences with all due diligence and precision as I endeavor to share a concise and hopefully entertaining account of a series of real events that occurred to me over the expanse of seven years or so, events that have inexorably altered my understanding of life and death, and indeed, of what is *real*.

  The reception of a live storytelling (the mode by which I am accustomed to sharing this true tale) and an account to be read are necessarily very different experiences. A reader cannot see the storyteller's facial expressions, hear intonations of a speaker's voice, nor notice fluctuations in pupil size, breath or gestures as she or he peruses the print. The reader is thus left to other devices to evaluate the verity of what is read, and at most might envision an imagined rendering of the narrator in the act of storytelling to help assess the truth of words writ, assuming the writings' style doth permit.

  I understand that the content of this tale will be difficult to believe even for the most open-minded amongst you. I will attempt to keep such factors in mind as this true-life account of multidimensional and mind-boggling implication flows from memory to fingertips to keyboard, and then to whatever medium to you, dear reader, and as I present my case with appeal to your deeper access to truth, free inquiry and discernment, as well as to your sense of literary pleasure.

Devotions in Yosemite

  It was pitch black in the tall stand of pines engulfing the campground, dark pillars holding up a slightly less dark sky. I had a sense of invisibility as I began to chant in a deep, billowing and sincerely devotional manner, "*Aum Namah Shivia, Aum Namah*

Shivia," over and over, differing tune and tone, pitch and volume as seemed to suit the *prana* flowing through my form. As I attained a thoughtless trance-induced euphoria, a miniature-helicopter-like-air-chopping-sound brought me back to my earthbound senses at the floor of Yosemite Valley.

With the proficiency of an old west gunfighter drawing a sidearm, I retrieved my flashlight from whatever pocket, flipped the switch and simultaneously drew a bead on the mysterious culprit with a thin beam of light. An extremely large beetle with a rather extraordinary set of antennae lay motionless on the forest floor. In its descent to the pine needle-strewn ground, the bulky insect had missed my head by mere inches. Seemed certain the creature's interruption of my impassioned intonations was indeed an auspicious *sign*—for lack of a better term.

Upon a closer inspection of this oversized bug bearing an intimidating set of mandibles, I realized its branching antennae were almost precisely analogous to the headdress on the *Siva Nataraj murti*[5] depicted on the cover of a book which I was carrying amongst my belongings titled, *The Only Dance There Is*.

The two to three inch beastie bore armor that reflected or refracted an array of colors, glimmering on the surface of the bug's deep black exoskeleton. Its two elytron (wing plates) and an armored sclerite (back plate) showed brilliant green and purple and blue and red under the narrow beam of light, leastwise in my recollections of the arrayal of colors vivid even under artificial illumination. The feathered antennae were black and branched out elegantly, likewise shimmering in the ray of light the flashlight projected. This beetle apparition held my attention for a number of minutes as I closely studied its colors and form before deciding to double-check my assessment of the antennae/sacred statue analogy.

I found my tent in the dark forest, pitched in Yosemite National Park's only walk-in campground aside from those far from roads on backpacking trails. No reservation was required at this site, and the fees were reasonable. For a combination of these and other reasons, this particular place to pitch a tent or hang a

---

5 A *murti* is a statuette or other devotional depiction of a deity; *Siva naTaraja* is Mahadeva—"Great God, The Destroyer"—as the Lord of Dance.

hammock was notorious for attracting hippies, hardcore rock climbers, and various other fringe elements amongst outdoor enthusiasts.

At one time Camp 4 was completely avoided by the park's transit buses merely for the fact that the people who were want to pitch their tents under the tall trees there had excessive amounts of fun—a clear case of discrimination. To offer an image to grant a glimpse of the raucous reveling this site had seen, I was told that during the seventies and into the eighties the tourists aboard passing transit buses often received a choreographed view of so many moons from far below the sky whilst driving by this locus of a somewhat wilder Yosemite camping experience.

In my cozy tent, sleeping bag already in place and a small *Ganesha* tapestry hanging above my pillow, I examined the photographic representation of a brass dancing Siva, a thin yet muscular figure surrounded by fire and crowned with a multi-branched headdress, four arms and two legs and posture in perfect yogic pose. I unhesitatingly concluded that the beetle's antennae and the statue's headdress were indeed more than mildly similar, if not nigh precisely same. Now I will concede, many features of religious representations are drawn directly from observations of nature. Nonetheless, the coincidence of my transcendental chant and the apparition of this beautiful beetle with the *Siva Nataraja* headdress antennas was enough to convince me of the auspicious nature of what I had just experienced.

Still in a devotional mood and mode, I lit candles and incense, smoked some herb and began to chant "*Ganesha Sharanam, Sharanam Ganesha,*" an invocation of the popular Indian deity who is responsible for the creation and removal of obstacles, among other things. After a few rounds on the *mala* I wore round my neck, I stopped to examine my breath and enjoy the altered awareness that comes from meditative states generally, and specifically from the resonant vibrations of a voice's voluminous Sanskrit intonations bouncing around a practitioner's skull and chest—quite a nice "natural" high.

As this euphoria waned, I experienced a sense of loneliness, and quite naturally associated this with my dearth of female companionship. I had been separated (for a second time) from at the time still-legally-wife for better than a year, and had not experienced any sort of significant satisfying intimate relationship since our parting. The energy I had directed into the aforementioned newfound ancient practices had gone a good distance towards transforming these sorts of immediate desires. I had just attended a wedding, however, and I met a beautiful and intriguing European woman (I've forgotten her specific nationality —Spanish or Italian, I think) on a backcountry trail and again in the campground who piqued my interest and sense of want for female companionship.

      In this mood and mode, I decided to ask via this divine remover of obstacles, represented ('present?' or perhaps better, 'presented') in the orange and brown and yellow died tapestry depicting said elephant-headed deity, if he might be so kind as to remove whatever obstacles might prevent me from a positive relationship with an attractive woman. "Nothing too committed, mind you Ganesh," to paraphrase my thoughts, "I'm not even divorced yet," though seems other reasons and events unmentioned and perhaps unmentionable had indeed already sealed that union's cessation.

A Neophyte Post-Hippie-Era Hippie Goes to Haight-Ashbury
      From Yosemite, I hitched a ride with a self-represented white-Rasta driving a rusty blue van to the nearest town with rail service, and from there caught a train to San Francisco—my first visit to the west coast since I was ten years old. I checked into the Green Tortoise Hostel, a lively bunkhouse in a neighborhood of strip clubs and trinket stores and a noted hub for world-travelers where one could stay for $20/night and feel fairly comfortable openly smoking marijuana (in the recreation room, at least) and sipping a beer whilst mingling with numerous and interesting world travelers. The hostel also served as a point from which one might embark on adventures to a number of destinations aboard one of a number of painted-green vintage greyhound-style buses converted to offer cuddle-puddle style sleeping accommodations for upwards of forty-three people.

      I soon set out to explore San Francisco's fabled hippy-mecca, the Haight-Ashbury district. Admittedly wearing rose-colored glasses (er, John Lennon style shades) as I walked up and down these streets, the once-homeland of the free-love, peace, and psychedelic movements, not to mention the origin of lots of good music, I scarcely noticed that the Grateful Dead were either dead or had moved to Marin or Sonoma County, that Janis and Bobby McGee were nowhere to be found (though Wavy Gravy was still hanging out), or that love-ins were just plain a bad idea with HIV a significant factor by the mid-1990's.

    It didn't even annoy me that the price of herb on the street was rather steep. A "haighth" (a Haight Street-purchased eighth-ounce of marijuana) is often up to a gram light, else up to twenty-dollars higher than the price to be found in California outside of this particular cutthroat marketplace (unless you "know somebody"). I was also not yet so immediately conscientious regarding the ironies of the commodification of 60's counterculture as I am now, and went about my days a very happy and high neophyte-postmodern-hippie wandering the Haight.

    Blissfully exploring this famed district of the city by the bay, I soon discovered Golden Gate Park's "Hippie Hill," a locus for drum circles and lounging in the sun popular with longhair types and counterculture sorts since at least the Summer of Love. Emblematic of this hill's history, some random dready informed me that an oddly shaped tree growing alone at the foot of this hill was made famous by a photograph of Janis Joplin sitting atop its branches. This tree is thus colloquially called "the Janis Tree." The rather short and bushy tree is said to be just big enough for "a girl and her guitar," though I've seen two or three climb out of this tree's tangled branches—girls and guys and not necessarily guitars.

    Other stands of trees surround the grassy hillside, home to a cadre of gutter-punks and the likes who are often the source of the infamously short bags of weed, and apparently not infrequently the perpetrators of violence after dark in this once gathering-place of peace protests and free-love. I made the acquaintance of a few of these and other regulars who hung out around the hill and at the Haight street entrance to the park, and thus maintained my supply of grass despite the steep prices, remaining comfortably high the whole time I was in the Bay area—as is only apropos for a recently-converted hippy's first time in San Francisco.

On one particular evening I remained on the Hill until after dusk, enjoying the evening sky's last light. As I began to make my way out of the park, I approached a shadowy grove of trees at the edge of the expanse of green grass. Though the sky was not yet without a reminder of the sun's setting, the trees obscured what little natural light remained.

In what seemed a mere moment, a shadow-obscured male figure approached unseen from my left side, said something I cannot precisely recall after placing a pistol to my left temple. I felt two concussions as I turned to retreat, my vision suddenly pixilating to a narrow tunnel—not unlike experiencing any significant bang on the head—and I was abandoned of my consciousness far before I hit the ground.

Next thing I knew I was standing on the other side of this grove of trees, just off Hippy Hill, disoriented and bewildered, but without the expected holes in my head—and it was now daytime!!

"What the fuck just happened?" I asked myself. "Did I dream that? 'BANG-BANG?' Did I sleep in the trees? I know I didn't go back to the hostel last night . . . what the fuck?!?!" I didn't even have a headache, and certainly no blood gushing out some hole or holes in my head.

I gazed around at the sunlit park setting and contemplated the absurdity of this most bizarre of situations, indeed quite dazed and confused (please pardon the cliché). After a few moments attempting to regain my bearings and composure, I noticed an attractive young woman sitting in an open grassy span. She was sporting a recently shaved-head and wearing a lacy white dress, and as her gaze met mine I decided to make my way towards the opening. Over the next few seconds, as I walked in the direction of this apparition, my cognizance of the preceding events faded from memory. Not until seven years later—perhaps to the day—would I recall the happenings of that odd evening, and specifically the percussive event which turned that nefarious night into day; led back to this lost memory by a mysterious woman, a mistress of disguise, who rather reminded me of this woman sitting on the patch of Golden Gate Park grass.

I sat several yards from this lovely figure in white and pulled out my notebook to write in my journal and work on some poetry. As I not so subtly smoked some sensimilla, I noticed she was taking note of me. A week or so later this first person encountered "on the other-side (?)" approached me during the Sunday afternoon drum-circle on Hippie Hill.

"Hi!" she said with a warm smile whilst offering me a small flower extended in her right hand, "my name is Aan—Angela . . . "

"Nice to meet you, I'm Jeffrey."

After half-a-moment of silence, I invited Angie to sit with me. She asked what I had been writing the other day. "Poetry," I told her.

"I write poetry too. I'd like to show you some sometime, if . . . if I have the opportunity."

Sort of randomly, she also told me she was into "role-playing" whilst we sat on the grassy hillside, enjoying the wild rhythms and melodies of drums, flute, and whatever other instruments were engaged in the weekly improv sesh, and sharing bowls of herb and joints with others sitting round us. I admit, I presumed she meant by "role-playing" some sorta San Francisco fetish sorta somethin'. I soon took a different interpretation of this statement, however—excepting of course when she brought out the maid's outfit complete with puffy petticoat one time . . .

Angie and I strolled to Strawberry Hill to ride a paddle boat around this hill's moat, ate some Middle Eastern cuisine, then headed to her studio apartment, just off lower-Haight. The first thing I noticed as we entered her domicile was *a large tapestry of Ganesh* on the wall at the head of her bed!!

"You might not believe this . . ."

I told her of my supplication to Ganesha in Yosemite several days previous, the much smaller *murti* tapestry of Ganesh at the head of my sleeping bag, and she told of having made a similar request around the same time. I soon moved my things from the hostel and ended up staying with Angela for about three weeks.

A couple of interactions in our short but sweet relationship became important clues informing my endeavors to discern the meaning of a bizarre storyline, clues later pieced together that would vex my already broadened paradigms and expanded consciousness.

A few days after our meeting, Angie showed me some of her poetry, apparently typed on an antique typewriter (judging by the font) on plain white paper. Upon examining these words, I realized they were in fact Ani Difranco lyrics.

"Very nice," I said as I handed them back, silently contemplating any number of scenarios regarding these indie-pop lyrics presented as personal poetry. *Is she a plagiarist? Is Angie really Ani—thus the mispronunciation of her own supposed name at our introduction? Is Angie role-playing as Ani Difranco role-playing as an anonymous person?* On another occasion I asked her to play the guitar that sat in the corner of the otherwise nigh empty apartment. She replied that she was "trying to give it a rest for a while."

After a few quite blissful weeks with this sweet and somewhat mysterious lover, I boarded the Green Tortoise bus for a ten-day cross-country trip to the east coast. After our parting, Angie apparently made a few attempts to contact me, and I likewise made a few attempts to call her when I was back in the Bay area. I haven't seen or communicated directly with her since, however, unless a mysterious woman I encountered about seven years after this in the Bay Area was Angie, yet again playing roles . . .?

Revelations of Life and Death: The Golden Gate?

Many miles and experiences later, I was in California holding tickets to fly from LA to Delhi. I was staying with my friend Joe in the Sebastopol area, an hour or so north of the Golden Gate Bridge. We were passing through downtown at dusk on a balmy yellow-sky Friday evening when I intuitively sensed I should check out what was goin' on at the bars. Tom, a friend of Joe's, stopped the small sedan at my request and I hopped out and walked round the corner to O'Connell's or O'Farrell's or some such local venue for drinking and dancing, music and other delights.

The chalkboard at the door touted the evening's band, "D'Gin" or some such seeming cipher. I've revisited potential meanings of this playful appellation, and come up with at least three probable intentions: Dig-In, Da' Gin (fermented juniper berries) and Djinn (genie), or some such clever derivation. I bought a pint of a local microbrew and danced my way towards the back end of the bar and towards the stage. The vocalist, a tiny little dready mama with a stellar voice, immediately made eye contact with me, raising one eyebrow to form a rather distinctive wrinkle on her forehead. She reminded me a bit of Angela, and was a perfect doppel to Ani Difranco—so far as I could recall either woman's appearance.

    Two of my friends from the area had fed me the information that Ani D. owned a house near Santa Rosa, was involved with a festival in Guerneville, and had been playing with an anonymously named band at small venues in the area. Ah, now everything comes into focus . . . ?

    The band on stage was by no means amateur, and I recognized some of the songs as Ani D's, though the very professional renderings were a bit different than any I had heard in recordings. The vocalist even executed a particular Ani stage move I had only seen performed as effectively by my good friend Star/Jessica, and of course by Ani D herself on video (I had not yet seen her perform live at this point, unless with an assumed identity on this evening in Sebastopol).

    Danced till first set-break, then sat at the bar. The mystery vocalist sat down a seat away and ordered a beer. I complemented her music and introduced myself. She told me her name was "MeMe" or "MiMi," pronounced like a repetition of the personal pronoun. The tenor of her intonation indicated an intended sarcasm, as if to say, "and you *know* that's not my name." We exchanged a few other pleasantries, then she abruptly turned her head in a manner rather like rolling ones eyes with the whole of one's head, and then walked backstage.

    Later I smoked a bowl of some NorCal heady-nuggets (very good marijuana) with some guys from her band and a few random others in the parking lot behind the bar. When I asked one of the band-members his occupation, he replied, "Oh, these days my life pretty-much just revolves around *MeMe*." The same sardonic tone seemed to convey the same subtle message: "and you *know* that is not her name."

Next day I investigate. At Incredible Records I leafed through the sizable collection of Ani Difranco CDs. On the cover of a more recent release, a portrait of Ani with dreadlocks bore a more than slight resemblance to "MeMe." An older album cover— from about the time of my SF love affair with Angela—showed Ani with a shaved head, and indeed I perceived certain similarities between this photo and my recollections of Angie's visage.

At a coffee house in Cotati later that day (or the next?), a woman I happened to engage in casual conversation mentioned a free Berlin show in Golden Gate Park. Still in investigative mode, I started to add stuff up: free concert by a powerful female vocalist from the eighties (think "Metro," not "Take My Breath Away"), and thus a likely influence on Ani; Golden Gate Park, the location where I'd met Angela . . .

Didn't find the show, but whilst sitting on Hippie Hill I noticed a short woman sitting to my left with a couple of openly affectionate lesbians in her company (fitting well respective M.O.'s for both Ani D *and* Angie—both self-avowedly bisexual). She looked directly at me and raised one eyebrow, displaying the same pattern of wrinkled forehead flesh I had noted on the singer's face a few days previous. I made bumming a cigarette and a loaded bowl my excuse to investigate at closer range.

This woman, no dreads and only an inch or so of hair on her head, told me her name was "Slide," then tossed her head away —like rolling one's eyes with the whole of one's skull—in the same manner as "MeMe" had done after our brief exchange at the bar. Hint: think of the TV series "*Sliders*" (plot deals with wormholes in time—*gate*ways to other-dimensional Californias), and perhaps also pertinent, recall "Marla Singer" in *Fight Club* standing in "the power-cave" in lieu of the gleeful penguin, takin' a puff of a cigarette and uttering only the imperative, "Slide . . ."

Slide walked off into the trees, and I wondered if perhaps her head-tossing gesture meant I should follow. Uncertain, however, I remained seated, continued puffin' with the others sitting there, then left the scene all the more intrigued as these strangely connected events continued to unfold.

Next day, again seated on the hill, I noticed a woman with the same body-size and shape who on queue stared back with the trademark raised-eyebrow-wrinkled-forehead-look clearly displayed. This woman had straight long brown hair, however, wore a non-descript light blue down jacket and blue jeans, and was in the company of some similarly conservatively clad college kids. She and I were the last two on the hill just after the sun faded. We exchanged a few slightly awkward pleasantries, then went our respective ways. I was quite certain this was the same woman as "Slide" and "MeMe." I was quite baffled.

Third day sitting on Hippie Hill, I once again encountered a woman whose face and forehead and body seemed certainly to belong to the same woman, in yet another guise. This version was sitting in the midst of a gathering of SFSFs (I learned of this acronym of an appellation from some acquaintances whose gutter-punkish paths had lead them to the company of the "San Francisco Scum-Fucks"). This manifestation of said mistress incognito had long straight black hair, wore black patent-leather from unsnapped newsboy hat to knee-length shiny leather boots, and looked straight at me with the same characteristic facial expression as the previous three *incarnations* (for lack of a better word).

Again using shared smoke to gain a closer vantage, I sat three or four persons away from this sexy leather-clad mystery lady. I loaded a bowl to legitimize my continued presence amongst this rather savage tribe, observing with an attempt at nonchalance. A few other park inhabitants joined the flock, including a rather rotund black man that bore a startling resemblance to Forest Whitaker who reclined just below me on the hill.

I had encountered this fellow quite a few times over the previous few days. Upon the occasions of our paths meeting, he would generally approach me asking for money or herb. "Hey, ya' got any weed? Gimme some weed," he'd say with a whiney nasal tone, or the same spiel, replacing "weed" with "money." In retrospect I recalled that years previous some random Rainbow hippie happened to have randomly mentioned that Ani D. and Forest W. were friends. Ah, now things come into focus . . . more absurdly yet!!

Whilst reclined below me on the hill this fellow began to fidget and then began to gyrate his hips in a rather grotesque fashion. I immediately thought of the fat demon Siva stands upon in *Nataraja* pose. Following this intuition, I turned the sole of my right foot towards this fellow. He started to squirm as if suddenly very uncomfortable, then cried out, "SIVA!" and then stood to his feet and walked away. *Just as I had thought! Ha, ha!!* A few moments later, a senior member of the gang, short but broad and burly, approached me.

"We decided we're gonna have a conference now, and it's time for you to move!!" he growled in a not unfamiliar, labored and deliberately low and gruff tone—the kind of sometimes artificially raspy articulation adopted by many crusty older homeless men or veteran A-campers ("alcohol-camp" at Rainbow Gatherings).

"I'm actually comfortable where I'm at," I responded, seated in half-lotus, and quite appropriately ending my sentence with a preposition, to which he followed with something quite like the imperative, "You better fuckin' move or I'm gonna fuckin' kick your head off!!"

"You know, this is a public park, and if you and your friends don't want to sit by me, you can move," said I, not willing to cow within view of this mysterious woman, genie, goddess, or whatever she was, despite whatever hesitations and trepidations instinct or conditioning might be want to elicit.

The whole of the crew, with the notable exception of the mysterious *femme fatale*, then began to hurl their refuse at me. Luckily the projectiles were McDonald's sacks and wrappers, plastic bottles and paper cups, and not glass 40oz. bottles, dirty needles or whisky flasks. In the midst of this barrage, the leather-clad lady leaned forward, looked my way, and said in a rather stern yet calm voice, "You should move." I gladly took the opportunity for a graceful retreat, yet left this scene with more questions and few answers. Who, and as importantly, *what* was this being, appearing in so many different guises? though not by given evidences a shape-shifter, perhaps a djinn? a goddess (and possibly even with a capital "G")? and certainly at least a masterful Mistress of Disguise.

Later that night at the Haight Street entrance to the park I was puffin' with some random hippie when a small dready kid not much over eighteen stumbled out of the dark, bleeding from a few places on his face and carrying himself as if he had broken ribs.

"Eight of 'em jumped me! Eight of the motherfuckers jumped me and beat the shit outa me . . . all I did was ask for a cigarette," he said, a few tears falling o'er bloodied cheeks from blackened eyes.

I wrapped a wool blanket around him, concerned he might go into shock in the chilly San Francisco evening air, and then tried to call emergency services. The injured individual then wandered off into the city night wrapped in the gray blanket before I could secure him some medical attention, to my slight dismay.

The next morning I made my way down Haight Street from my bed in the bushes deep in the park. A few blocks down Haight I encountered a young couple moving things into a moving van. They stopped me and asked if I wanted to make a few bucks. I obliged them, and spent somewhere near an hour carrying tables and chairs and TVs and so forth down a narrow flight of stairs. The fellow was moving back to the Midwest, Michigan or Ohio or some such. After emptying the apartment we all stopped for a smoke.

As we stood in front of the stoop and I had a chance to study faces, I thought for more than a moment that the female of the pair looked more than mildly familiar, save that she was three to four inches taller than the figure I had been encountering, and she didn't quite give me "the look," though had the short hair of "Slide," a newsboy hat (plaid wool and not black patent leather, snapped closed) and she *almost* raised her eyebrow appropriately to present the by now psychically imprinted or leastwise well memorized forehead wrinkle pattern.

I walked away nearly certain I was delusional, thought it must be merely my poor mind was imagining this face's repetitive apparition. Had someone dosed my morning coffee? Had I slipped over the fine line between insightfulness and insanity? genius and mental degeneration? I bought a cup of coffee and smoked a bowl to think it over.

That evening I was yet again sitting on Hippie Hill, taking no warning from the violence of the previous day and evening. The sun was nearly set, and there were at most a couple of other people remaining on the green grassy slope. I was about to get up to leave when I noticed the woman I had met whilst moving furniture earlier in the day. She was on the hill at about the same elevation as I, and twenty to thirty yards or so to my left.

She turned her head to look my way, and lifted one eyebrow to fully form "the look." Because of the bend of her knees, the cuffs of her bell-bottoms were lifted enough to reveal that she was wearing elevator shoes (if the proper term for the then-hip super-thick-healed footwear) with THREE TO FOUR INCH SOLES!!!! I was NOT delusional in my earlier identification: it was indeed the same woman! She immediately stood and started down the hill towards Haight Street, towards the grove of trees (where seven years previous . . .). I decided I had to ask, needed to clarify, must understand . . . WHAT THE FUCK?!?!?!

I caught up with her at the edge of the trees.

"Hi! So how did the rest of the move go?"

"Oh, fine," or some such said she.

After a couple more unsubstantial sentences were exchanged, and before I had the chance to ask her anything of her "true" identity or connection with these other uncannily similar figures, I was suddenly blindsided by a blow to my left lower lip from a fist flying from out of the shadows. Only mildly fazed, I managed to do some sort of fancy wrist-lock with my left hand as my shadowy assailant drew his fist back for a second punch, and then responded as automatically with three quick rights to his head. This was a rather uncharacteristic response, by the way, as I am generally non-violent by nature and I am not trained in any martial art.

Still grasping my assailant's wrist as he was reeling from the punches I had delivered, he exclaimed rather dazedly,

"Hey, that's not fair! You're not s'pose ta' grab somebody's hand, you're just s'pose ta' beat 'em down!!"

"Oh, I'm sorry! I didn't realize there was some unwritten code to street fighting," I replied, rather more calmly than I would have guessed I would've, considering the situation.

"But . . . those were some good hits!" he added, extending his hand almost as if not of his own will or volition. I grasped his hand, gave him a half-hug, and said, "Well, I love ya' brother."

"Well, I don't love you!" he said, retreating a step or two, perhaps afraid I might try to kiss him or something.

"That's OK, you don't have to," I said as I started to walk away. Of course the mystery woman had left the scene by this point.

A few steps into the trees and further towards the tunnel that leads to Haight Street, another fist came out of the darkness, striking me in the same spot on my already bloodied left lower lip. I did not even stop to face this second attacker—among other reasons, because I assumed more black-clad SFSFs might materialize from out of the woods to take me on as a pack, as they had with the dready kid the night before.

As my head was buzzing from the combination of two punches, vision a bit blurred, a memory returned that shook me to the core: seven years previous and just before I had met Angela, it was not two punches, but *two bullets* that were delivered to my head at this very spot. I had been lured back to this site, perhaps *precisely* seven years after my initial altercation in this precise location, to have my memory restored—to be granted the realization that I had passed on to "the other side," or some such shit. Overwhelmed by this bizarre realization, I quickly made my way down Haight Street, and I have not returned to Golden Gate Park since. Since and at that moment of realization knocked back into my head, I have sifted through many other memories and from various evidences have been given cause to wonder: has this sort of thing happened to me before? since? Indeed, after a good bit of retrospection and contemplation and reflection on certain past events, I believe and have good evidences, it has . . .

I walked hurriedly down the nearly deserted street, still trying to put things together, tears more than once falling as my steps carried me down Haight towards the east. I checked into a hostel, and next morning took a bus to Cotati. As I hiked towards Sebastopol from the bus stop, I noticed a large and conspicuous banner hanging from a privacy fence next to and facing the highway. It read, "YOU ARE MISSED, JEFFREY!" Yet another clue, hint or allegation strewn before my path, whether to clarify or misdirect . . .

For the next three weeks or so I stayed at Joe's. Before this fateful stay in San Francisco I had already missed the bus to pick-up my passport in time to catch a train or plane or bus in time to get to LAX in time to board my non-refundable courier-flight to Singapore to then fly to Delhi to begin a trek to Mount Kailash, so I decided to go to the National Rainbow Gathering, a hippie thing held somewhere in the National Forest every summer since 1972.

To offer a glimpse inside the mist-shrouded and mysterious camps of these many and variegated magical peoples who migrate to alternating states' wild places each summer for this celebratory rendezvous: wander with me now, if your imagination will allow, down a mountainous dirt road, sometimes only one lane-wide. You'll notice stone cairns denoting that you're on the right track, else indicating where to turn. At main gate you'll be met by someone or other likely wearing tie-dies and uttering the traditional greeting "Welcome Home," and likely offering a hug and maybe a toke off a joint.

Between parking and the main meadow you may encounter "A-Camp," the only place where alcohol is acceptable at a Rainbow Gathering (one of very few basic guidelines or "rules" at Rainbow Gatherings other than common decency and respect). This is certainly the least *mellow* fire-circle to sit around at night. Said group might be described as not unlike bikers without hogs to ride and who also happen to have heightened environmental consciences,[6] else as gutter-punks who left the gutter behind for a seat by a rushing mountain river, but couldn't yet leave the 40oz back in the city. Bus Village(s) are obviously located where there is viable parking, thus also towards the outskirts, and are often site of a veritable art exhibition with VW Bugs and Buses and even sailboats soldered atop old school buses, as well as other modern gypsy-style hippy wagons custom-designed and embellished as if the certain product of an intense acid trip.

---

6   A-Campers tend to be among the last to leave "clean-up," and can certainly be lauded for their efforts in separating recyclables from compost and other refuse in spite of (because of?) the "alcohol vibe" presented 'round their space.

After a mile or two hike towards the interior of the gathering, you'll notice an increasing density of tents and hodgepodge campsites with Buddhist prayer-flags or tie-died tapestries bearing depictions of Hindu deities or Jimi Hendrix or a Grateful Dead bear or peace signs flying from tree branches. Music from distant drums or from a flutist making merry whilst wandering in a nearby field of flowers or spilling out from a guitar held tenderly by some brother or sister kickin' it by a smoldering log or the din of some random crew crying out "We love you!!!" in order to elicit the same peace-cry from some other kitchen or fire-pit circle, else some likely synchronized combination of these sounds meets your ears as you get closer to main meadow.

Kitchens begin to appear randomly amidst the forest's kaleidoscope camouflage, complete with cooking-fires, countertops built of woven sticks, and sometimes earthen-ovens to bake pizza or brownies for the masses. Community fire pits also increase alongside the trail, and all sorts of beautiful people start to manifest out of the forest greenery and the shadows of tall trees. Naked earth-goddess-mammas wearing only glittery body-paint and fairy-wings walk by, gazing at backpack-clad newcomers with exceedingly dilated pupils and blissful smiles as they offer the appropriate "Welcome Home," and often offer a bare-breasted hug to whatever random homecoming hippie, male or female. Keep in mind, however, this is no free-love fest in the late-60's sense, and respect and reverence accompanies the nakedness here, through and through. Adults and children play in the field and forest, and wild people in many states of dress and consciousness sit and dance 'round wild drum circles that often last all night.

If you pass by Yoga Meadow, you might see a certified *tai chi* master giving lessons for free next to an *Ashtanga* yoga instructor, likewise teaching willing practitioners an ancient healing art for no charge. You would almost certainly hear chants of "Hare Krishna . . ." if you passed near the ISKCON tent (they make really tasty if over-sweetened Indian food, and pretty descent chai, by the way), hymns to Jesus if you happen by "Jesus Camp," or perhaps pagan chants to Mother Earth or a Hebrew prayer or random (or synchronistically spoken) Sanskrit mantras issued from some circle or other within the greater circle of the gathering site.

Laughter and kind greetings and the smell of weed are in the air just about everywhere, and an overall harmony generally ensues in the midst of so much diversity. I've never yet heard of a skirmish between the Jesus-campers and Fairy-Camp (gay/lesbian camp) at a gathering, nor of any pitched battles between Serenity Ridge (an AA/Twelve-Step kitchen) and A-Camp.

I admit I have yet to see a Halal camp pop-up at such an event, though I once happened upon a Kosher camp called "Jerusalem Kitchen" at a National Rainbow Gathering. Indeed, I'd imagine there'd be a much better chance of peace in the Middle East if you sat Jerusalem Kitchen down with whatever Islamic crew might consent to come to a Rainbow Gathering—"Mecca-Camp," maybe (yes, there is certainly such thing as a Muslim hippie). Simply fill a hookah with some good Lebanese hash and passed around some mushroom tea, and then let these peace-loving tree-huggers come up with the solution to the Palestinian/Israeli conflict. Else perhaps bring Israel's Knesset together with the Palestinian National Assembly on a small tropical island and dose the falafel or matzo for a similar outcome—though likely with a higher dosage required.

In the somewhat-center of this site of several thousands camped together peacefully there is a large meadow with a "Peace-Pole" posted in the middle, symbolizing the central theme of these gatherings. Food is free here, though everybody's s'pose to lend a hand where they can. Exchange of cash money is anathema here (unless to contribute to the "Magic Hat" fund for food and other necessities), and credit cards are not accepted. Trade-circle is the central marketplace, where blankets laid-out display hand-made drums, blown-glass pipes, hemp everything, tools and cool hippie clothes and chocolate bars—*for trade only*. Cannabis is the most stable currency (though that's the case in the U.S. generally), weed is smoked freely and reverently everywhere, and psychedelic explorations are not discouraged—though drugs are not allowed.

Shanti-sena, or "peace-force" (à la Gandhi), made up of anyone and everyone at a gathering, keeps good order and deals fairly with conflicts. If any responsible adults happen to hear someone call out this Sanskrit mantra they are obliged to make a beeline to the scene of whatever conflict to help resolve, and might be noted that the mere intonation of these syllables is supposed to invoke peace. Nonetheless, the Fed's can't seem to stay away, sending in the LEO's with firearms to harass the peaceful under the guise of "protect and serve." These "forest-cops" with their side-arms are often told, generally politely, that we don't much appreciate "guns in our church," and these intruders are always preceded by calls of "Six-up!!!" to let others down the trail know they ought to extinguish and pocket all pipes and joints till the nuisance passes. Other Forest Service personnel who sometimes show up, biologists or botanists or water-quality surveyors and so forth, are generally received as less intrusive guests than the ones who think we need policing and who carry pistols into our peaceful assemblies and places of prayer.

I have actually heard of more than one "defection" from the Fed's ranks to the freak-side. Indeed, I've been made privy to multiple reports of forest rangers deciding it wasn't too late to "tune-in" and so forth, stripping off light-green uniforms and joining their long-lost family in a joyful reunion (often after having been offered a tiny piece of perforated paper or a chunk of chocolate covered fungus).

All in all, this rag-tag gathering of peaceful dissidents maintain a pretty tight ship, with no leaders and no designated or elected representatives, no centralized planning to speak of, and consensus as the primary "rule of order." On the Fourth of July, upwards of twenty to fifty-thousand freaks stand in a massive circle round the "Peace-Pole" to utter the sacred syllable "AUM" (which is, by the way, the root of the Judeo-Christian "Amen," and Muslim "Amin"—there is a subtly pronounced "ñ" at the end of AUM) intended to promote world peace and harmony.

By the time clean-up crew is gone, scarce a trace of these thousands is left to sully the wilderness scene, and even skeptical forestry bureaucrats and field agents are generally surprised that a bunch of pot smokers and trippers are so fucking conscientious and such responsible stewards of the land. No fire pit is left intact, shitters and compost holes are buried and concealed, trails unmade and reseeded with native seed, and every last trace of human habitation or litter is remediated or removed. You'd be hard-pressed to find even a single cigarette filter remaining amongst the natural forest floor debris by the time we're all gone.

Anyways, a few days into my stay at this particular National Rainbow Gathering, which was held near Mt. Shasta that year, I was walking along the road at the edge of the site when what did I spy but a familiar small-framed woman with short hair sitting by a tree, singing blissfully to herself and any who might happen to hear her. As she noticed me approaching she ceased her song, reached out her right hand with index and pinkie finger extended and exclaimed (one eyebrow raised in characteristic expression),

"San Francisco says, 'What's up, yo'?!?!'"

Before I had a chance to formulate a response, she continued, "C'mere, c'mere, I got somethin' for ya,'" beckoning me to approach with waves of her hand.

She rummaged through her belongings and retrieved something in a small square plastic package.

"Here, you might need to give this to somebody sometime, er somethin'." It was a reflective emergency-blanket, still folded and in the wrapper!

"Sit down! Sing somethin' with me!"

I sat to her left on the side of the dusty road and attempted to recognize the lyrics of anything I might know as she tried out a number of well-known tunes, but to little avail—I've only a very few popular songs committed to memory. We abandoned this shaky endeavor as a couple of other hippies happening by stopped to chat. I stood and walked on as she conversed with these others, uncertain of how precisely to perceive this last (certain) encounter with said mystery woman.

By the way: just a little ways down the trail a fellow camper, wet from head to toe from some likely trip into the creek, just happened to asked if I happened to have anything to help him stay warm on his hike back to his camp. I gave him the still packaged and folded reflective-emergency-blanket and continued towards Main Circle, skipping-on-down the trail.

Afterthought for the still skeptical . . .

Mind you, dear reader, in case you had your questions: I was *not* under the influence of any mind altering substance during these encounters, save a bit of weed, and on occasion non-intoxicating levels of alcohol. Neither of these could have altered my perceptions to the degree necessary for this to have been some series of delusions or illusions—save as illusion is what all of human experience is at some level, as some religions contend. Only towards the end of my stay at this gathering did I very reverently receive some smoke of DMT (said substance having been derived from *Valerus* grass or the root bark of a mimosa tree, by the way), a potent hallucinogen which does have the capacity to produce visions potent enough to be dubbed "delusion." Oh, and I also chanced to share in a cozy chat with Ram Das/Dr. Richard Alpert at his campsite—speaking of psychedelic spirituality and so forth—though didn't try any of the goodies likely to be found nearby.

This narrative of events is true, as much as any set of experiences I have known. Many of the conversations writ here are quoted verbatim, and all are at least very close approximations of the represented verbal exchanges. I have examined many scenarios that might render these series of events in some other guise, and no alternative explanations add up as well as what I have faithfully represented in the preceding, humbly offered for your consideration, dear reader.[7]

---

[7] Perhaps I should note: certainly should this narrative become published—which I fully intend—then it is not an unlikely scenario to expect, that someone or other with inside information comes forward to help me to fill in the blanks, and if by some odd chance you are that someone or other, please feel free to contact me to tell what you know of this twisted tale's truths and turns, else those principles of *maya* might help explain these events and experiences.

Towers, Trips and Tornadoes

    The vintage green greyhound bus with the words "Green Tortoise" stenciled on the side stopped after a full night of cruising, parking near the base of a great monolith misnamed "Devils Tower." Indeed, the popular title associating this large rock formation with the Judeo-Christian-Islamic embodiment of evil is not at all the proper name for said place. The current popular name is in fact a misinterpretation of the Lakota appellation meaning "Bear's Tower" or "Bear's Lodge."

    We had embarked on this journey from downtown San Francisco in the shadows of skyscrapers, man made promontories of concrete and steel, a stark contrast to this great granite rock reaching towards the sky, which in fact rose high from the erosion of the earth around it and thus did not actually rise at all, save when molten and deep underground. Nineteen or so travelers, mostly students or recent graduates from Europe, Australia and New Zealand, myself plus a couple more American hippies, and two designated and salaried drivers boarded the renovated antique coach to take the slow (if still somewhat scheduled) route across the northern United States. We had left the tall buildings behind, and where we now stood the only thing scraping the sky was a big rock that shall yet stand when the Transamerica Pyramid has long since fallen.

    Nineteen or so non-traditional tourists disembarked, stretching in salutation to the morning sky as we stepped out into the fresh-air and sunshine of my home state's wide-open spaces. On the somewhat-scheduled agenda of our tour was a circumambulation of this grand promontory, sacred to Native Americans for many, many moons (though only recently adopted as a location where prayer bundles tied with red ribbons dangle in pines growing on the slopes around the sacred tower's base, many likely asking that the white man goes back where he came from), and as a locus to where suburbanites in Bermuda shorts and Hawaiian shirts drive their RV's and SUV's as a summer vacation destination, often on their way to or from Wyoming's other top two tourist destinations, Yellowstone and Jackson Hole, or to neighboring Montana or South Dakota's Black Hills.

Several of us decided to make the sacred circumambulation, which oddly is counter-clockwise. This is an aberration from most sacred circular journeys that I know of—at least in the northern hemisphere—with the exception of the Bon Po pilgrimage around Mount Kailash, the primary abode of Siva and a center of devotion for Hindu, Jain, Buddhist and Bon Po alike, and is a promontory even recognized by Muslims as something of a sacred site.

I departed from the rest of the group, wanting some semblance of solitude as I went about this act of sacred reverence for this renowned rock not quite so lofty or high as Kailash, chanting Sanskrit mantras as I paced the well-worn American Indian trail. Though my choice of sacred song might seem inappropriate considering the context, Lakota, Cheyenne and other plains tribe languages actually contain numerous close cognates to Sanskrit words, vestiges of the influence of ancient Indian settlers (i.e., from the Indus Valley of the subcontinent now called India).

Indeed, Columbus wasn't wholly wrong then he called the inhabitants of the so-called New World "Indians." This is also evidenced by architectural similarities between Inca, Aztec and Mayan Temples and those of ancient India, as well as by the numerous cognates to Sanskrit words scattered throughout many (if not most) Native American tongues.[8]

---

8   The Lakota Sioux word for "sun" is *anpétu wi,* which quite obviously corresponds to the Sanskrit word *anapayati,* which translates, "before the sun makes a start." As the sun rises in India after it has risen in America, this is clearly a cognate, and a reminder for the early settlers of where they were in relation to their original homeland. The Cheyenne word for "sun" is *ése'he,* which corresponds to the Sanskrit word *asti,* which translates as "setting sun," i.e., the direction to India. Cheyenne for "moon" is *Taa'é-esehe,* quite close to the Sanskrit word *taiSa,* a term denoting a particular full moon. The Aztec call themselves *astika,* which is a cognate of the Sanskrit *astika,* which translates as "one who believes in the existence of God/another world," Maya is the Sanskrit word for this illusory reality and Maha Maya is the Hindu Goddess of Illusion, and the Apache call themselves *"Inde,"* i.e., really "Indians," people from the Indus Valley.

According to a commonly repeated version of the Native American mythology regarding the origin of said significant geological formation we were circumambulating on this summer's day, a group of sisters were being pursued by a giant bear, desperately seeking refuge from the mighty predator's wrath. Hoping for a miracle, they hopped on top of a felled tree's stump and cried out to whatever god or goddess or benevolent spirit, which promptly caused this stump to rise into the sky to deliver the maidens from danger. The great bear clawed at the sides of this elevating log, resulting in the deep grooves that run from top to bottom of the purportedly petrified stump, and the sisters—varying in number according to various accounts I've encountered—then proceeded to ascend into the heavens to become some constellation or other.

Perhaps the spaceship that hovers above the tower in *Close Encounters* was the triumphal return of these sisters to whence they left this planet. If it is so, 't would be rather telling of their assessment of the state of things on this once sparsely populated, unpolluted, wild and free land: the spaceship returned to the sky.

After circling this great igneous phallus, we reboarded the Tortoise and drove on to the Pine Ridge Reservation, where we stopped to meet the westbound bus and to partake of Indian tacos at the home of a Lakota family. According to one of our drivers, a Green Tortoise tour bus had once wandered off the intended path and "randomly" ended up at this homestead. When they sought directions back to the highway, the resident family offered to feed the bewildered batch of hippie tourists, as is the custom amongst the truly civilized peoples of this world. Ever since, this spot has become a regular stop for Tortoise tourists, and thus a helpful source of income for this kind Lakota family living on an otherwise exceedingly impoverished reservation.

As the sky grew dark from an approaching storm and the waning of the day, both groups started to set up tarp awnings from the sides of the parallel-parked buses, anticipating a shower. I refrained from assisting in what I figured a futile task, recognizing in the approaching clouds the signature of a mighty gust-front. As the first drops of rain descended, a wind increased to the point that the rain, also increasing, began to fall as much horizontally as vertically. I now joined the crew attempting to wrestle the tarps away from the fierce gale. After somewhat effectively folding and stowing the tarps, all piled back into their respective buses.

We had ample room and ample alcohol (our crew had purchased copious amounts of booze and beer in anticipation of our rendezvous with the westbound bus), so we started to party inside our temporary traveling home. I rolled up several joints or "spliffs," a mixture of marijuana (SF kindbuds) and tobacco mixed with other smokable herbs (American Spirit "Pow-Wow Blend") and some hashish.[9]

A few of us started to dance in the bus, and as the rain slowed we decided to pile out into the cleansed night air, spinning ecstatically to Rusted Root's "Send Me On My Way" in ankle deep water and mud. Among those who joined in this rapturous dance was a beautiful young British woman in her early twenties whose name eludes me, and yet who I rather fancied amongst this party which maintained an exceptionally favorable gender-ratio (from a straight male's perspective, that is). This lithe yet curvy English girl would often comment that my appearance reminded her of "Grizzly Adams," and with a gleam in her eyes which told she might have had a want to wrestle, Indian-style.

As we wildly danced, I remember this lovely figure's long and very dark brown hair, doused and flying round her lily face as she spun. I've recollection of her relishing the raindrops moistening her skin and dousing her dress, barefoot and free as she and I and several others spun round-and-round like Sufis in this storm's waning and by then only light rain. This ecstatic dance and transcendent hints of romance in this deluge's demise might well characterize what compelled and propelled my early journeys in general, the freedom to truly appreciate life's beauty and the Divine from outside the bounds of stodgy tradition and liturgy, convention or pretension or pretense of propriety, to find and make those moments worthy of literary and artistic praise and transcendent gratification.

---

9 Actually I ought to note, the term "spliff" is an American hippie misusage of the Jamaican/Rastafarian term, which refers to marijuana buds rolled in a marijuana leaf with no admixture of tobacco.

The next day we were scheduled to take a seven-and-a-half mile hike in the Badlands, a large section of barren sandstone hills that rise from the South Dakota plains. As most of my fellow alternative tourists made their way to the Lakota family's house for breakfast, I decided to check out a line of trees that stood about a quarter-mile from the house across a brilliant green meadow. I had a want to bathe, you see, and knew that in this country, water and trees are generally found together.

A dog that followed me to the creek had markings indicating that his ancestors had likely accompanied the people of this tribe for many, many moons. As I stripped and cautiously climbed into the cold clear knee-deep water, the dog sat patiently waiting on the creek's bank, his or her gaze alternating between me and the surrounding area as if standing guard. I have little doubt this canine was serving as some sort of spirit-guide-dog, and that what I discovered upon stepping out of the purifying waters was indeed quite intentionally placed.

In a round and rather ripe patty deposited beside the stream by some bovine fertilizer factory I noticed several small parasol-shaped growths of a dark-brown hue complete with purple-brown gills. I knew from my amateur but well enough informed mycological knowledge that these were almost certainly *Cilocybin dungophilus*, a rather mild form of psychedelic shroom. I plucked most of these diminutive mushrooms, assuming they were indeed meant for my consumption and leaving at least one or two for spore. I sampled one to see if a bellyache ensued, then later downed the rest as we arrived at the visitor center at the entrance to the Badlands.

The sky was overcast and the air was hot and humid, sure signs of more storms in this often parched land. I again went my own way as the majority of our group started on the scheduled hike. I turned off onto a side trail and found a nook between two barren sandstone hillsides where a small arch had formed from erosion. I sat next to the arch and gazed at the vividly verdant valley below and at the astonishingly brilliantly colored automobiles passing by on the two-lane paved road. As I sat I smoked the remainder of my hashish on some bright-green-red-haired-purple-Cush nuggets, enjoyed whatever whimsical dissociative daydreams and contemplated the wonder of it all, etc.

The mushrooms had kicked-in, though due to the rather minimal psilocin content—i.e., compared to the commercially grown *cubensis* mushrooms I normally consume when I do shrooms—I knew this would be a rather mild trip. A pleasant yet not overwhelming alteration of vibrations. After a while sitting and chanting a few Sanskrit ditties and being bemused by the sight of toy-cars trekking the two-lane down below, I decided I'd better try to catch up with the rest of the crew doing the hike.

After returning to the main trail and a few more short stops and side-trips to stare at the pretty rocks and wonder, I noticed a distant rumble of thunder coming from behind. As I quickened my pace down the trail, it seemed but moments until the flashed of lightening and claps of thunder had overtaken me. Only a light sprinkling of rain was falling as I noticed that the intermittent noise of thunder had given way to a constant rumble. I turned to look to the left, and watched in awe as an immaturely formed funnel started to descend on a mesa at the edge of the valley.

"I may be trippin' but I ain't trippin' that hard!" I said or thought to myself.

The small funnel was falling on the mesa at a forty-five degree angle, kicking up dust and making an awful roar. As I gazed at this terrible wonder of nature, I soon realized the funnel and the wall cloud from which it had descended were heading straight towards where I stood. I turned and quickly continued down the trail, picking up my pace to a fast-walk.

After a few minutes not watching the progress of the spinning mass of clouds, I turned to see that this once poorly formed cyclone had taken the shape of a thin pair of legs. After a few moments to convince myself of the verity of what I was viewing, I concluded that indeed, my assessment was correct: a very powerful double-funnel was descending on the trail a quarter-mile or so behind me.

At this point I knew it was time to run, to run away with all due haste from these terrible anthropomorphic whirling winds that had now changed course from the original angled path and were quite definitely following me down the center of the valley. I was being tailed by a pair of giant legs, not quite walking behind me in the Badlands, and seemingly threatening to kick the shit out of me in the midst of this dry dusty valley. Or perhaps—to offer an appropriately trippy image comes to mind—imagine Wiley Coyote being chased by two sexy legs clad in fishnets and a short skirt with puffy white petticoats descending from the sky and riding on roller-skates.

I must have been at the least a slightly silly sight to see, as well: a skinny, bare-chested pale-skinned man in short-pants with bushy long-hair and an oversized-beard in size 13 hiking boots swiftly running away from a two-legged tornado, all whilst singing an imagined Native American song in falsetto: "Hay ya, hay ya, ya, hay ya . . . ."

After having run upwards of a couple of miles, I stopped to evaluate the progress of my pursuer. At first I couldn't make out the form of the tornado, though the freight train like rumble was still sounding. As I refocused, I realized that the whirlwind was no longer a tight double funnel, but had become partially transparent as it was now over a mile-wide. It is possible my moderately altered perception caused me to misgauge the breadth of this beast, but not my much. I watched in wonder as what appeared to be objects the size of trees (or at the least large limbs) were slowly circling in this monstrous vortex.

Again I proceeded to run, glancing from side to side to try to find some deep eroded ditch or other shelter from this storm's rage. I ran and ran, then paused once more, turning to see a great tower of wind and clouds, rain and hail and dirt rising from earth to sky, not so wide as before, but now a solid black pillar somewhere between a quarter and a third-of-a-mile wide.

I contemplated this form as like the sky and earth in tumultuous lovemaking. I thought of the great linga of the Destroyer and the yoni of the Wrathful Goddess. I thought of the power and majesty of the Divine, at least emblematically manifest as a column of two-hundred plus mile-an-hour winds, dirt, water and random debris spiraling 'round in the Badlands, and by all appearances quite intentionally following me down a dusty worn-sandstone valley.

Again I continued down the trail, and finally found shelter from this mighty vortex beneath a bridge. The tornado passed my safe haven with a roar, and continued to follow the general course of the trail. I immediately thought of the other hikers and those on the bus, which was to meet us at the end of the trail, asked whatever presiding agency that these be spared from the fury of these terrible winds, and then hurriedly hiked the remainder of the seven-and-a-half miles.

As I reached the trail's end, I found that the rest of the crew was indeed safe, obliviously preparing lunch on picnic tables. I immediately told of my experience with these seemingly divinely directed winds, only to be chastened by an indictment of my altered mental state,

"Oh Jeffrey, your just tripping!"

The other Tortoise tourists had experienced some of the winds of this storm, as well as a torrential downpour, but had been bypassed by the actual cyclone. When we stopped for fuel, however, an alert came over the radio warning of a large tornado in the Badlands area, verifying my assertions, and assuring me that the mushrooms I'd eaten weren't stronger than I'd assumed. Under an eerie green and red stormy sky, we reboarded the bus and continued on towards Chicago.

Circling a sacred tower. Spinning ecstatically in the rain and mud. Ingesting mushrooms that might readily be recognized as resembling a funnel dangling from a wall cloud. A tornado that seems to convey consciousness. I guess all this adds up and makes perfect sense, assuming you can detach yourself from the teachings you've been taught that tell you life lived and the mystical are unrelated, if you learn to unlearn those lies that maintain this material world has nothing to do with imagination or spirit or the sublime, and forget those purported "common sense" maxims that tell you that tales of a someone encountering the truly magical else meeting manifestations of the Divine are merely fairytales and fantasy. It sure makes sense to me. Now as to precisely what it all means . . .

Sasquatch in the Snoqualmie

Long before the white man wandered into the wilderness of the Rocky Mountains and to the west, the native peoples were aware of the existence of another intelligent hominid sharing the forests, and they generally respected and revered these cryptids as close cousins and even brethren (despite scattered stories of certain tribes that rather fearfully portray these mysterious mythical beasts). The Yakama tribe called these shy furry forest dwellers *ste ye mah*, words which denote "a spirit hidden by the woods." The Quinault refer to these behemoths as *tsadjatko*, and the Salish language names them *saskets* (thus the English derivation "sasquatch"), both of which translate into English simply as "the giant" or "giants." The Lakota call them *shiye tanka*, or "Big Elder Brother." The Tillamook (the tribe, not the cheese-makers) named them *yi dyi'tay* (not V*alençay* nor *fior de latte* nor *cheddar*), which means "wildman." Indeed, there are stories about and appellations for these massive yet nonetheless elusive animals throughout the lore of North American Indians.[10]

As any average American boy, I was fascinated by tales of encounters with Bigfoot. Episodes of *In Search of . . .* and various books from the Laramie Public Library inspired my youthful imagination and embedded a proverbial itch deep under my skin to seek out evidences proving the existence of this secretive species. I devoured reports regarding unexplained sightings of said cryptid, certainly a favorite amongst the menagerie of monsters and mythic beasts that trod the forested paths and swam the dark depths of my youthful imagination. I decided somewhere around the age of ten that I must indeed someday have an encounter with the mythical sasquatch.

Fifteen years later, give or take, I was with two others hiking back to base-camp in the wilderness of the Upper Sauk River drainage in the mountains above Darrington, Washington (an established hotspot for sasquatch sightings), when a chill or tingle rose up my spine, and I felt compelled to utter a proclamation of

---

10   For an apology for my unabashed use of this seemingly politically incorrect term, see footnote [8].

my prescient sense that we were going to "have an encounter." My companions and I were clearing trails of old growth deadfall and brush in the lush rain forests of the Cascade Mountains, and of course talk of sasquatch was regular fare for late-night chats amongst our crew whilst we passed pipes or joints, sipped beers and shot the shit 'round the firepit.

On this day, as my coworkers and I were casually chatting about the subject of sasquatch on our hike back to camp, said sensation of the presence of prescience pleasantly stimulated my central nervous system, alerting me to the gravity of a mini-revelation.

"We're going to have an encounter!!" I announced excitedly as Jonah and I and a local kid on our crew were marching down the trail, laden with two-person (crosscut) saws, axes and bow saws. "I just know it!!" I added with a rather giddy laugh.

Jonah and I had met at a coffee house in Bellingham, Washington a number of months previous. We chatted and played some drums, smoked some herb and became fast friends. It was Jonah who had discovered this amazing employment opportunity when he and a friend had been forced to abandon their intentioned backpacking trip covering a section of the Pacific Crest Trail, as the pair and all their gear got soaked in a storm of sleet and cold rain up in the high country. He and his companion had thus been forced to follow an alternate trail down to the nearest Forest Service road, and upon reaching the trail head happened to encounter a man and a herd of goats wearing saddles and loaded with saws and axes and winches and such. In spite of weariness and a wish or want to return to civilization, the two saturated hikers stopped to inquire about the oddity of saddled goats. Gary the goat-herding Forest Service contractor offered employment on the spot.

Meanwhile, I had been biding my time on the sidewalk in front of Stuart's Coffee House in downtown Bellingham, waiting for *something* to happen. In spite of the mostly pleasant company of other birds of the same feather—un- or underemployed hippies, ravers, punks, freaks of whatever flavor, students, and various and sundry sorts of coffee addicted (mostly-) potheads—I was feeling anxious, and sensed somehow that Jonah's return would herald an end to the rut I had slid into in this cloudy city in the northwestern corner of the continental United States.

As soon as Jonah arrived at Stuart's one sunny midday, just returned from the mountains to the southeast, I was already ready to go. We made a few last minute arrangements, Jonah said a few-hours long hi-and-bye to his girlfriend Cristina, and we hit the road sometime around midnight. We were bound for the Sauk River drainage, twenty-miles or so southeast of Darrington, Washington, a wilderness area where stands of enormous old growth timber still touch the sky in the lush rain forests on the western slopes of the Cascades.

After cruising through Darrington, a quaint hamlet immediately surrounded by picturesque towering peaks on three-sides, we met the end of the pavement and continued into the forest on a wide dirt and gravel road in the dark of night. Jonah kept his eyes open to search for the turn into the trail head campground whilst we blazed multiple bowls of beasters (British Columbian Cannabis) and jammed out to Jimi Hendrix or Dead Can Dance or some trance tune CD of Jonah's played on the stereo. Erstwhile entranced by the rhythms and vibrations of the road, Jonah realized we had missed our turn after we wandered winding up several switchbacks, so I spun the truck in a quick U-turn and we started back down the zigzagging road.

Jonah cautioned me to slow just as we reached our turn, which was at an exceedingly sharp angle from the truck's trajectory. As I tried the turn after something like a second of hesitation, I had to bring the truck to a halt as the 1963 Dodge Power Wagon's turning radius was quite a bit too wide to complete the turn in one motion. We were facing the forest, sitting perpendicular to the proper direction of traffic on the dirt drive that led to the trail head, when suddenly I had the sensation that we were rolling backwards. I pressed harder on the foot brake and engaged the parking brake at the same time Jonah uttered an urgent appeal,

"BRAKES!!"

"The brakes are on!" I replied to his anxious plea with an equally anxious response.

We were not rolling. The wheels were quite firmly planted on the hard-packed light-brown dirt drive, and yet we both continued to feel as if we were moving backwards. I gazed as if in a trance at the trees directly in front of us, which appeared to be moving away, but in a continuous motion that never quite caused them to recede into the distance. Jonah reported the same sensations, both visually and in terms of the sense of inner-ear balance.

It seemed to both of us as if we only lingered thus for a few minutes before I put the truck in reverse, then completed the turn. Shortly after we parked for the night, however, we noted that the drive from town to this site had taken well over an hour. Upon later clocking the distance of this drive—and even factoring in the fact that we'd passed the turn on this first time traveling to the trailhead—we concluded we had lost somewhere approaching an hour whilst we'd observed this anomaly of a forest repetitively or continually fading back from our perspective, both seated firmly on the bench seat of the Miraculous-Beast-Shanti-Mama.

Had we been abducted by aliens? Was it a "vortex" or a "wormhole" or some such time-space anomaly we had experienced on this mountain road during the dark of night? Had we perhaps entered a portal into another dimension? Certainly the extraordinary experiences we were to have over the coming weeks working and playing in this enchanted rain forest would lead us to conclude that one or another of these odd options was indeed a distinct possibility.

Next morning we met Gary, his partner Lucy, and their goats. Gary had long graying hair in a ponytail, and wore the appropriate facial hair to match his occupation. Lucy had slightly curly mid-length dark-hair, and as I recall from our brief meetings a rather pleasantly curved figure (and no goatee or other ungulate-like characteristics, I am happy to report). The pair had been contracted to clear several kilometers of trails here and elsewhere in Washington and were quite pleased we had shown up, as apparently good help was hard to find in this particular neck of the woods.

Our job was to remove deadfall from across the trail and cut the brush alongside to a few inches in height. Some of the fallen trees that blocked the pathway into the high country were upwards of five to six feet in diameter, and were no little task to cut through and winch or leg-press out of the way of hikers and horses (and goats) hoofing it up or down the mountain. Granted, these were not redwoods or giant sequoias, but as this area was designated wilderness we were required to use manual saws and axes on the still massive fallen trunks. Though this obviously required an extra expenditure of human labor, the relative quiet of a crosscut saw compared to a six-foot long chainsaw allowed us to encounter wildlife which otherwise would have hightailed it to the next valley over.

  Just past the trailhead was a small swamp filled with ferns and devil's club, a wide variety of funguses, mosses dripping from tree limbs and quite a number of species of aquatic plants growing in the still pools of water. Old growth cedars and Douglas fir grew to great heights above the marsh, rendering this part of the trail darker than pitch as soon as the sun would set behind the high peaks and allowing only a little sunlight to filter through so many layers of needled boughs and fringed fronds above even at high noon. A boardwalk and small bridges made up the better portion of this lower stretch of the path into one of the most magical patches of forest I have yet been blessed to experience.

  After this marshy fern-filled portion of the pathway, the corridor through the massive moss-embellished trees ascended sharply into a much younger forest. A steep scree slope to one side, and a likewise steep decent to the river beneath and to the other side, the trail twice crossed rushing spring- and snow-fed creeks that were tributary to the larger flow in the valley below. On one occasion we watched a small black bear scurrying up the rocky slope, rather startled by the scarcely seen sight of humans on this lightly travelled trail.

  The packgoats were generally a bit reluctant to cross the rushing waters of the rivulets, and would often hesitate at the banks with the proverbial stubbornness of a mule. These billies and nannies would scarcely even lower their bearded muzzles to partake of the clear cold drink, as their desert-dwelling ancestors had adapted to acquiring most of the moisture they required from whatever vegetation they might manage to locate in the barren scrub of their homelands in northern Africa, and the vegetation here in the Pacific Northwest rain forest was saturated. The parched and sawdust covered primates accompanying said cloven-hoofed beasts of burden, however, were always happy to arrive at these streams after long hours of sawing and chopping and winching variously sized logs and limbs and lumber out of the way and to one side of the trail, splashing the cold and refreshing flow on soiled faces and arms and even sometimes chancing a case of beaver-fever to taste of these revitalizing waters.

On the day of my prescient epiphany, we were heading downhill and had just crossed the second stream, carrying on with the usual bullshitting and banter, when my intuition indicated the certainty of the coming encounter. Indeed, Native American lore tells that sasquatch are "spirit beings" and not mere animals, thus I'm supposing it likely this spiritual beasty transmitted the psychic message that let me know of his or her intentions to visit.

That night, as Jonah and I sat next to a roaring fire, sipping tea and smoking herb and cigarettes after a filling meal of brown rice and veggies, I began to get the feeling that we were being watched. Several times I scanned the forest around us with my headlamp, focusing the beam of light on a particular point between two trees where I sensed our voyeur was located. Jonah commented that I was wasting my batteries, so heeding his advice I turned off the lantern. No sooner had I set this headlamp down on the ground beside me, when a booming "CRACK" resounded through the forest from nigh exactly where I had suspected someone or thing was watching.

Now, this was no ordinary din in the darkness. Something exceedingly large had quite obviously broken an exceptionally large branch. We had been cutting and chopping and breaking and dragging all manner of lumber by saw and axe, hand and foot and winch, from one-inch-thick sticks to fallen trees nigh six-foot in diameter cut through twice and winched away to clear this trail of obstacles, and the noise this breaking branch made in the still and dark night indicated something quite exceeding heavy had either stepped upon a freshly fallen tree or limb of no small girth, else had become night-blinded by my lamp's light and had thus broken a large unseen limb on a standing tree. I immediately hopped to my feet.

"HOLY SHIT!" I proclaimed in surprise, "Jonah, that was something really fucking big!"

Jonah still sat, staring into the darkness.

"C'mon, man. Let's get in the camper, dude," I urged, as if the thin aluminum sheets, fiberglass insulation and pine paneling that made up the camper's walls would prevent a thousand-pound-plus beasty from getting at us if it had the urge.

"Naw. If it's a bigfoot, I wanna meet it," Jonah said somewhat nonchalantly.

I continued to adjure that he join me in the illusory safety of the piggyback house on wheels, until I finally enticed him inside to smoke a bowl. I turned on some mellow tunes at about half-volume on my CD walkman with remote speakers and we sat there casually puffin' some nuggets and philosophizing as was our usual fare, till suddenly a din that at first seemed the thunder of a distant explosion sounded over the stereo's volume. I immediately turned off the tunes, and quietly uttered,

"What the fuck was that?"

"I dunno," was Jonah's simple reply.

"Was that an explosion? What the fuck would be—" my query was cut short by another "BOOM," or perhaps more accurately, a heavy "THUD" that shook or vibrated the camper, à la *Jurassic Park* when the footsteps of T-Rex sends shock waves through a glass of water sitting on a table.

"Oh shit!" I said with a worried whisper, "What the fuck was that?"

"Uh . . . I dunno," Jonah answered, likewise in an alarmed and under-the-breath utterance.

The sound and vibration had issued from just the other side of the thin walls of the camper, right next to where I sat. Something exceedingly heavy had seemingly stomped upon the forest floor, something quite massive that stood mere inches from where I sat upon the lower bunk. Neither of us even dared peak out from behind the curtains to see what had made such a monstrous noise in the night. I was quite certain that were I to move the curtain aside, I would be staring at a hairy chest at seven feet off the ground, and Jonah's want to meet bigfoot had met with a wariness of things that go bump in the night—especially really big things that can shake a nearly three-ton truck with the stomp of a foot—and the wariness won out.

    We sat petrified in the silence for a few minutes, till said silence was broken by four or five more heavy bipedal footsteps that proceeded to the back of the truck. We sat still for nearly half-an-hour more, listening intensely before either of us had the guts to look out of the windows to see what we might see. We heard a few more noises, the clattering and clanking of some pots and pans we'd left on top of the picnic table and assorted other slight dins and disturbances in the still of the night. When we finally dared to look outside, we saw nothing suspicious, and then went to sleep after another bowl or two to counter the adrenaline. Jonah didn't sleep in his tent that night, and took the top bunk instead.

    Next day when we awoke, I noted that the pots and pans and utensils were still all piled together in the largest pot as we'd hastily left them the night before, but were moved from the table top onto the bench of the wooden picnic table. We offered an account to the others, who reported they'd had a quite quiet and undisturbed sleep. Though I had some suspicions someone had played a trick on us, upon testing whether a mere human might be able to stomp or drop a heavy rock on the ground to manufacture the sort of sound and vibrations that would shake a three-ton truck and camper, we concluded this was not a viable explanation. We even took turns climbing to the side of the pickup bed then leaping off and onto the forest floor to try to make even a tiny vibration detectable to the other, seated on the lower bunk inside. Indeed, neither of us could even tell when the other outside had hit the ground, both endeavoring as much force as our respective weights could create upon stomping or leaping down from five feet high.

    Gary informed us he had to go to town to get some supplies, so we concentrated on clearing brush from the sides of the trail not far from base camp. As we weren't venturing far into the forest we didn't bother to pack lunch, and instead returned to our respective campsites to replenish and rest during our midday break. As we then began to hike back up the trail to resume working, walking on a side trail that later met the main, I spotted a large brown humanoid-shaped figure through a corridor where the undergrowth was absent, standing and staring straight at us from some seventy yards away.

"Whoa!" I said, lifting my hand to halt our group's progress, *"What is that?!"*

Jonah and the local kid who was working with us stopped in their tracks to attend to my alert.

"There's something up there!" I said, squinting to attempt to make out the details of the tall thing I was observing in the dim forest light, which again, appeared to be the dark brown shape of a humanoid standing and facing my vantage.

The local kid, whose name I can't recall with certainty, said he saw the same something from another vista, a few yards ahead. As I started towards his perspective he likewise started towards mine to discern if we were indeed viewing the same something. Whilst no one was watching for no more than a few seconds, this bogey took the opportunity to make him or herself scarce, for upon returning to my original point of view I noted that whatever had stood staring at us had made a hasty withdrawal, and local kid said the same of his sighting. We immediately started towards where whatever it was we'd seen had stood, and upon arriving at said spot, right next to an alternate trail sign, I gauged that what I had viewed (judging by the height of the trail sign and such) must have measured between eight and nine feet tall. Local kid agreed, and still in investigative mode, we started up the side trail towards the top of Lost Mountain.

The trees along this trail were tall and thin, and though the sun was shining, only patches of the forest floor were illuminated by rays unfiltered by broad-leafed and needled boughs. A distinctly magical quality imbued the light and air and sounds we experienced as we stalked the tall, dark, and assumedly furry beast we had briefly viewed from below. I felt like a native brave, hunting some illusive and magical totem animal as we walked with slightly crouched postures, gazing side-to-side and stalking this specter with stealthy strides, thoroughly enjoying this playful excursion in search of sasquatch—now that we were in the light of day.

After hiking a mile or more with no further sign of our quarry, we decided we ought to retrace our steps and return to work. Just as we began the descent, we heard a call echoing through the woods unlike any animal's vocalization I had ever heard before. I have spent a great deal of time in the wilderness, and have ravenously consumed every nature program I've happened across on television since early childhood, from Marty Stauffer's *Wild America*, Mutual of Omaha's *Wild Kingdom* to pre-cable National Geographic televised specials to the Nature Channel and Animal Planet. I've fished and hunted from the mountains of Wyoming to the hills of Oklahoma, studied birdcalls from bird watching guides and time in the field, listened to Elk bugles echoing in the misty fall mornings of the Rocky Mountains, observed various species of owls—the source of sometimes ominous seeming sounds in the forest—in both daytime and night, and hiked in the hills and high country from the West Coast to the East. This resounding mid-pitched "hooooooooooo" fit no category of creature call I had ever heard or read of, and conveyed a quality that seemed to indicate it issued from an exceedingly deep and billowing chest. Perhaps the closest analogue I can think of would be a howler monkey's eerie cry echoing through the rain forest, except as one long and unbroken sound.

    We paused to listen for a second call, and I decided to mimic its sound to see if I could elicit another. Sure enough, a second sounding followed, a bit closer and louder than the first. We resumed our hike down the trail, trading calls as the source seemed to follow alongside at a distance. By the time we reached the turn to our trail the calls had again grown quite distant, so we returned to our work trimming shrubs and removing overhanging branches from the sides of the trail.

    Cristina, Jonah's girlfriend at the time, and several others from the Bellingham coffeehouse crew came up to visit and camp with us on various occasions, and we made a couple of trips back to the city to replenish supplies and socialize, but had no more encounters with sasquatch in the Sauk River drainage. We did, however, have a somewhat more questionable and less up-close and personal *possible* encounter on the occasion of a little "trip" into the woods near Mount Baker on one weekend-off, and also experienced a few other amazing and anomalous incidents at our worksite, such as observing odd little blue lights in the swampy section of the trail which would dart through this darkened old growth section of the forest like tiny dancing stars, and chancing upon a sasquatch totem embossed on the burled trunk of an ancient tree.

    The other possible "encounter" with sasquatch occurred on the occasion of a reggae festival held annually at the River Farm, a longstanding commune about twenty miles towards Mount Baker from Bellingham. We picked up a batch of the Stuart's Coffeehouse crew on our way, and after arriving and wandering the festival grounds purchased a couple of ounces of boomers (shrooms, magic mushrooms, fungus of the genus Psilocybin, don't ya' know) and distributed these amongst our cohorts. After a while hanging out in the camper, we decided we wanted to wander in the woods to play and explore. Unfortunately, however, the forested area around the festival was off limits, so we agreed to take a little drive to a spot where Jonah and I had searched for chanterelles on an earlier occasion. I had personally only eaten a (relatively) small amount of fungus at this point, by the way, as I had the foresight to recognize I might have the need to get behind the wheel.

    Once we arrived at our destination, our crew of nine hopped out and started to wander up the winding trail that led to the top of a heavily forested ridge. The first section of this trail was thickly wooded with willow thickets and various other deciduous trees and undergrowth, and as the ridge cut off the sun, the area was quite enveloped in shadows. We played amongst the thickets, and then found a circle of nine large trees where each of us took a seat, leaning against his or her chosen trunk. After several minutes of quiet meditation and intoning a group AUM or two, we again started meandering up the trail. Jonah and I decided this might be a good place to experiment with the sasquatch call we had heard and learned to imitate on the aforementioned occasion, and were much encouraged to do so by our companions. We took turns making the long wailing call, pursing our lips in a simian fashion as we did our best simulation of the sounds we'd heard a week or two before and a hundred-miles or so to the south.

We continued on the narrow pathway, and at the first switchback heard a most peculiar noise issuing from a bit beyond this turn in the trail and through an impenetrable thicket. Said odd sounds seemed somewhat like those made by cows, yet more like an imitation of cows than actual bovines. We all agreed on the unusual nature of this din in the dark forest, and I immediately recalled having read a book as a child that claimed sasquatch often imitate cattle "mooos" when traveling in a group to mask the noise of multiple massive and heavily laden feet treading upon the heavily littered forest floor. We continued past this first switchback and these "cows" seemed to be following our progress, a bit behind and upslope from our trajectory.

One of our crew decided to run up ahead to see if he might surprise our stealthy pursuers around the next switchback. He soon came barreling back down the trail to excitedly report that he had startled "something really big" that was bedded down up ahead. Jonah and I went ahead to check out the bedding area, and noted that indeed, something large had flattened a significant area of tall grasses. As we rejoined the rest of the trippers at the second switchback, the crew consensually concluded it was time to turn around and head back to the camper. Whatever was tagging along turned back towards the first switchback precisely when we did, always just out of sight and continually uttering off-tone bovine-like vocalizations. The family of big beasties had somehow continued to evade our gaze, leaving us with a mystery will never be solved.

Now I will admit, auditory hallucinations and distortions are part of the package when magic mushrooms are ingested. Nonetheless, a couple of significant facts caused me to believe it *likely* that what we were hearing were not four-legged domesticated bovines, but a tribe of sasquatch coming to our calls. First of all, cows are by no means stealthy—especially when in the numbers we heard, and can easily be approached even in the wildest of settings. Second, the fact that all of us agreed that what we were hearing sounded more like something *pretending* to be a herd of cattle than actual cows seemed to add weight to this assessment. Still, this "encounter" is obviously to be regarded as more suspect than the encounters Jonah and I had previously experienced for the simple fact that mushrooms do undeniably alter mental and sensory faculties.

After another day or two off Jonah and I returned to work in the Sauk River drainage. Cristina joined us for this stint in the wilderness, collecting conifer cones for seed to sell for a reforestation project of the Schwarz Wald in Germany whilst we worked on the trail, as there was a woman in Darrington paying fifty-bucks a burlap bag-full. During this span in the big woods, I was blessed to see one of the little blue lights Jonah had seen on a few occasions in the swamp just after sunset. Unlike fireflies, these lights were exceedingly fast fliers, and were not intermittent in their bioluminescent display. Said anomalous flying lights would only appear after deep darkness had fallen in this magical marsh, swiftly soaring in spiraling erratic patterns between the tall thick-trunked trees and ferns and devil's club. The little light I observed zipped across the trail a few yards ahead as I was slowly making my way through the darker than night shadows under the old growth cedars, then performed some amazing aeronautical acrobatics, looping and spiraling away and deeper into the swamp.

Insofar as other encounters with suspected faeries, whether or not this adds any credence or context to the aforementioned account, once whilst engaged in shamanistic play with a group of friends from Laramie next to a pile of boulders known as Eagle Rock, a lovely sprite named Mandy laughingly led me to a bush from which sang something that sounded precisely like the flying faeries in the 70's cartoon movie *Wizards*. Mandy also once dragged me into the women's restroom at the Ranger Bar, led me into a stall and pulled her jeans down to display a large tattoo of a winged faerie on her thigh. I also believe I glimpsed one more Cascades faerie before we left this forest, out of the corner of one eye.

We soon finished cleaning this section of trail and moved on to another sight nearby. We remained at this second location for only a week or so, and then packed up to depart from the Sauk River drainage for good, as there was no more trail to clear. Of notable discoveries at this second site, Jonah and I happened upon a large forked tree that bore a massive burl about five feet in diameter on its trunk that bore a certain similitude to a primate's face—and specifically rather resembling an orangutan's visage—with two large symmetrical eyes, a continuous furrowed brow, and a decidedly simian mouth and chin clearly portrayed through the bark and burls of this totem tree.

    On the day of our departure, I sat beside the river to chant and meditate and to say goodbye to the magical wilderness of the Cascade Mountains and to offer thanks to the kindly and playful creatures and spirits we had encountered amongst the ancient trees of the rain forest. I paused from my chanting to take some deep breaths and contemplate the wonder of this delightful and mystical place, perhaps a few tears of joy falling onto my cheeks, when out of the corner of my eye I spied something flying by a few feet to my right. Translucent lacy wings conveyed this tiny creature up and into the branches above, and I swear I saw two tiny human-like legs dangling from this flying form. Indeed the forest's magic was seeming offering a parting appearance via said slight soaring emissary, responding to my grateful sentiments expresses in chants and *pranam* by offering a magical farewell, a gracious goodbye, conveyed from this ancient forest's wondrous, wild and weird inhabitants to one merely open enough to see and believe.

From Rain Forest to Desert: Activism, Capitalism and Peyote

Olywa. That's hippie/anarchist/freak-speak for Olympia, Washington. Jonah and Cristina and I had just departed from the magical old-growth forests of the Upper Sauk Wilderness, where Jonah and I had been employed by a pack-goat packing goatee sporting Forest Service contractor clearing trails of deadfall as big around as a man is tall, encountering bigfoot and faerie and bear-folk and livin' the good life. We were on our way east, but whether to first go south through Oregon, California and Arizona, or straight east through Idaho to Wyoming was yet to be determined.

I was hangin' out in the parking lot of the local food co-op, waiting for Cristina and Jonah to finish stocking up on healthy organically grown environmentally conscious chow. We'd already hit the food bank to fill the cupboard in camper, and were waiting for a half-pound of boomers to serve as our bank account for the road. In Olywa, magic mushrooms are less expensive than just about anywhere else in the country, thus offering a significant return on the investment. Psilocybin cyanescens purportedly even propagate as volunteers on the lawn at the Olympia city hall and the fire station, no less.

As I stood smoking a cigarette, a lovely and rather voluptuous young woman with dark-brown hair and rosy cheeks approached and immediately extended a flier towards me, introducing herself as Sarah. She proceeded to explain the plight of the Diné (Navajo) that the federal government was attempting to evict from an area of the reservation in Arizona called Big Mountain.

"The government enacted legislation over twenty years ago that forced the removal of several hundred Diné families from their land at Big Mountain, and though they claimed this was to resolve a land dispute between the Diné and Hopi, it was just another case of kicking native peoples off their land to gain access to minerals. The Diné tribal leaders had refused to cooperate with the coal company that wanted to mine on their land, so the coal company's lawyer—who also just happened to represent the 'Hopi interests' in the case that went before Congress, which should be considered a conflict of interest—anyhow, this lawyer went to the Hopi government. The Hopi already had a big coal mine on their land at Black Mesa that was run by the same company—you know the songs about 'the company store' in Appalachia? Same company. They don't even pay the Hopi miners minimum wage!!

"Now there are now only a few hundred Diné, mostly elders, who refuse to leave their land at Big Mountain . . . kind of sparse land that they'd been pushed onto after getting out of the concentration camps they were held in during the late 1800's. Hitler even studied these concentration camps to devise his own version fifty-years later. These people are really tied to the land they were resettled on a hundred years ago—they even bury their umbilical cords in a corner of their sheep pens.

"A number of outsiders are currently living with these elders as human-rights observers and helpers, 'cuz most of the young people have left the land. The government resettled about 14,000 Diné residents to a place in New Mexico that was the site of a large nuclear waste accident, and the cancer rate there is somewhere around twenty-percent. Is there any way . . .would you be able to help out?"[11]

At about that moment, Jonah and Cristina stepped out of the co-op, groceries in hand. I looked at them with a big grin on my face.

"What?" said Cristina with quizzical intonation and expression.

"This is Sarah. She was just telling me about some *Native Americans elders* in *Arizona* that need outsiders to come live with them . . . in ARIZONA!"

---

11   This conversation is a vague reconstruction, as I cannot recall the exact words exchanged, and may contain an amalgamation of information from various sources regarding the situation at Big Mountain. Some of the words and certainly the purport closely represents Sarah's presentation to me in this parking lot in Olympia. I endeavor to be exceedingly honest and accurate in such tellings as a service to you, dear readers, and likewise to maintain academic, spiritual and textual integrity. I will attempt to be as precise and historically accurate as I might within and outside the bounds of quotation marks, but I cannot be held to the perfecting standards of an eidetic savant, so bear with me.

Jonah and Cristina looked at each other, then turned back to me with knowing smiles. Jonah and I had spent long hours in deep conversation at base-camp while we were doing trail-work, smoking copious amounts of kindbuds and cigarettes as we conversed into the late night, and among many topics we covered was the possibility of spending some time with indigenous elders before those with traditional wisdoms and knowledge were all gone to whatever happy hunting grounds, or in the case of the Diné, pastures.

As I already mentioned, we had been undecided as to whether we ought to swing south through Arizona, where neither Cristina nor I had yet explored, or straight through Idaho to Wyoming. This encounter and invitation seemed to us a certain sign that we were destined towards the deserts of the American Southwest. A short while later our investment showed up, and we began one of the best journeys of my life, and I assume among the most memorable for my companions, as well.

I had met Jonah and Cristina at Stuart's Coffee House in downtown Bellingham amongst a motley crew of caffeine junkies and potheads that frequented said scene. Jonah had shaggy blond hair (or may have already had dreads), wore glasses, was constantly carrying a shiny metal dumbek with a Kokopelli sticker stuck to the side, and was generally a young man of few words. Cristina, who hooked-up with Jonah not long after I met each separately, was a short-framed bouncy-mousey x-raver chick with curly light brown to dark blond locks (not dreaded) who also wore glasses. Actually, maybe "mousey" is not quite the proper adjective, as her demeanor might better be compared to that of a bunny. Her nickname was "Thumper."

Cristina was quite excited that the woman who had served as messenger of this calling was named Sarah. We stayed for a night or two with another Sarah there in Olywa, and Jonah and Cristina had a friend up in B-Ham (Hippie/Anarchist/Freak-speak for Bellingham) who was significant in their match-made whose name was also Sarah. Cristina had a thing for the repetition of names as signs, which I must admit I have contemplated increasingly in my travels since as potentially important indices of mystical signification and synchronicity and of a person's personality.

After reorganizing the Miraculous-Beast-Shanti-Mama (1963 four-wheel-drive Dodge Power Wagon W-100 complete with cab-over camper on back and an orange and yellow smiling faced sunshine freshly painted on the passenger-side door by Ellen in Bellingham) we started south. First designated stop was Portland, Oregon, where a friend of Jonah's was attending Reed College, among the most progressive institutions of learning in the United States.

We wandered around the campus, and I couldn't but compare the composition of the student body to those with whom I had attended college at Oklahoma Baptist University. Though the quality of the liberal arts learning at my alma mater was good enough to get me into the University of Chicago for grad school, freethinkers were few and far between amongst the matriculated population. I had found a small cadre of liberally minded friends after my disillusionment with the Baptist delusions which had held sway in my mind during my first few years at said institution, mostly English, History, Anthropology and Theater majors —"liberal arts."

At Reed College, freethinking was the rule, not the exception, and I overheard intelligent and interesting conversations at nigh every turn. As I sat on the patio at the campus coffee house, sipping a cup and smokin' a likely weed-spiked hand-rolled American Spirit cigarette, I heard one undergrad mention Derrida, and noted titles on students' books that resonated with both my university and radical-hippie-freak heritages.

Jonah and I decided to test some of the mushrooms, for quality control, you understand. I ventured out of the camper, and discovered I was hardly alone in my psychedelic frame-of-mind. It seemed one out of four or five of the students whose paths I crossed were in the same state. I was invited in to an apartment to smoke some nugs and hashish with a small party of upperclassmen and women, then set out again, feeling less self-conscious in my altered wanderings than was usually the case when tripping in an urban setting. At least in pockets like Portland, *we got the numbers . . .*

Jonah had stayed in the camper with Cristina, who decided not to partake of our taste-test, and when I rejoined them we proceeded to make impromptu music with whatever instruments we could make out of what household implements served the purpose. Jonah seemed content to make a water-drum of his Nalgene bottle, and I proceeded to bang wildly on pots and pans, and Cristina may or may not have accompanied on the dumbek. Jonah and I both had drums, but this makeshift use of items meant for other purposes seemed more befitting our magic mushroom state of play. At least this is what I recall of said trip, though memory-recall and mushroom-consciousness are not perfectly commensurate states.

We headed towards the coast after this, and then drove south to Coos Bay, Oregon, home to Merlin and Mike (at least I believe Merlin's traveling companion we'd met in B-ham was called "Mike," a stocky non-descript Korean fellow who came to town with the colorfully tie-died skinny hippie kid who called himself after the mythical mystic sorcerer of King Arthur's court—long time ago . . . that is, referring to my imperfect memory of names, though King Arthur's day was obviously long ago, too).

We spent only a brief time in Coos Bay, rather unimpressed with what welcome we received there. At a shopping center parking lot at the outskirts of Crescent City, California, we traded some shrooms to restock on herb, no sooner pulling up with said intention than two heads happened to walk up to make the deal. This is what's called "road magic," by the way. After this brief stop we continued on to the next well known stop on the northwest hippie-trail: Arcata—Humboldt County, that is. Green-gold. California-tea. Yeah, we loaded up the truck and were off to find some weed . . .

The Arcata area, and Humboldt County in general, is one of the most prodigious pot-growing regions of the country. The outdoor herb cultivated there is about the best to be found east (west?) of the Hindu Cush. After the logging industry (thankfully) lost steam in the region, marijuana took its place as the linchpin of the economy, and is by far the county's largest cash crop—though for that matter, marijuana is the largest cash crop in the whole country, for those of you who didn't know.

We immediately headed for the plaza, center of much activity amongst activists, anarchists, hippies and trimmer-wannabes. "Trimming" buds off the fifteen-foot Cannabis trees that grow so well in this climate is a major draw to the area for impoverished traveling potheads, come harvest-time. Wages were around $10 to $15 an-hour, plus all the leftover "trim" (leafs and small "popcorn nuggets" not on the central cola buds) you can carry, and maybe an ounce or two of heady nugs as a bonus, or some like combination of compensation. Pretty fair for unskilled labor. We had some hopes of doing a bit of trim work ourselves, and thus attempted to meet a grower or someone in-the-know on the plaza.

Food-Not-Bombs serves on various days of the week on the plaza, and so we figured we'd catch a free vegan/"freegan" lunch and likely make some contacts, too. After our ritual of morning coffee and cigarettes (with the exception of Cristina, who drank tea and didn't smoke cigarettes), we found a spot to squat in the plaza. We were informed by some dready kid that in the center of the square was a digital camera that circled the periphery of the scene to take photos—according to him, as surveillance of the so called "criminal" activities of the peace-crowd. Though the cops might have a look at what this camera records—certainly a potential infringement on rights to privacy—so can you or I, as is the case with so many public places these days, as a web camera broadcasts the scene worldwide. Nonetheless, if I owned a pellet gun . . .

Though the federal government realizes full well that to no small degree the marijuana trade benefits the national economy, they still insist on making things difficult for so many otherwise law abiding citizens who believe that "every green and seed bearing plant . . . is given to us to use," or something like said injunction from the Torah/Old Testament, else who realize the truth that Cannabis was actually much more anciently utilized as a sacrament by yogis, *sadhu* and the likes. The local government in Humboldt, however, mostly turns a blind eye to this most important economic booster to the community, and generally the cops here only bust people for possession who are otherwise perceived as a nuisance.

If I recall correctly, we camped that night at the city park with the big redwoods. Numerous squatters make the depths of this park their home, where one can even make a temporary dwelling of a hollowed out stump big enough to fit an oversized SUV. Next day (or was it the day after?) we started on our journey again, with the next intended destination Honeydew, purportedly the locale that started the Humboldt cultivation craze.

Cruising through Humboldt State Redwood Park on a narrow winding road that meanders past some of the tallest and girthiest trees on the planet, we decided to stop at a campground near the summit of this little highway sometime around sunset. Quite a blessing this turn turned out to be, as the magic of the road would have it, indeed. We awoke the next day to discover that next to a picturesque river there was an apple orchard, presumably planted by early homesteaders of the Redwood Empire.

Numerous varieties of just-ripe *pommes* dangled heavy from overburdened limbs, red and golden and dappled-mixed-colored. We filled the food-service buckets we'd acquired for an earlier entrepreneurial endeavor ("Three-Guys-Pies," which turned out to be two-guys—me and Jonah, as the other guy dropped out—plying Tibetan blackberry and night-picked blueberry pies at music festivals back in Washington). We ate Humboldt apples for nigh the next two months. Apple pie, apple strudel, apple pancakes, apples stir-fry, apple-you-name-it, we ate it. As it turned out we made a much larger score of Humboldt-grown apples than Humboldt weed, only ending up with a quarter-ounce of the latter.

Such is the life of the post-modern nomadic (not so much hunting) hunter-gatherers like our little band. Weed, wildcrafting, and wandering in search of someplace resembling the home we know must be somewhere, where food isn't shipped from some other continent cultivated by peasants without the land to grow their own, nor covered in poison, where nature is respected and revered, real community exists, spirituality isn't only what's proscribed by books written by crabby old men from some ancient foreign land, centralized government stays out of the lives of everyday peoples—we can well enough police ourselves, thank you—and "freedom reigns" isn't just a spin of "the authorities are free to probe your personal belongings and political beliefs at will, despite Constitutional protections, for whatever they want." Those things, and just for the love of adventure.

We stopped only briefly in Honeydew, which turned out to consist of little more than a post office, a gas station/general store, and if I recall correctly, one or two bars. We continued down the road to a small community nestled along the Lost Coast called Shelter Cove, where we watched an eerie fog roll in on a chilly cobblestone beach. After a coffee-stop, we started up the steep climb back towards Honeydew and the Interstate. The truck was underpowered and struggling, thus despite my better judgment I put the truck in low four-wheel drive (something you're not supposed to do in an older 4wd vehicle) to gain the power we needed to crest the hill. We succeeded in the ascent then traveled across the central valley with scarcely a pause and on to Tahoe, where we did little more than gather some giant pine cones, and then proceeded up an even more treacherous incline to the south.

Chugging up towards the mountain pass above Tahoe, the Miraculous-Beast-Shanti-Mama was huffing and puffing, and I am not certain but that she wasn't uttering in her engine's strained labors, "I think I can, I think I can . . ." I wasn't in such a storybook mood at the time, however, and proceeded to curse up a storm. Cristina cautioned me that casting such expletives at the vehicle and at the offspring of female dogs and so forth was perhaps not the best mode to invoke assistance in our current dilemma. I had once again locked the hubs and the levers engaging the lowest of six gears to try to eke out the might we needed to reach the summit. Just after the road leveled and the shoulder widened, we suddenly lost all power, brakes, steering, and nearly lost the left front wheel as a bearing had blown, almost eaten to the core. I used the e-brake and guided the truck to a safe halt on the shoulder.

"Thank Goddess we made it to the top!" commented Cristina.

Indeed, had these mechanical failures occurred only a hundred yards passed or further, we would likely have plummeted hundreds of feet to our certain demise. Jonah hitched a ride to the next town, and returned triumphantly in the passenger seat of a tow truck. We had the truck towed to the nearest mechanic, which happened to be in the then "zero-tolerance" state of Nevada.

We ended up stuck in Gardnerville, Nevada, living out of our mechanic's parking lot for the next several days. I was able to have the means for the truck's repairs wired, but we still needed some cash for living expenses over the next few days. We happened to notice the billboard at the local high school touting "Drug-Free Week," yet had only one means of currency or trade beyond twenty dollars or so in Jonah's wallet, just the sort of ironic Hollywood scenario setup one might expect after such an epic breakdown.

While enjoying some pie and coffee at an all-night diner, Jonah and Cristina struck up a conversation with a young couple that was interested in purchasing some mushrooms. The male informed them that he was on probation, and the female was still in high-school. I told my companions that I wanted nothing to do with such a risky sale, especially considering the age differences, but that they could do as they liked. The pair bought a quarter-ounce, and expressed interest in acquiring more.

After the bearing came in and the wheel was back on, we still had an issue with an underpowered engine. We met the probation-violator alone at a local park to make some gas money for the road. After checking at a couple of the local auto-parts stores for the proper plug-wires to fit the slant-six that powered our mobile home—to no avail—we decided to park in front of the all-night diner till morning when we could try another auto parts store.

Instead of immediately hopping out of the truck, as was normally our habit once stopped, we lingered listening to tunes on the CD player. Whilst we sat, Cristina noticed a girl and an older woman standing in front of the café.

"Isn't that the girl we sold the mushrooms to?"

"You guys sit tight, I'm going to check something," said I, leaving the motor on as I proceeded out the door and around to the back of the truck. I unlocked the camper door, not with anything particular in mind except to look nonchalant as I surveyed the scene. I glanced around the parking lot and noticed a rather rotund fellow wearing a western-style button-up shirt and blue jeans standing at the open door of a blue Chevy Blazer. In one hand he held the microphone of a two-way radio, into which he clearly spoke the words, "Ten-four on that location."

"Oh shit!!!!" I uttered quietly as I quickly closed and locked the camper door.

Swiftly circling 'round the truck, I made my way back into the cab, slammed the door, and eloquently exclaimed my concern.

"Oh shit!!!!"

"What? What?" said Cristina with a worried tone.

"Oh shit! Oh shit! Shit! Shit! Shit!"

"What? What? Jeffrey, you're scaring me!"

I drove the hobbled truck out of the parking lot and turned towards the hill leading out of town and back into California, adrenaline and an emotive response somewhere between fear of jail time confinement and Dukes of Hazard thrill coursing through my veins and brain. The blue blazer followed us out onto the highway. We prayed and chanted vehemently as the underpowered pickup struggled to make it up the hill. "I think I can, I think I can, I think I can" we repeated to encourage the not-so-little beige truck with an orange sunshine painted on the side. She replied, if not in so many words, "Nope, I sure can't."

I made a quick U-turn, not certain whether or not we were still being followed. We then turned off the highway into a suburb at the edge of town and onto a long paved road past dozens of sleepy suburban abodes. After a couple-hundred yards or so I noticed a set of headlights behind us that bore a nigh certain resemblance to those on police cars.

"We're being tailed. Oh Shit!" I uttered as I watched the lights in the rear-view mirror.

We turned left at the end of the main road, then onto a dirt road at the end of the pavement that diverged into numerous four-wheel-drive trails proceeding out into the desert. Normally I am quite averse to such desecrations and destructions of the landscape. On this occasion, however, I was quite grateful that as the ominous lights tailing us started the second turn, the driver of said vehicle of the law decided better than to try to pursue a high-clearance four-wheel drive truck into the labyrinth of desert trails. As we watched him/her cease the pursuit from the vantage of rear-view mirrors, I started to bounce up and down in my seat.

"We got away!! We got away from the cops!! Hee hee! Haw haw!"

Jonah immediately joined the celebratory proclamations, though it took Cristina a few minutes to recover from the trauma before she half-heartedly joined in. We stashed the boomers underneath a juniper, careful to leave no tracks by hopping from bush to brier to the tree, then camped for the night. Next day, we rewired the plugs with functional cables and went on our way, retrieving the shrooms on our way back to the relative freedom of California. Nevada has since shed the "zero-tolerance" attitude, I might add, a factor which had certainly increased our edginess as we endeavored to evade potential incarceration.

For our next stop we discovered some delightful hot springs near Mammoth, a copious flow called Hot Creek where we basked in the slightly sulfurous waters and shook off whatever symptoms of PTSD from our close brush with prison-time. We encountered only one other party at these springs, a retired couple in an RV on their way to Baja Mexico with a load of stuffed animals to pass out to the children they'd encounter down there, as they'd told us had been for some time their practice on said seasonal migrations.

When we ran out of fresh water whilst at the springs, Cristina knocked on our neighbor's door to request a quart or so. On our drive out just a few minutes later, a six gallon water container was placed conspicuously in the middle of the dirt road blocking our progress, increasing our water storage capacity significantly as we prepared to head into the deep desert, as well as quenching immediate thirst. This less overtly supernatural providence is road magic, too. Indeed, it's pretty extraordinary how much generosity and kindness is to be found amongst the folks you meet whilst trusting yourself to the wild wandering paths of the open highway. Indeed, encountering vehicles of compassion becomes almost commonplace (though never taken for granted) once one surrenders to the experience of the road, and upon learning the art of free-form travel.

We descended from the mountains and into Bishop, then stocked up on food and water for a much-anticipated expedition in Death Valley. After our routine coffee house quest, a good night's sleep, and our ritual morning cup and smoke, we made a turn towards the east.

    With a now fully functional Miraculous-Beast-Shanti-Mama, we headed from high mountains to deep desert, slant six roarin' like a bull and wheels rollin' smooth like we were riding on a cushion of hot desert air. Our primary destination was Saline Valley Hot Springs, an oasis in the low desert encompassed by Death Valley National Monument. The Saline Valley area was a later addition to the National Parks Service holdings, which caused a bit of an uproar amongst the desert rats, hippies, wild-people, and everyday adventurous sorts that had traditionally frequented these springs during the cooler months of the year.

    National Parks Service oversight generally means limits on camping, among other strictures and restrictions of freedom—whether well advised or no. Due to popular outcry, however, a sort of compromise was reached, such that many of the usual sorts of limits were waived, and other than the occasional appearance of the National Parks System logos on the occasional pickup or SUV cruising by, the place was pretty chill.

    A virtual village annually springs up at Saline Hot Springs come the fall, and many reside there for months on end, basking in the hot waters and creating an impromptu community until the heat of the following springtime drives most to wherever they called home for the rest of the year. RV's with enough clearance to venture the sand-dune hazards of the two-rut road leading in, VW buses, extreme four-wheel drives, and any number of other odd vehicles line the road near the two wellsprings of hot and drinkable water from October to March or so, and maybe some in the summertime, too, though the place is certainly much less appealing then with triple digit temperatures and scarce any shade.

    On our way in, I couldn't resist the thrill of hitting the dunes, perfectly spaced, at just the right clip to almost or just slightly catch some air. It was necessary, after all, to maintain a certain speed to prevent the trucks rather narrow tires from bogging down in the soft sand, regardless of a want for thrill seeking.

    With each rise we would whoop and holler and scream with delight as we felt temporary moments of weightlessness when we crested the little hills (more than a few times bumping heads on the roof of the cab) whilst blasting funky trance tunes on the stereo as we rode this roller coaster ride in the dark desert night. As we again met the ground after each instance of experiencing 0g, the deep sand softened the blow on the trucks suspension, and the leaf springs and springs in the seat bounced us back up for a secondary thrill.

Cristina had her fill after one particularly hard meeting with the ceiling, so I let off the accelerator. It was of course too late for the contents of the camper, which were strewn all over the floor and lower bunk. Cleaning up broken eggs and flour and vegetables took a fair bit of time and effort, but it was worth every minute for the thrills of the ride.

As we started towards the springs through a groomed thicket that surrounded the pools, a group of revelers emerged from the line of tall bushes. At first glance, I saw a rather rotund fellow with a dick that seemed far out of proportion, making me feel momentarily self-conscious, though I am not at all poorly endowed. On second glance I realized he was wearing a rubber-molded costume that appeared disturbingly realistic in the fading light. His companions were also wearing some semblance of costumes. It was Halloween, something we had not even given a thought or at least no mention as we were quite out of touch with civilization's mode of timekeeping.

My sense of masculinity reassured, I wandered into the oasis to find a nice pool with room for me to climb in to enjoy the night sky and soothing hot waters. Jonah and Cristina went off in search of their own private pool.

As we awoke the next day, I was quite impressed with the sight of the spring and the vista surrounding this oasis. The valley is nearly devoid of vegetation except directly around the pools, where palm trees and perennial thickets grow, as well as smaller trees and shrubs and flowers planted by industrious villagers over the years. There are several pools of various sizes and shapes, a kitchen wash station, and a claw-footed bathtub idiosyncratically installed for one's bathing pleasure at this wondrous oasis. Fairly steep banks rise at either side of the valley. A large peace sign made of lighter-colored stones graces one of the sides of the basin, and a small landing strip for light aircraft can be seen on a plateau half-way up the valley's slope. The sun was pleasingly warm on my unclothed skin as I stood surveying my surroundings, but not at all too hot for another dip in the springs.

We made the acquaintance of a number of colorful characters during this hot springs sojourn, ranging from the typical desert rat species to young hippies like ourselves to retirees too adventurous to stick to the paved roads and clothing-required or gender-separated pay-springs in Death Valley itself. We drove further up the road to briefly check out the upper springs, then after three days or so at these oases, drove (or dove) into the depths of Death Valley proper.

We had only eaten mushrooms on a couple of occasions since we started this adventure, mostly relying on them as a source of income. Death Valley seemed an appropriate place for a group vision quest, and so we searched the map for someplace to spend some quality psychedelic-time, preferably well away from the main highway. We decided on a particular canyon with an appellation that sounded promising, and took off in four-wheel drive on yet another treacherous path into the wilds of Death Valley National Monument.

At one point the road dropped down a steep embankment and into a dry riverbed with water-worn stones the size of basketballs half-protruding from the sand. Yet again, despite a much more ginger attempt at negotiating a desert trail (now marked only by small strips of plastic tape left by parks service surveyors) the contents of the camper were soundly tossed about from icebox and cabinets and onto bunk and floor. After a snail's pace crawl up the riverbed we stopped at the gaping mouth of the canyon.

We spent a night that night so quiet it made the solitude of even the high mountains seem like a wild party. We were below sea level and the air was heavy and thick, despite minimal humidity. I believe I came to understand the oxymoronic expression, "the silence was deafening" during the dark of that deep desert night.

The next morning Jonah decided to climb up a steep-sided rocky peak on the right side of the canyon before our ritual ingestion of sacred soma.[12] Cristina and I anxiously watched as Jonah trod the treacherous cliff-sides on the rocks above. Soon he disappeared from sight.

    Setting aside my concerns, I gathered some round river rocks and made a mushroom-shaped pattern about fifteen feet long on the canyon floor, placing the three-eighths of an ounce or so on a rock situated in the center of the area which figured as the cap. When Jonah returned from his expedition, we said a few AUMs and then each walked up the stalk of the mini-Nazca-style monument to pick our portions. After some improvised ritual we proceeded to munch these magic mushrooms with all due reverence.

    I was never fond of eating any sort of fungus until I established a habit of occasionally (and at times almost excessively) ingesting the psychedelic sort, which by the way are not particularly tasty—if ya' didn't know. Upon the realization of what good they can do for a soul, however, I have not only learned not to gag when chewing up the psychedelic sort, but have developed a taste for the "edible" varieties, too (of course, I have also since adopted the practice of drinking my own piss, an Ayurvedic elixir called *Sivambu*, the "Nectar of Siva"—in case you had a want to know).

    After a bowl and somewhere between fifteen to thirty minutes, the boomers started to do their work. My knees became wobbly, a clear sign this was to be a powerful journey. Before the trip came on too strong, we decided to hike up the canyon to explore its secrets. After a short distance, the canyon's sides closed in and grew vertical, not over twenty-yards from wall to wall. We continued up the winding dry riverbed, enjoying the increasingly fluid colors and textures of sand and stones and water-worn rock walls as we randomly wandered to and fro, as trippers are prone to do.

    Around one particular bend in the canyon, we discovered an entrance to a small cave. The entryway was a perfectly shaped

---

12   One of the interpretations of the "soma" of the Vedas is that the sacred substance described was indeed none other than psychedelic mushrooms or some mixture including these funny little fungi.

vaulted passage, and a short stoop of a porch even rose from the canyon floor in front of the quite homey looking grotto.

We had to venture inside, of course, and were quite enjoying this nifty little hermit's hideaway until we noticed that at the back of the cave there was a narrow crack, just large enough for a thin man to pry his body through. Jonah, who was more often the risk-taker, declined to slide in to explore what mysteries the fissure held. He said he had a bad feeling about it. Not heeding his advice, I slid my body in and up to explore the shallow crack.

As I peered into the dimly lit end of the cave, I discovered a shelf about five to seven feet long or so just below shoulder level. Upon the shelf was what appeared in the dim light to be a person-sized glowing chrysalis-shaped form. A bit startled at this sight else perhaps admittedly by my altered perception's reception of said sight, I quickly retreated, and with one look at my expression or perhaps at something I said in my surprise, else some strange sense of dread that followed me from the narrow fissure, the other two joined me in a swift retreat for the door.

Jonah and I sat down on the stoop, quickly distracted from the apparition in the cave, and Cristina soon proceeded to rant about the sorrows she felt in this desolate place. "It's so sad," she kept repeating, until finally she took her leave of this odd and mysterious desert locale. I do not at all mean to belittle her response, mind you. After she retreated to the camper, Jonah soon following, I felt something approaching the deepest and most mournful solitude I have ever experienced in my life as I sat bare-chested upon the hermitage's stoop.

I shortly returned to the truck as well, only to realize I had left my favorite shirt in the spooky cave. It was one of those short sleeved *kurta* imported from India that have multi-colored patterns around the V-neck and hem and sleeves and are not uncommonly seen at Dead shows and like venues. I decided to go back to retrieve this item of clothing, which I rather distinctly remembered having removed whilst in the cave. Upon a thorough search, however, I could not find one shred nor thread of cloth. As we later discussed this phenomenon, we agreed that who or whatever resided in the mysterious chrysalis must have taken the shirt as an offering to compensate our invasion of his, her, or it's resting place.

Back at the mouth of the canyon, the odd phenomena did not let up. We all three watched what clearly appeared to be an exceedingly slow-flying missile cross the canyon just a hundred feet or so above our heads. Shortly thereafter we observed two or three unmarked white "planes" that appeared to be swept-wing fighter-jets spiraling in an odd vortex of rising air and dust several miles away.

I might discount my perceptions of the later two anomalous occurrences, had I not had two corroborating witnesses by my side. Though the "hallucinations" caused by psychedelic mushrooms may be explained to the satisfaction of scientists by what is known of neurochemical reactions in the brain, that three persons witnessed the same oddities is enough to convince me something extraordinary had indeed occurred. Regarding the glowing chrysalis, as I was the only one to see this strange sight (though I did see it again upon returning to the cave), I would allow more room for a more "rational" interpretation, and perhaps my perception can be explained as merely a visual hallucination transforming an ordinary rock into the enclosure of some odd or extraterrestrial creature.

Soon Cristina's sense of something not being right returned, and as the overcast sky grew rather menacing, I became somewhat concerned that a downpour upstream might produce a deluge in the narrow canyon that could easily sweep us away to miles down the dry wash. We loaded up the truck and started to retrace the trail to exit the danger zone. I was probably still tripping too hard to responsibly drive under normal circumstances, though I negotiated the path exceedingly slowly as we returned to the steep incline that led out of the riverbed.

I was a bit over-concerned at the prospect of mounting the rise up and onto the level ground above, so Jonah hopped out and ran downstream to see if there was an easier exit. In my altered state of perception the fifteen to twenty-foot slope, though indeed better than 45 degrees and rather uneven, appeared as daunting to ascend as Mount Everest.

I was a bit short with Jonah when he returned, as he gave a rather bewildered blank stare when I asked if he'd found a less intimidating path to depart from the riverbed, shrugging his shoulders as I waited for some sort of response regarding his findings. I was very anxious to leave the venue of a potential flash-flood behind, fears certainly somewhat accentuated by my state of mind, as boomers are prone to amplify certain emotions.

The few drops of precipitation I recall observing on the windshield, a rarity in this nigh the driest of deserts, would have raised my concerns to some degree in whatever state of mind. Though I have never seen a desert wash filled with a significant flash flood torrent from a deluge upstream, I could tell from the deeply gouged banks of the dry riverbed that this was no place to be during such an event, if a beautiful flowered sight to see afterwards.

After some more confused deliberations I decided the better part of valor was just to go for it, though I believe I asked Cristina to hop out in case I rolled the truck on the treacherous incline. I gunned the motor in low, and as the truck's hood aimed at nothing but sky I let out a holler, adrenaline plus serotonin released from the ingestion of mushrooms mixed to make my head spin as the truck crested the rise. The Miraculous-Beast-Shanti-Mama leveled out, and I could once again see the ground. We had made it, and though the feared downpour didn't manifest, we all felt relieved to leave the sunken elevation of the wash, and even grateful once we again reached paved road. Usually paved roads were the ones we were happy to leave behind.

After one more night in this deep desert valley, we headed towards so called Sin City. Quite a startling contrast to go from the wild and strange solitude of Death Valley to the bustling and densely populated madness of the gambling capital of the world.

Cristina's father was attending a conference in Vegas, so she and Jonah stayed with him at a posh hotel whilst I strolled the strip for amusement. I don't recall having done any more gambling than to drop a few quarters in the slots, if that. Traded some mushrooms for a bag of herb, and mostly wandered around watching the flurry of businessmen and women taking advantage of business trips to indulge their whims, observing school teachers and shopkeepers sublimating suppressed instincts by the thrill of watching a ball spin around a wheel, and wondering which couples were to be counted amongst innumerable extramarital flings for which this glittery city is so well known.

    I found a drum circle in Sunset Park I had heard touted as one of the nation's largest regular gatherings of urban hippies—certainly the highlight of this stop for me. Sat on a slope and shared some smoke with a local couple, enjoying the tribal rhythms and watching lovely hippie mommas spinning and swaying to the groove in long flowing flowered skirts.

    Yet again I pondered the contrast: less than a mile away, people were frantically fighting the odds to get hold of fortune's wheel, to grasp at the version of the American Dream Hunter S. Thompson critiqued so poignantly; and here in this expanse of grass and trees was a lake with only partially domesticated ducks floating past in lazy synchrony, fish swimming freely underneath their webbed-foot paddles, and sitting upon green grass and dandelions a gathering of only partially domesticated people seemingly want to remember those simpler rhythms that used to time humanity's lifeways, dancing to drums made of logs and stretched skins, partaking of smoke so long a part of human life we have neurological receptors built to take nothing else, and staring at the sky and earth and water with primal memories rising to the surface even amidst the nearby neon lights and sounds and machines and money-madness of Las Vegas.

    Granted, the grass and trees and lake were artificial, in the sense that these would soon wither and die and evaporate as soon as human oversight was lacking. Still, this semblance of a more natural being-human soothed my soul a bit in the midst of the flashing, buzzing, whirling, clink-and-clatter.

    As the red sun sunk below the desert horizon the drummers and dancers departed one by one, and I returned to the belly of the Miraculous Beast Shanti Mama, soothed to sleep by the echoes of deep booming djembes, varied pitches of dumbeks, ashikos, tablas, congas and bongos still rumbling in my thoughts, and visions of these ancient rhythms flashing in subtle patterns under my closed lids.

    I looked up a cousin that lived in my deceased aunt's condo, and had a drink with her and her brother, and may or may not have smoked a bowl or joint with them. After respective family reunions, I reunited with my traveling family and we quickly departed from this odd oasis in the Nevada desert.

Our next designated destination was Prescott, Arizona, where Jonah's brother Josh was studying forestry at one of the local colleges. After a short respite at his home, Josh led us into the first deep cave I had ever explored. The Jerome cave is a rather unassuming hole on the side of the highway between Prescott and Jerome, a once ghost town with a very interesting story of revival.

The town called Jerome is built on the side of the slope that leads from Arizona's pine-covered high country down to the desert below. The highway winds through this hillside town, once a mining community which was revived by some hippie colonists back in the seventies. I was told that the long-haired squatters once got caught communally cultivating a crop of cannabis next to a stream that proceeded from the opening of an abandoned mineshaft. The authorities of course confiscated the crop (which likely found its way into the stashes of some of the arresting officers, assuming the plants were mature). The penance these would-be growers ended up serving was merely some hours of community service: they were court ordered to make improvements to their own town, with state funds. Not bad as penalties go for an otherwise unjust prohibition and a faulty penal code restricting the farming and use of a God and Goddess given green thing.

The cave called Jerome is a fairly roomy and straight hole into the ground that proceeds about a quarter-mile through a small mountainside's solid rock interior. We walked into the darkness till meeting the cave's abrupt end, then sat to smoke a bowl, extinguishing all sources of illumination with the exception of intermittent flashes from a BiC to burn the contents of the bowl as we partook of some tasty Prescott homegrown.

Whilst the lights were out and after the pipe had made a few rounds, we heard a thump, then another din in the darkness between our seats and the exit. Now, whether one of my three companions had thrown a stone to startle the rest, or whether we had some unexpected company in the depths of that mountain, I cannot say. Regardless, we immediately ceased our session and headed back towards the light of day, my companions all seeming equally startled.

Our next stop was yet another steaming geothermal flow, Verde Hot Springs. If you had not noticed, dear reader, our group was very fond of sojourns at hot springs, those wondrous gifts of this planet's geothermal processes, bubbling pools of healing waters which once again show that nature provides all we need, if we might just adjust our wants to what is natural. There is little better than to sit in steaming waters while symmetrically fractaled flakes of snow fall from the night sky, else to enjoy the cooling twilight after a long and sweaty mountainous trek by plunging sky-clad into mineral waters heated deep in the belly of the earth, aching muscles and bones soothed whilst watching the sun set over a still snow-capped peak. Mama Earth's amniotic fluid, blessed succor proffered by Ma Prithvi[13] Devi.

Verde Hot Springs was at one time a resort where the likes of Al Capone purportedly hid away from the hassles of business, bootlegging and robbing banks. The only way in was by a long, rough and winding four-wheel drive road, else by riverboat. The resort was closed and boarded up sometime in the fifties.

I was informed by a campground host that after the resort had fallen to ruin from years of neglect, it was, yet again, a band of industrious hippies that decided to make a community of a beautiful site others had let fall to the wayside. They lived in the remnants of the hotel and blissfully basked in the sun and sweltering waters of the hot pools—until, that is, officials from the Department of the Interior decided they weren't so fond of these free-living peoples, as has been an unfortunate attitude characteristic of "civilized authorities" for millennia. Not so lenient as the local courts in the Jerome case, the Forest Service decided to ensure once and for all that this settlement couldn't continue in its communal ways on the banks of the Verde River. According to my informant the feds dynamited the hotel, leaving only ruins that rather reminded me of remnants of an ancient Roman bath.

---

13   "Prithvi" is perhaps the most ancient known name for Goddess Mother Earth.

Two pools still exist on the tiled floor that remains, several feet above the river's flow. One is nestled against a rock-face and is quite deep, about four or five feet wide and fifteen to twenty feet long. One can float in this pool whilst listening to the rush of river water below, or sit in the smaller pool which has a small shelter built around it, various whimsical paintings and at least one AUM symbol decorating the mini-bathhouse's walls.

We lingered here for a few days and met a number of fellow hot springs aficionados who had come to bask in the warm waters during the increasingly cool fall weather. A couple of young dreadies soon showed up, and we shared a few sessions with this pair and some of the older heads of the earlier generation of hippies who were likewise camped at the campground downstream and across the river from the ruins of the resort.

Kaili and her boyfriend Travis were awaiting the return of their ride, another wandering wild woman with whom these two had been traveling with since their departure from Carbondale, Colorado. When the third party returned, a small drama ensued.

Kaili's boyfriend had apparently previously hooked-up with the van-drivin' momma, and the two had decided they were now the couple, leaving Kaili in something of a predicament. She ended up choosing to travel with us, which was rather to my liking as I was a bit weary of being the solo third companion traveling with a rather amorous couple. Not that I held any presumptions that Kaili would end up my lover, though I must admit I was not closed to something of the sort.

Kaili was generally amicable, intelligent and witty. She was rather short, yet somehow fit all due curves on the contours of her abbreviated figure, and wore a smile sweet as honey found following bees from a field of flowers to the hive. Her pleasing visage was framed by an attractive set of dreads adorned with blown-glass cylinders and skull-beads which oft did rest upon well rounded breasts. I believe I can say that Kaili was not much unlike her near namesake, Kali, though Kaili had no skirt made of arms (unless she kept same well hidden in her backpack), was rather light skinned compared, and did not decapitate anyone whilst traveling with us that I am aware of . . . She slept in her mummy-bag next to me on the top bunk with her dog River, a black labrottie mix, somewhere in the mix, but nothing quite happened between us despite the rather cozy accommodations.

    We traveled from the springs towards Montezuma's Castle, an Anasazi cliff dwelling quite familiar on the Southwest tourist circuit, though decided to take a short side-excursion before going to the National Parks administered monument. We turned south and down a dirt road a few miles before the "Castle," parked the Beast Mama, then hiked in to a small river that backed up against some cliffs. Jonah was certain we'd find some dwellings there, and indeed as we arrived at the river we found not only a number of pristine ancient homes of the Anasazi, but perhaps the most amazing tree I've ever encountered.

    I am uncertain what species this magical green wonder was, but its growth was uncanny. The base of the tree was ten to fifteen feet in diameter, though the greatest breadth of this kindly ancient one only extended up a few feet off the ground. There were several large limbs that branched out from there, and two flat 'porches' on which one could lounge. A large diameter hollowed out limb added to the jungle-gym pleasure of this wondrous living thing. River-dog got a thrill from climbing through the angled hollow, as did we humans in our play upon this extraordinary tree.

    One growth we found rather interesting or comical was an extension of the tree towards the base that grew in a small square, rejoining the trunk near where it had exited and leaving a void in the middle. I decided it was the toilet seat for the shaman who had once made an abode amongst the tree's welcoming branches, though there were differing opinions amongst our crew.

    The dwellings across the creek were small, and the walls that enclosed these living spaces had largely crumbled. We sat in the living-room of some family long since passed on to whatever afterlife the Anasazi disappeared to upon departing this world, smoked a bowl and offered some tobacco and pondered the lives of these mysterious people that left little more than pottery shards and circular ceremonial structures called kivas and shelters of varying sizes on the faces of thousands of cliff-sides throughout the

Southwestern United States.[14] The Diné, as we later learned, are very wary of the artifacts left behind by the people they call the "ancient ones," and have taboos about disturbing any of the shards of pottery or tools strewn all over the desert floor of their lands.

Our visit to Montezuma's Castle, though quite a spectacular structure to see and consider, was somewhat anticlimactic considering the experience we had at the less frequented site a mile or two away, and especially as the actual "castle" was already closed for the evening once we arrived. We did encounter a small rattlesnake along the trail, which we took as another auspicious sign, perhaps granted by a spirit of "the ancient ones" as an indication that despite our pale skin it was sensed that we were of kindred-spirits to these people who carved out a living so lightly upon the land, so long ago.

We decided against a stop at the nearby famous meteor crater and headed straight on to Flagstaff, where we were to seek out the support staff for Black Mesa Indigenous Support, the activist group that was working with the besieged Diné elders at Big Mountain. We found a likely coffeehouse, of the sort so often the gathering places of those who would resist the inequities of the system, discuss poetry and conspiracy and the news not reported by the mainstream media, and likely the right place to find our contacts to place us with a family on the rez.

Macy's European Coffeehouse was indeed the place to be, and we shortly met a pair who were exactly who we sought at this Bohemian hotspot. We also met a rather interesting fellow there who went by the name of "Anu," who later accompanied us to our host family's home. He said he had taken his name from a Tibetan mantra, but the name is also, rather curiously, the name of an ancient Syrian deity.

Soon we headed to the rez to make our home for several days with Willie and Sarah Begay. Recall, from earlier in this tale, that it was a woman named Sarah who had enlisted our help in the

---

14   The word *Kiva*, designating the round half-underground ceremonial structures found throughout the Southwest, is quite clearly derived from the Sanskrit words *ki* ("anthill") and *va* ("dwelling"). Indeed, the Indians of the Southwest were truly Indians, descendants of colonists from the Indian subcontinent.

co-op parking lot in Olywa. Another interesting "coincidence" is the fact that Jonah had worn a thrift store scored pinstriped mechanic's shirt for a good portion of the journey that sported the name "Willie" on a patch on the left breast pocket.

    We cruised through Tuba City, then on to the disputed lands. We pulled up to the Begay homestead and Anu introduced us to our hosts, who came outside to meet us. Che ("grandfather") Begay was a kindly, short and stocky gray-haired man with thick glasses and eyes with pupils that usurped nearly the entirety of the place that's normally granted to irises. Mesuna ("grandmother") Sarah was a rather intense woman, fitting well the images in so many paintings of stately elderly native women depicted in the popular "Southwest" genre. Their youngest son who resided at the Begay homestead from time to time, who we came to call "Willie the Younger," was a gaunt man who wore two long braids.

    The main house was fairly modern in its construction, but several *hogans* were strewn about the property (if "property" is the proper word to describe the lands inhabited by people who did and do not share European notions of land-ownership). *Hogans* are traditional Diné houses, seven-sided structures with a roof that peaks at the middle with a small hole in the center to release smoke from the hearth fire. We were assigned to stay in what we were told was a ceremonial *hogan* that was across the road and up a hill from the main house. My three human companions, Kaili's dog River and Anu slept in the *hogan*, and I stayed in the camper.

    Our tasks were to help around the house, chop wood for the coming winter, cook, and herd sheep and goats. Rather than watching for coyotes and cougars whilst wandering the hills with these wooly flocks, we were instructed to keep a wary eye out for the Bureau of Indian Affairs cops that had been harassing the holdouts to removal since Congress decided to side with the Hopi government (who were, as previously stated, playing pawns of Peabody Coal Company—as I came to understand, most Hopi elders were actually against the forced removal of their Diné neighbors). Were we to see BIA trucks we were instructed to herd the livestock into the canyons to make them less easy to "confiscate"—read: rustle and hold for ransom.

Almost immediately upon stepping foot on the red sandy soil of Big Mountain, I felt as if something significant was quite altered of the atmosphere there, compared to where we four came from. Indeed, the very air of the place had a distinctly different quality from that to be breathed on lands usurped by the white man.

I soon noticed that a subtle mode of communication ensued between us and our host family that somehow superseded the need for a common tongue, and that this "knowing" even transmitted into interpersonal communications amongst our crew. I sensed a different sort of sensitivity to my surroundings and generally altered sensibilities as I went about my chores, swinging an axe to split logs needed by the Begay family to stoke their fires for the coming winter, and chewing ephedra ("Mormon Tea") whilst walking with the sheep and goats across the hills and mesas and through the arroyos and canyons of this sparsely vegetated and beautiful land.

On one day when I had not yet been assigned any particular tasks, I stepped out of the upper hogan and suddenly began to hear the sound of a chant that seemed to be of the Diné tongue. The sound came out of nowhere. I looked around in every direction, perhaps expecting to see Che, who had sung something that seemed the same as this melody whilst driving his pickup to check on his herds of goats and sheep and cattle whilst Jonah and I rode next to him on the bench seat.

After perhaps five minutes or more, I noticed a figure coming over the rise of the hill from the direction of the main house below. It was Che Willy Begay. He didn't say anything to me as he walked past, a few feet to my right. He was gazing at the ground and singing the very song I had heard a few minutes before, but at rather a subdued volume. As he passed, he glanced in my direction with a slight turn of his head, lifted his shoulders as a gesture to admit his jest, and seemed to let out a little chuckle.

How he had thrown his voice across fifty-yards or more and over the rise of the hill on a breezy day, I cannot say. This instance seems rather emblematic of the manner in which the realities of indigenous peoples and the very atmosphere created by their lifeways differ from those places and social realities where magic and mystical truths have been stifled by so much doubt and ill-attention, by hurried and thoughtless lives lived in pursuit of the so-called American Dream, and by the intentional dissimulation and propaganda promoted by whatever presumed authorities.

That night whilst our crew and Anu sat in the hogan sipping juniper berry tea, I shared an account of what had happened a few hours earlier. After finishing my tale, Anu chimed in about how sound travels differently out there in the desert and so forth, seeming attempting to call into question the credibility of my account. An uncomfortable silence ensued, soon broken by the sound of three or more voices that began to sing from the midst of the fire burning inside the potbelly stove. I refrained from saying anything, as I was not inclined to be made to look the fool again. Cristina was the first to comment upon this anomaly.

"It's so sad! Can you hear it? It's so sad!" she said in a lamenting tone, and Kaili and Jonah made comments confessing that they heard these songs too, as did Anu. I began to weep as the voices grew louder, singing what was certainly a song of sorrow, perhaps about the loss of freedom and land and dignity suffered by whatever indigenous voices projected from the flames.

At least two other instances among many magical happenings that transpired during our stay with the Begay family are worthy and fit to mention. Both were occurrences surrounding the occasion of a Native American Church meeting that was being held for the children of area Diné families.

On the day before the ceremony, Jonah accompanied Che Begay to kill a ewe to be consumed by those gathering for the occasion. He later recounted that before slitting the sheep's throat with a sharp knife, Che Willie sang a song which Jonah said he assumed was to thank the spirit of the animal or his ancestors or the spirits of the land (the only "gods" the Navajo know, as I've been told of their beliefs). After this ceremonial chant, according to Jonah's report, as Che had cut the throat of the wooly ungulate he seemed to have been thrown back by some unseen force, uttering a grunt or moan as he was struck by the spirit of this member of his herds or by the pain elicited in this creatures death, or some such sympathetic transformation of the violence done.

On those infrequent occasions when I have partaken of the flesh of animals since this telling, I generally give consideration to this intense example of empathy with the being whose death gives life to those who will consume it's flesh. Indeed, if the meat industry were so thoughtful and compassionate as traditional peoples in their treatment of animals I would not so oppose this currently violent and mean-spirited business.

Kosher and Halal rules dictate a minimal infliction of suffering in the slaughter of livestock. Many Native American traditions insist upon prayer and ceremony as gratitude to the spirits of the animals they kill to feed and clothe the people of their tribes. Family ranchers generally give personal if not affectionate care to their herds. It is only in the cold and heartless modes of modern industrial society that the suffering of these sentient beings that feed and clothe is considered of little to no consequence to well trained and desensitized consumers and livestock workers.

Another significant experience I had personally whilst staying with the Begay family was a dream that came to me on the night of the peyote ceremony. Oh yeah, I had forgotten to mention that the NAC meeting for the kids was a ceremony where they were to ingest this powerful psychedelic. I fell asleep in the camper to the sound of a drumbeat, a simple *bum-bum-bum-bum-bum* which varied only slightly in tempo over the whole expanse of the night. In my dream, I had a vision of a short stubby cactus with a button on top that was surrounded by a bright white light, the beat of drums continuing in the background even in REM sleep. That was the extent of this dream, but it told more than so many more complex symbols contained in the average mystical vision I've chance been granted.

It has become clear to me that the primary reason that "ordinary people" do not have so many extraordinary experiences (or don't talk about or take due notice of them if they do), and why average urban or suburbanites don't experience mystical happenings on a regular basis is that those venues have been largely closed by modern society's collective mind, which has seemingly forgotten the beauty of our ancestor's ways, however distant in the past, else compartmentalized such into books of fiction, fantasy and movies. There was a time when *everyone's* ancestors lived closer to the earth, when dreams mattered and visions were revered, a time before some point somewhere along the way when somebody decided to replace these ancient and abiding ways with a want for consumer trinkets and mostly mindless entertainment.

The consensual reality we have built like walls around our spirits has too much stifled the playful possibilities of life lived as an adventure, as a beautiful holistic encounter between mundane and mystical, matter and imagination, culture and nature. Many people have been tricked into somehow believing that playful creativity and want for magical adventures ought to be left behind by the time they attain second grade, and that their reward for such stoic acceptance of institutionalization is some pie-in-the-sky to be had somewhere after this life. Properly practiced, these two things need not be separate. Responsible living and adventure, rejoicing in being alive and taking care of business can peacefully coexist. Life is meant to be savored—responsibly and mindfully, mind you—and truly *lived*.

This journey was perhaps the best of my life thus far, wherein adventure and magical synchronicities, signs and stories to be remembered for a lifetime were manifest, and friendships were forged that have few comparisons before or since. I have wandered many, many miles thereafter, assuredly gaining wisdoms I did not have during this blissful journey, and indeed have acquired a great many deeper knowledges through many (often less pleasant) circumstances and experiences. Nonetheless, these months wandering from rain forest to desert and innocently playing our way across the American west shall always be amongst the fondest of my memories, and continue to serve a reminder of the playful benevolence and innocent magic of life on the road. Perhaps I should end the telling of this true tale by quoting one of Jonah's favorite phrases: ". . . and a good time was had by all."

The World Is Not What They Say It Is

The circle of cropped grass was expanding bit-by-bit by hours of frantic if rhythmic efforts in a semi-concentric patchwork of red willows and tall grasses and wild mint, all save the scrawny stick willows hewn to just above the root immediately surrounding the hut, which grows as the grasses recede. A hairy man bending down bare-chested, blade in one hand and a bundle of long grasses in the other, utters resonant intonations of an ancient tongue as he goes about his labors. Ancient words rhythmically chanted in time to the rhythms of his work as the tall grasses are harvested, as has been done from time immemorial to fulfill a need for shelter, with a similarly primeval respect for ritual. This seeming anachronistic figure is simply cutting grass to enclose a small thatched hut as a haven from the oncoming cold of winter, though indeed might evoke presumptions of a prehistoric context. Overt appearances, however, are often but a single view of a multifaceted formation or a compound manifestation.

The gathered bunches of grass are bent towards the base, then woven into the willow-stick frame and left to hang like shaggy blond hairs on the head of a Nordic wildman. Slowly the gaps are filled, and the tangle of sticks and straw begin to resemble a home, if humble and somewhat cramped. The red-bearded-long-haired-thin-framed-pale-skinned man pauses to assess his labors. He scratches his head and then his balls, unassuming and not the least self-conscious (though perhaps a bit self-aware). No one is watching. No one, save a few of his fellow tribesmen and women, birds, beavers, muskrats and mice know the whereabouts of his small abode, concealed in a maze of willows just a few yards from the river, framed a few steps from the water.

The hut is shaped like an igloo, except unlike an igloo the door is constructed on the side of the dome, and the odd structure is built around a larger species of willow tree, concealed just a few dozen yards off of the paved trail at the edge of Optimist Park. Joggers in their Nike running shoes, cyclists, in-line skaters and power-walkers regularly pass by the unobtrusive entrance to the narrow winding pathway that passes through the thicket and leads to this partially domesticated wildman's humble home.

Bunches of sticks tied together with grass are hung as odd ornamentations in the red willows that grow straight towards the sky from the moist ground. Glow in the dark stars and other oddities dangle on strands of hemp, decorations designed to delight those with whimsical imaginations, and to deter the meddling of those who might not take so kindly to a squat situated in the midst of a public park, a homestead hidden just upstream from the West Garfield Street bridge and only a couple of minutes walk from regular and titled homes of stucco and brick and plastic-siding wherein regular tax-paying Americans spend their tired evenings watching glowing screens displaying other people's lives, factual or fictitious, that are generally more interesting than their own.

The hut has a fireplace built with rocks left over from a city project along the paved greenbelt trail, a counter top attached by hemp string to one side, a plastic crate half-buried in the cool clay underneath the counter for food storage, and a single mattress folded lengthwise to make a couch sitting atop some wood pallets. Under the extension off the dome is a double-mattress elevated on pallets as a bed. The mattress is covered neatly with sheets and several blankets as insulation from the increasing cold of night.

Underneath thatching, the ceiling is covered in a layer of scavenged bubble-wrap to seal against rain and melting snow. One long window is left uncovered by straw to match the suns progress across the southern sky. A two-burner alcohol burning stove sits atop the counter, and various utensils dangle from the woven willow wall above. A small kitschy picture hangs over the hearth with an inscription that reads, "One touch of nature makes the whole world kin," a quote from Shakespeare's *Troilus and Cressida*. A transferred plastic image of a sparrow on a tree-branch adhering to one side of the decal script completes the embellishment of this faux-wood panel.

During my small austerities building this abode in the most-of-the-time solitude of this section of the river, biding my time with various yogic practices, I began to find the boundaries between self-and-other dissolving as never before, *tejas* ("fire") well stoked from sun salutations, *mantra* and trance whilst harvesting the tall grass and thatching. On one occasion as I was feeling particularly high from intense chanting and the onset of a beautiful sunset, I shifted from mantra to pop, and started to gleefully sing "all you need is love . . ." and imagined in my ecstatic trance that other souls could hear or at least feel my jubilant devotions and blissful state of yoga. A train started into town about that moment, and I decided to see if I could share my joyful intentions with the engineer. I swear to you, after I sang in both voice and mind "all you need is love," the train's horn sounded in perfect time to the following five beats of this well-known anthem, "du, du, du du du."

This strange construction was home to a displaced wildman for somewhere around three moons, till as so often happens to wild peoples the authorities of the so-called civilized folk came to roust him from even this unassuming hovel.

Sitting and sipping suds at the historic Buckhorn Bar, I noticed a blond and a redhead I'd not seen there before. The blond introduced herself as Blair, the redhead as Catherine (though whether with a "K" or a "C" I can't say). They told me they'd met in Africa whilst serving in the Peace Corps. The redhead said she was from my mother's father's hometown, a mostly Mennonite community in Kansas. She said she wasn't a Mennonite. I don't recall where the blond was from. A skinny sharply dressed fellow was bouncing between the two, seemingly weighing his options for later in the evening.

After another drink or two, the four of us made our way to the "wigwam," as I had come to call my hut in the swamp by the Laramie River. I had some shwag to smoke (Mexican-grown compressed marijuana, for those not hip to the jargon) and invited these new acquaintances to join me on a jaunt over the footbridge and to the Near Westside and through Optimist Park to my "primitive" abode.

I swung open the thatched woven-willow door, and we each ducked under the door frame to make our way into the wigwam. I started a fire in the stone and mud fireplace and lit some candles, and we enjoyed some smoke, passing a pipe and coughing and laughing. We had each consumed copious quantities of alcohol, and as there were two of each gender and orientation near the same age (at least by all appearances), the natural coupling ensued. Catherine and I began to make-out rather madly, whilst the other pair half-heartedly kissed a bit. Catherine decided to spend the night after Blair and her partner had departed, rather soon after our passionate drunken tongue-tangling had begun.

Not the next morning, but the morning after, I awoke to a loud if shaky-voiced proclamation and command proceeding from the periphery of my "yard."

"Laramie police! This is the police! Come out! Come out right now!"

Before going to sleep the previous night I had heard the nigh unmistakable sound of a squad car door slamming shut—cop car doors make a particular and discernible din as they are closed, if you grow accustomed to listening. I slid out of bed and pulled on a pair of pants. The shout was repeated.

"Just a minute, I gotta put some clothes on," said I.

As I opened the door and made my way outside, I was confronted with the sight of a fully uniformed cop half-crouched with his pistol drawn.

"Put that silliness away," I said with a wave of my hand.

"Oh . . . sorry," he uttered, seemingly a bit embarrassed at his overreaction.

I suppose the bundles of sticks dangling from the willows on the pathway might have startled him, perhaps with images from *The Blair Witch Project* in mind as he made his way through the winding willow-lined pathway. I should perhaps have told him, Blair had only stayed very briefly at the wigwam, and had departed two nights previous. I was officially evicted by the head of City Parks a few days later, but my endeavors at least received a nice front page write-up in the Boomerang titled "Wigwam Worries," and a follow up, too.

Several days later, "homeless" once again, I spent the night at Catherine's apartment. We had met at the bar, and went to her place to smoke a bowl of some nuggets—homegrown *Cannabis indica* this time, the dank. During an intimate moment later that night, as I was looking up and into her eyes, something happened that I cannot quite explain to this very day. Gazing at her face mere inches from mine, her visage suddenly morphed into the visage of the last woman I had known in that precise position, and then became again the face of the woman I assumed I was sharing intimacies with. I said not a word, though my eyes may have dilated and my mouth may have fallen agape in surprise. Then gazing down at me, eyes ablaze, she asked or stated rather matter-of-factly, "Oh, you saw my face change!?"

"You're a fucking shape-shifter!" said I—no pun intended.

"Ah, cheap magic trick," she replied with a broad smile.

I once watched a shape-shifting lycanthrope run across the road on the Navajo (Diné) Reservation in Arizona, slammed on the brakes of my truck to avoid hitting the beast. Less than twenty yards or so in front of the pickup, this large hairless green-glowing elongated canine creature with human-type musculature scampered across the dirt road and into a ditch. I've seen many a mangy coyote and have a respectable knowledge of wildlife, and this was nothing yet described by modern science.

One of the Diné kids that had guided me to a Hopi lady's house to buy some shwag told me, in response to my surprised utterance, "What the fuck was that!?" that the strange creature we had viewed was a "Skinwalker." The Diné believe that shamans who have dealt with dark-magic sometimes acquire the ability to morph into these lycanthropic, part-coyote creatures. I have also encountered other suspicious persons I suspected to be of the shape-shifting sort, on at least one other occasion. Perhaps it also warrants mention that I once awoke after a night with another quite beautiful and rather crazy lover, squinting at the sunshine only to gaze down to notice a suspicious and rather large suction mark with a scab in the middle on both my forearms, which left some rather funky temporary scars (not sure whether t'was she or her cat was the vampire). Never before or since, however, have I encountered such a reality shattering phenomenon at such close range as that night in Catherine's bed. The experience had first hand with said wild shapeshifting redhead has convinced me, perhaps more than any other single momentary happening, that the world is not what they say it is.

In Search of the Beloved

Brightly colored veils were a blur, or was it my vision that was smudged by a rush of transcendent desire, elation elicited by this encounter sublime? Entranced by rhythmic motions conveying transcendent love stories and mystical secrets superlative, beautiful bare belly and swaying hips expressing movements and vibrations as ancient as the first pangs of desire, those most primal longings that bring forth and maintain existence itself. Shakti.

I remember rich purple, shimmering gold and soft pink—though I could be mistaken regarding the precise shades. I remember beautiful dark locks of hair flowing like a night waterfall under an ocher moon, wistful brown eyes and sparkling visage expressing emotion in certain time with body's certain movements, facial expression matching mood and motion, and breasts and belly and buttocks swaying and trembling so perfectly timed to the smallest increments of the drum's beat.

Every muscle and curve and strand of hair and cloth and step and even breath seemed to move in such idyllic synchrony as one would expect only of a dream or psychedelic hallucination or Hollywood special effect. And her laughter! Her lovely laughter fell upon my ears like the peal of the perfectly tuned bells of an Himalayan shrine, like the sound of a mountain waterfall echoing off canyon walls, like the song of a spring breeze blowing o'er bright green spring leaves and bearing the scent of jasmine or lilac or apple blossoms, as melodic and genuine and pure as laughter can be. She seemed unreal, beyond mortal, a Goddess, unapproachable, unavailable, and it seems, unforgettable.

I was still a young man (in spite of having served—before I began to regain my wits and instincts—as the pastor of a church where most of the congregation was two to three times my age), and thus hadn't the least clue of how to behave in the presence of one such as this, most beautiful of belly dancing baristas, likely the loveliest to have ever graced this world.

I think I stopped for a coffee at Trinity Coffeehouse (formerly Muddy Waters Coffeehouse), and then began to hike down Grand—or would moving to the East on that particular street be hiking "up?" That is, considering the layout of Laramie, as addresses ascend as one proceeds in the direction of the Laramie Range (on the East-side of the tracks, that is), and as the elevations rise at a steady pace from the river towards the Sherman Hills. These sorts of directional and geometric and geological factors tend to figure into the way I have learned to think since exploring and examining so many sacred-ways of so many peoples, and I've found that to literally read the lay of the land indeed might grant some surprisingly valuable clues to whatever given puzzle.

I recognize these habits might be labeled "neurotic obsession": i.e., constantly calculating and emotively cross-checking time, place and persons in an envisioned web of experiential reality—past present and future, and across the span of my travels and imaginings and visions, and via all possible and likely connections between faces and places known and imagined, and always hearkening to an understanding of Divine good and whatever applicable mythological archetypes and spiritual teachings. Most the time these are nigh subconscious and peripheral contemplations else merely musings, save when the riddle at hand seems to beg the question.

Regardless of what epithets might be applied to these practices of perception, I have in fact discovered that geography can be read, in the manner stars might to some degree be read, to map certain aspects of a destiny. And indeed, I have some exceedingly complicated questions to answer, and would avail myself of whatever tools I might, in good conscience, to find answer to certain riddles have vexed me in recent years as I continue this journey through space and time aptly or inaptly titled "life."

Lay-lines of relationships and places visited and the more obvious and generally acknowledged points of geo-spiritual significance can be treasure map to any number of gems of understanding and esoterically emplotted secrets, and even sometimes to physically manifested booty . . . so to speak. Layers of signification even overlay the patterns of city streets, whether or not these are intentional or inadvertent. And indeed such significances are sometimes intentional, as was proven to my satisfaction when I encountered a plaque in downtown Sandusky, Ohio that told that the layout of the streets was designed to represent the Freemason compass—a group who pay no little attention to sacred geometry, often imitating various ancient modes of geometric and geographic conjurings (which said occultists then adapted to their particular and peculiar philosophy) as they designed many of our cities. The streets and important buildings of Washington D.C. are likewise arranged according to certain geometric patterns designed by this group, certainly with intentions to do *something* . . .

    A more abiding and natural manifestation of a "geographic constellation," or perhaps better, "earthen pictogram," is represented in the topography surrounding my purported place of birth. There are three mountain ranges that extend into southeast Wyoming (the Sierra Madre Range, the Snowy Range, and the Laramie Range), that when viewed from above are clearly the three prongs of a *Trishul* (the proper Sanskrit and more ancient term translating to the vernacular as "trident"), which connects to a *danda* ("staff") which extends south in Colorado as the Front Range. This Trishul appears to be held by a large cloaked and bearded figure which can be seen sitting in lotus or "Indian style" and facing east, comprised of mountain ranges and valleys and bodies of water from below the Four-Corners region and up through western Colorado and eastern Utah. Check it out the satellite photographs, if you doubt me. A more well-known and revered example of a natural geographically manifested sign is found on the southeast face of Aum Parvat, a great mountain in the Himalayas that displays a massive ॐ symbol in the snow on one of its slopes—which of course offers the riddle: which came first, the symbol or the sound?

    This particularly fateful journey to Quebec and the Eastern U.S. certainly proved as much a trip through warped time-space and lines of fate and memory as a mere cross-country tour that happened to take nearly three years to complete. And I must say, it's not always easy to maintain one's bearings on such an adventure (or misadventure, depending on one's perspective), even with some insight into the subtle features of the map or the sky. It is more than likely there are many layers of hidden signification inscribed upon the landscape, dimensions of potential travel not represented in any atlas I have yet encountered nor in any construction I have yet read of or figured, primordial inscriptions formed of earth and water which have had subtle effect and esoteric bearing upon the outcomes of my journeys and destinations—and likely upon yours, too. If there's a way to read these, all the better for the time-space traveler trying to find his or her way to a destination, whatever that might be. Perhaps something like a *Hitchhiker's Guide to . . . Eternity*.

If you find yourself traveling much, try to take note of the geometries between whatever points on the map become significant to your life story. See if there is not indeed some subtle symmetry there, shapes drawn on the dot-to-dot puzzle of your life journeys. Then like looking at a Rorschach inkblot, give an eye to reading the meanings in and of your patterns of personal migration. More fun than reading tealeaves.

I guess this won't work for you more sedentary types who've stayed near hometown for your lifespan, unless you've the patience to plot your patterns of movement from home to work or school or market, café, church or temple and whatever day-to-day steps you take to see if a meaningful design is revealed in and of your paths and habits. Patterns will likely emerge that will offer you much insight into certain life questions.

My intention was to hitchhike to Cheyenne and then hop a train from the convenient rail yard, located just off of the capital city's downtown. Though I could have hopped a train from Laramie's yard, I suppose I thought it more appropriate to depart from her hometown, or something to do with the lay of the rail lines as the line from Laramie forks, one track cutting south through Ft. Collins and the other east through Cheyenne. Before I made it past the UW campus, a fellow I knew mostly from the Buckhorn Bar pulled over and offered a ride.

I was wearing a pack my friend John had ordered custom made at Atmosphere Mountain Works downtown. He decided he didn't like certain features, and so passed it on to me. Zunaka, the wolf-dog that had accompanied me for several years, was traveling with me in tow—or was it I was in tow?

Ed dropped me off at the gas and Greyhound station about two or three miles from the edge of town. Before trying for another ride, I was approached by a man with salt and pepper hair. It was "Dr. Bill," former principle at the prep school I had attended as a child. He didn't recognize me at first. I told him of my plan, and he offered me some cash to help on my journey. I thanked him, and after a smoke I started to walk down the highway. I threw out my thumb to get some help over the hill to Cheyenne, and very shortly was obliged as a kindly middle-aged woman in a Subaru who pulled over to the shoulder and opened her passenger door.

I parted with my kind hostess after the mountainous passage, disembarked at the edge of downtown Cheyenne, then hoofed it towards the train station. Though I can't recall the precise date, it was either late January or early February (I'm leaning towards it having still been January) 2005, and fortunately for my purposes the weather was unseasonably warm. The sun was out, though high clouds lingered. I had reasonable clothing for the current climatological conditions, blankets and tarp, munchies, dog food, some herb, corncob pipe and tobacco, and plenty of water. I had less than two hundred dollars in cash.

Having never been on a freight train for any distance I was quite enthused at the prospect of riding the rails, if perhaps a tad ill prepared logistically and otherwise for all the implications of what I would experience over the duration of the coming long journey. I was also excited at the prospect of a meeting with Leslie, mere weeks away—assuming all went well with my voyage and that she was amicable to my humble intentions.

I was going east to seek the company of a particular woman purportedly living in Montreal who I had decided might be of some importance in answering one of those "What does it all mean?!?!" sorta questions (à la John Cusack in *High Fidelity*). She was a mysterious and beautiful barista and belly dancer I had encountered years before, and had become a figurative Beatrice, Kali Ma, and yoga guru in my imaginings (and certainly in at least some imaginings, tantra-yoga teacher or the likes), an idol or icon or *murti* in my mind's envisioning.

Having experienced certain premonitions in early October that something might not be well with this woman I had never really known yet could not forget, I decided perhaps it was time to bring some fruition or closure to my feelings and perhaps offer whatever assistance she might require of me, assuming my prescience was accurate. I thus endeavored to brave riding the rails and the winter's cold to venture on the least planned and provisioned journey of my life, just to chance that I might again be granted an encounter with this woman, to take hold of whatever possibility that a connection missed might have meaning still. All this in spite of the fact that the extent of our communications previous to this journey were limited to such exchanges as:

"Coffee?"

"Yeah—er, no . . . perhaps I'll try a chai today."

Yet experiences that occurred in the following years led me again and again to imagine this figure as somehow significant in my spiritual path, and perhaps bearing some importance otherwise. I found I couldn't shake thoughts of her even when I tried, continuing to find imaginings and daydreams of her lingering in my mind, randomly and inadvertently finding likenesses of her visage in the faces of women I encountered throughout my journeys—and not necessarily (or at least not always) by my own intention. Through relationships and love affairs with more than a few beautiful women over ten years or so, Leslie had remained something like an ideal expression of the Feminine Divine incarnate, at the very least in my imagined renderings.

This is of course not difficult to do with a figure who's somewhere afar. I intended to brave bridging that distance, as I'd reached a stage of confidence in myself—and in Self—that compelled me to take the chance something of meaning might manifest, else I'd at least likely be granted an audience with someone at least imagined Divine.

Around the time I first began to unconsciously exhibit (ehem) certain signs of being *sadhu*, she danced a dance of such subtle movement, such seductively charged grace displayed during belly-dance performances given at a local coffee house (where she was also employed), I could only later render this apparition as at least very like an incarnation of Parvati, and specifically resembling said Deity in the myth wherein She was encouraged to seduce Siva, as the other Gods feared the fierce *tejas* (fire) raised by the Master and Progenitor of Yoga.

Zunaka and I hopped the fence just a bit east of the downtown station and I found a train that was at least heading in the proper direction, judging by which end the engines were on. As I lifted my seventy-five pound furry companion and my pack and myself aboard the container-car I felt an exceptional exhilaration, a liberation of being freed from even the burden of maintaining a gas-guzzling vehicular domicile as my mount (most of my previous journeys were aboard an old Dodge Power-Wagon with a camper on back and an orange sunshine painted on the passenger door, the which I had sold shortly before this trip), and thus in my reasoning unattached to the karma of war and exploitation of earth and people attached to said energy source.

As the diesel engines began to pull, the links tightened in domino sequence till I felt the many tons of metal under my seat jolt forward, wheels randomly screeching and whining, metal frames groaning as this snake of metal started on the well-worn track towards the direction of the sun's rising. I reclined and lit my pipe to celebrate this auspicious departure, first journey by freight-rail, and as I had deemed this quixotic quest, "last big off-the-cuff adventure." Of course, whether or not this actually proves to have been my last such impetuous and scarcely planned departure for the unknown remains to be seen. A certain amount of preparation and assurance of provisioning, more than I had secured for this endeavor at least, seems wiser now than then. I am no enemy to moderate creature comforts, even if I do undergo the occasional intentioned austerity, and the sometimes unintentional privation.

I had imagined this journey not unlike others previously, as part cross-country exploration and part ritual transformation. Yet certain factors were unique, as the theme of this adventure was romantically (for lack of a better English word, though the Sanskrit word *bhakti* might better fit) as well as mystically motivated, if with the rather humble romantic goal of sharing coffee or tea and a chat (likely at most, was my presupposition) with Leslie. I wanted at least a moment or two to offer thanks for the inspiration, and to ascertain whatever further significance might or might not present itself, with the intention of then touring the Northeastern United States and perhaps enjoying some additional explorations of Eastern Canada. And as is the case with any of my endeavors, I had in mind a willingness to play whatever role I might to better whatever I might for others in the process of my movements and actions, if only by thoughtful acts subtle or small, smiles or a kind word, sacred intonations, or by whatever means come my way as I walk through this or other worlds. *Karma-dharma, sevA*: duty in action, service.

By an hour out of town, bundled up in bedroll, I fell asleep to the hypnotic rhythms of the train—a sometimes jarring vibration of metal on metal that nonetheless becomes a sort of lullaby—and to the cold kiss of the still frigid winter wind, only partially blocked by the containers stacked in front of our perch. I slept a strange sleep—dreams in transit or transit in dream.

Awoke late at night in a large switchyard somewhere in central or eastern Nebraska to a disturbingly-orange-lit reality, to the sound of trains slamming together and broken apart and switched to other lines, and to a sky as dark and starless as any I've seen. Zunaka and I hopped off to stretch and piss, then made it back to our berth just in time to evade the yard-bulls as they rolled by, spotlights scanning the cars in search of . . . me?

This large yard was a disorienting place to awaken, and the more startling upon realizing the yard bulls are on the hunt, slowly cruising the narrow spaces between trains, scanning with piercingly bright spotlight beams between the heavy pale hue of discomforting pink-orange floodlights and patches of gray shadow. The scene was reminiscent of the metallic wasteland depicted in *The Terminator*, but instead of hovercraft searching for stray humanoids, it was a white pickup truck cruising between the tracks that sought stowaway humans hiding amongst so many tons of steel.

The first time they passed I was not seen. Two or three times more the white pickup passed by, a track or two over. Second time they passed directly beside our chosen berth they did not find our hiding-place, as we both lay flattened on the tail end of the piggyback container carrier. The third time I was spotted.

The man who caught sight of me gazed my direction for only a second, then turned away, perhaps attempting to pretend he had not spied our illegal perch. It could be that he sympathized with a hippie-cum-hobo desperate or crazy enough to ride a train across the Upper Midwest in winter. Perhaps he just didn't want to deal with the paperwork, but I think I sensed compassion, inasmuch as one can read intentions on the face of another at a glance, at night and in a passing vehicle. Despite the paranoia of Homeland Security and the Patriot Acts, on-the-ground administrators of the system's rules are still, for the most part, human. Most of the time . . .

Train started again, slowly accelerating until we were safely on the move and out of view of the railroad cops. As I lay under the again visible sky, I pondered how I might approach some possible meeting with Leslie, not wishing to appear *"the stalker"* and so forth. It is not so easy to determine those lines these days, as remnants of the chivalric tradition gave way to Victorian propriety, and the latter (the "free love" era notwithstanding) to extremes of sensibilities that, while to some degree justified as measures of protection of personal privacy, have also made it difficult to express the deep and heart-felt devotions of a love-stricken fool. Likely a significant portion of those endeavoring a romantic gesture by standing beneath his or her beloved's window whilst holding up a boom-box playing "In Your Eyes" get arrested and slapped with a restraining order.

These mores and strictures and lines in mind, I envisioned how I ought seek out and approach this heretofore unapproachable maiden. Leslie and I had not been acquainted beyond the most casual of interactions, after all, lest some subtle communications or remembrances I thought I'd sensed or recalled from her days as barista at Coal Creek Coffee were more than my imagination or wishful thinking.

Once I had overheard her not small voice declare, "I feel sorry for Holly." Holly was the name of my wife at the time, and I wondered if somehow this woman knew of my carousing behavior, oft enough displayed for public view at the Buckhorn and other local bars, and was indirectly chiding me for my misconduct. She also made various rather crass (or at least blunt) remarks to her coworkers that seemed meant for my hearing, and even almost overtly directed towards me, as well as uttering other random statements that seemed well fitted to circumstance in my life—certainly beyond what might be labeled "coincidental." Though later I would be informed this wasn't quite the case, at least as far as conscious intentions were concerned, and that I had in fact been a scarcely noticed part of Leslie's reality while she worked at Coal Creek, such factors perhaps prove irrelevant to synchronicities noticed, other than to denote said statements were not *consciously* or *intentionally* offered for my ear. Synchronicity needn't be noticed or deliberate to exist.

Innuendo *at best* was thus the only real communication I had carried on with this astounding woman, yet I was no longer willing to let fear or irrational inhibitions overcome my want to understand the important questions of this life, nor to dissuade me from seeking the company of this woman who had become my "Beloved." Regardless of fervor, however, I had in mind all due respects and restraint.

Indeed, my intentions were quite honorable, if not downright chivalric. I had no plan to do other than to politely request Leslie's company for a cup of coffee or tea—seemingly apropos considering the circumstances of our slight acquaintance—and was of course fully willing to accept a "No" with grace and repose. Regardless of the outcome of this potential encounter with this woman at least once glimpsed as seeming vessel of the Divine Feminine incarnate, I intended to convey every due respect and consideration.

I had contingently maintained a wish to wander about in the Northeast, after all. This was one region of the lower 48 I'd not yet seen in all my journeys, excepting a couple of weeks in New York City at the end of a cross-country trip on a Green Tortoise tour bus, and a few months spent in D.C. This journey would thus offer additional opportunities for exploration, assuming nothing of substance came of my meeting with Leslie—and as I've stated, I made no assumptions of her whatsoever. Indeed, I'd have plenty to see and experience on this voyage, regardless of whether any fruition turned out to be destined for the more quixotic features of the quest.

The train was rhythmically rumbling, grumbling and singing a cacophonic symphony to accompany my meandering thoughts. I ate some of what remained of my food, opened Zunaka's feedbag and shared some water with my white wolf-dog companion. I lit my pipe, and then covered my head under the felt blankets that insulated my reclined form—covers made from perhaps hundreds of recycled bedspreads (and who knows what) of the sort given away at homeless shelters and other charitable places, and further shielded myself from the wind under the tarp that encompassed my cowboy-style bedroll, Zunaka curled at my feet. I was wearing two or three pairs of pants, a couple or three layers of shirts and two coats as well as blankets and tarp. One of the two coats was given to me by Chloe.

Chloe was instructing a yoga class I had regularly attended on First Street whilst I lived in a wigwam by the Laramie River in Optimist Park. Chloe had been raised in a home where *murtis* of Siva and Krishna and Devi (Sanskrit for "Goddess") as various Avatars were displayed for devotion. Chloe worked at Trinity Coffee House (previously known as Muddy Waters Coffee House), which was across the street from Coal Creek Coffee Company's downtown coffeehouse (where I had first encountered Leslie). Chloe's mother Julia was Leslie's belly-dance and yoga instructor in Laramie years before.

Shortly after first meeting Chloe, she and I and a mutual friend who also happens to be named Jeffrey (aka Monk/Squirrel/Baba Ananda Vyasadev) went to a small party on the outskirts of town, and I discovered upon arrival that Leslie was present. It was a hot tub party, and of course people in the tub were likely not wearing clothes. Despite my appreciation for communal bathing *au naturale* under a starry sky, I didn't get wet with Leslie and others that night. Had I braved such an intimate setting with still secret object of devotion on that occasion, Leslie and I would surely have conversed, and I would likely have never embarked upon this adventure to request her company for a cup and a chat.

Chloe means green buds of grain, and is another name for Demeter, Greek goddess of spring and such things, and mother to Persephone, maiden kidnapped by Hades in the well-known myth.

I almost invited Chloe to dinner at my wigwam, but never quite got the words out after early morning the yoga class she taught. Maybe for the better, as I'm not sure my *dal* and *raita* or vegetable *bajji* would've impressed her much. She grew up in a home with a stepfather from India who I hear is a great cook. Chloe gave me a purple Marmot parka—she liked to ski.

Now the wigwam, as it turns out, was a rather pivotal locus in the inception of this journey, or at least in reckoning the subtle and esoteric factors that frame said trip. I had spontaneously decided to build this shelter whilst smoking some herb with friends Hans and Naomi under a rather prominent, if still well hidden willow tree near the Laramie River. Surrounded by red willow thickets (a non-branching straight stick sort of willow), this octopus-branched tree was well known to some area pagans, to pot-smoking high school kids over the years (of course), as well as serving as a campsite to various hippies and hobos and area drunks from time to time.

The first phase of construction was a lean-to wall woven of dead red willow sticks and set against the base of the short trunk, then woven together with the tree's lower branches and thatched with the abundant tall grasses growing nearby. Hans suggested these grasses might be of the genus Phalaris, thus containing DMT, but I had no interest in chemistry experiments at the time, just a want for shelter.

I found a full-size mattress next to the dumpster behind a local furniture store, and placed it on some pallets under the grassy structure. I later added a dome to one end of the lean-to, woven from branches of the main tree, saplings that grew in a convenient circle, and many dead red willow sticks. The structure was made waterproof with recycled bubble-wrap, also from behind the furniture store, and thatched top to bottom save for a bubbly translucent window that allowed in light from the sun's low winter passing.

Much of my time was spent searching the area for dead willows and patches of tall grass and chanting various Sanskrit chants, as is my practice, whilst I worked. I had plenty of time to spend on constructing my hermitage, as my only other obligation was as a cook three-days-a-week at the Laramie Soup Kitchen, where I utilized the donated tofu and various vegetarian items the other cooks would overlook to feed our patrons.

For heating and cooking and entertainment I built a fireplace of rock and mud with a cast iron top surface for heat radiation and on which I could set a pan or fry flat bread. The chimney protruded through the south wall. I mudded around the fireplace and lower portions of the entire structure to prevent the whole thing form inadvertently going up in flames—an obvious hazard with a grass hut. A two-burner alcohol stove sat atop a salvaged counter-top that I attached to one wall, pots and pans and utensils hanging above, with a half-buried plastic bin underneath which served as an icebox. A single mattress and some pillows were placed along one side of the dome as a couch of sorts, and a rug lay atop some cardboard as a floor. Home sweet home.

During my sojourn in this closest thing to a non-motorized home I had known for years, I decided that I ought to change my white wolf-dog companion's name to something more appealing to my personal aesthetics. He was given to my care several years previous with the name Zeus, a mythological figure from a mythological paradigm for which I maintain little affinity. I chose the name *Zunaka* from a Sanskrit lexicon, which is both a proper male name and a word meaning simply "dog," and which maintained a similar sound to what my white wolf-dog traveling companion was accustomed to hearing when called.

Less than two weeks later I just happened to be reading the *Upanishads* and just happened to come across the statement, "and Angira taught *Zunaka* the secrets of Brahman (the abiding Nature of reality/Universal Divine Person)." Seems I had chosen dog's new name well. In later research, I discovered that the willow tree —one of the primary materials and framework of the wigwam's structure—is associated in Greek mythology with the deity Zeus, as well as Hecate, witch goddess of the Greek underworld who is associated with Hölle, etymologically related to "hell" and to my x-wife's first name, Holly.

Signs and symbolic and synchronistic shit of all manner, shape, form and modes of delivery have become given realities since I began my path as a mystic madman. Situationally relevant mythology and memes and ancient memories have often enough manifest as undeniably prescient and pertinent writings on the wall, and mind and matter and motion and coincidence convey extra-temporal communications that often prove to be at least informed outside opinions, and sometimes offer concise and astoundingly accurate predictions and visions regarding my *sitz-im-leben*. This has not, however, detracted from the importance and scrutiny I grant to *each-and-every* signal and sense stimuli with seeming significance—for even some signs which appear as certain, veritable writing on the wall, can deceive and mislead. Generally those signs that have proven most reliable prognostications or subtle level indications have been those connected to *sanAtana dharma*, though whether due to personal expectations or the intrinsic truth of said paradigm is of course debatable.

    Discernment is vital, and awareness of tantamount importance if one chooses to look beyond veils and the officially sanctioned and popularly received visions of reality. Even misleading indicators can often be read (between the lines of esoteric semiotics and deceitful or mistaken impetus or intention) to offer clues to whatever riddles one is seeking to solve. The writing is indeed on the wall, in the clouds, in patterns of tealeaves spilled, dreams remembered and contemplated, and nearly everywhere—if one has the eyes (or *eye*) to see.

    I have had thousands of experiences I've scrutinized in depth that indicate 'tis not merely a material world, and material and spiritual are not so separate as many assume. And yet, there is certainly something to be said for non-attachment to the potential distractions of seeking to uncover that which is occulted, and sometimes much wisdom in paying no mind to the mystery's plot in order to maintain a meditative state of mind, not to mention sanity . . .

    Much preferable, of course, to maintain a somewhat oblivious and blissfully entranced state of consciousness (or perhaps better, "*mindful* yet blissfully . . ."), more in tune with nature than human intrigues or *lila*. At times, however, it seems even a would-be, dilettante of an *sadhu* needs to attend to these latter factors, to dive into the mire of sometimes fucked-up humanity and the confusing riddles and intrigues of *maya* in order to fulfill dharma.

This is reminiscent of a Japanese Buddhist proverb a friend named Tom in Santa Fe told me once. A man living in the city who grew disgusted with the drunkenness and debauchery he observed retreated to the mountains to seek enlightenment. One day upon some high peak, 'poof,' he became enlightened. And just what did this austere ascetic do upon attaining this elevated state of being? But of course, he returned to the city to engage in drunkenness and debauchery.

Early in the construction of the wigwam I began to have premonitions and other sorts of signs and sensations presented me which told me that Leslie, beautiful and beatified figure (in my personal constructions at least), was facing some potential threat to her well-being. I prayed some prayers, after my own fashion, and performed some rituals intended to protect her, after my own fashion.

"Don't mind me, but a humble (dilettante-of-a) *sadhu* squatting in this city park and carrying out ancient tantric rituals," or perhaps, "What, you've never met a crazy sorcerer living in a swamp? I thought every shadowy willowy thicket at the edge of any given village was supposed to be inhabited by at least one holy man or wizard or witch!"

I had various random visitors whilst whiling away the days and nights in my humble hut, most of who either offered to share some smoke, else gladly received my invitations to join me for a session by the fire. One of the more memorable visitations to this unusual abode was a pair of travelers presenting themselves as British tourists. They accompanied me from the Buckhorn and through the thicket one night to smoke or merely to see my hut, I can't recall which. One of the two was a bit o'er concerned about spiders, so we stayed only briefly.

The arachnophobe with the British accent was a beautiful movie (television?) star blond who told me she was an archaeologist, and that her name was "Claire," and she kissed me oh so sweetly on the walk towards her room at the Sunset Inn on this interesting evening. I only mention this event as I've recently become a fan of the TV series Heroes, and the Claire I met at the Buckhorn, led to my wigwam, and with whom I later shared a kiss bore more than a slight or merely coincidental resemblance to

Hayden Panettiere, the actress who plays *Claire* Bennet, the indestructible cheerleader. Sometimes the lines between art and life get rather fuzzy, if not downright tangled, twisted and even dread-locked.

Friends and other passersby would irregularly, randomly, and frequently stop by, and on more than one occasion I was able to offer shelter to someone in need of a temporary place to crash. This was something of what I had hoped to accomplish: to create a magical, sacred, pure, and safe yet wild habitat in the middle of a city. Only shared my wigwam bed with one woman, however, before a policeman showed up, gun drawn, to inform me I had to abandon my home.

"Laramie police!! This is the police, come out right now!!"

I pulled on a pair of pants and swung the door open, emerging from my cozy cottage to intercept a blue-clad gun-toting civil servant who was wearing an expression that gave me the impression he expected the Blair Witch to emerge from the spooky hut in the scary marsh. Blair was actually my erstwhile lover's best friend— if I recall correctly they met in Africa whilst serving in the Peace Corps, and Blair had left the wigwam once Catherine and I started making out, and thus was definitively not present. Admittedly, I had hung some spooky stick-figures in the trees amidst the many glow-in-the-dark stars and other appropriate seeming ornamentations, *murtis*, odd decorations, and two mildly menacing scarecrows I had constructed in my yard for kicks, so I suppose one could understand his paranoia.

"Put that silliness away," I said as I assessed his posture and the position of his firearm, in hand and presumably ready to fire, though not quite pointed at me.

"Oh, sorry," he exclaimed as he returned pistol to holster.

I ended up going to the local newspaper and receiving reasonably fair coverage of the incident of my eviction on the front page, but was still forced to leave my home by the river a few days later.

Catherine and I spent one more night together, this time at her house, a month or so before I set out for Montreal. This night, or more specifically a few short moments during this night, would prove to forever alter the lenses through which I perceive reality, already a good distance removed from most folks' paradigms after several years of crazy hippie-style mendicant mystic meanderings.

As we were on her bed that night, Catherine assumed a position atop me, and as is the custom in such circumstance I gazed at her face as she found her pleasure, legs bent on either side of my thighs and hands resting on either side of my shoulders. She opened her eyes and stared down at me, and whilst gazing up I quite clearly viewed her visage morph into the visage of my most recent lover previous, and then transformed back into the face of the woman I thought I was having sex with. I said not a word, though my eyes may have dilated or my mouth may have fallen agape in surprise. She continued to gaze into my eyes, and then said rather matter-of-factly,

"Oh, you saw my face change," a mischievous smile scarce contained upon her lips.

"You're a fucking shape-shifter!!!" I exclaimed, with no pun intended.

"Ah, cheap magic trick," said she, and only scarcely interrupting her rhythmic circular motions upon my lap and linga.

Once a person sees such a feat at such near proximity, any number of givens regarding the nature of reality are called into question. Quite simply expressed: *I have seen someone change her appearance into a different form at less than two feet from my face; therefore, shape-shifters exist; therefore, I can have no certainty that anyone is exactly who or what they seem.* Yet another case of the ground not existing where I once assumed it ought. This realization would certainly influence my assessment of later encounters with Leslie, and for that matter, my interpretation of every person I meet and face I see. Oh well, there goes so called "reality."

I had encountered a shape-shifter on at least one other occasion, I might note. This incident occurred on the Navajo (Diné) reservation in Arizona, though not at anywhere near this proximity. This particular southwestern mythic beastie was at the healthy distance of fifteen yards or so from my vantage, and I was safely inside my big burly four-wheel drive pickup, the Miraculous-Beast-Shanti-Mama. Upon viewing the huge, hairless, green glowing human-like canine run across the road, I cried out in surprise, "What the fuck was that!?!?!" One of the Diné teens that had guided me from Camp Anna Mae to a Hopi woman's house to acquire a quarter or half-oz. of shwag (bricked marijuana) casually responded with the answer I believe I already knew, as I had been introduced years before to the lore regarding this particular mythical beast when a teacher at the prep school I'd attended read to our grade school class from a book of true-life scary stories one Halloween.

"That was a skinwalker," he said casually, as if to say, "Oh yeah, here we commonly see lycanthropes cutting across the road in front of vehicles in transit after dark—no big deal." I have seen many a mangy coyote and have a respectable knowledge of wildlife generally, and what I viewed quite clearly as it crossed the dirt road was unlike any species I might know or imagine. The only possible and rather unlikely explanation for the apparition would be that what we had viewed was a cougar who had denned in a cave of uranium or radium, thus the loss of hair and green glow, though the length of the snout I succinctly recall would not fit with that theory and the movement of the creature was not at all catlike.

Amidst the rumble and sway and vibrations of my mobile berth I moved in and out of a strange sleep, a state in which normal time and space seemed distorted or warped, and dreams and waking were not so separate as they most often are whilst not in-transit, and especially in-transit in a mode not really meant for moving people. Just before waking I had dreamt that I was walking in some nondescript dimly lit urban neighborhood. Approaching on the sidewalk from the opposite direction was a man leading a horde of zombies. I leapt high over this seeming threat, and then awoke.

The train had stopped in a city or town. After nearly two days aboard this segmented serpent of steel, we dismounted well after dark and began to seek an open restaurant or convenience store. As Zunaka and I started down the neighborhood street, I noticed a man approaching on the sidewalk. It was definitely the man from the dream, though thankfully there were no zombies in tow—unless they were invisible. We exchanged nods in greeting as we passed in opposite directions under the glow of dim streetlights.

I soon discovered we were in Iowa, not far from the Mississippi, and found a late-night diner where I might sit on a padded seat, eat, drink coffee and recuperate. I soon regained my land legs, and shortly ceased to feel as if my body was vibrating. I ravenously consumed an omelet and hash browns, and drank quite a bit of coffee before returning to the tracks.

The train we had been aboard was gone, and another was parked in its place. We hopped aboard a grain hopper car, which are often built with a convenient platform on the tail-end that is protected from rain and snow and wind. Some of these sorts of rail cars even have a compartment one can climb inside between the car's shell and the interior grain bin, a cozy if grungy cubbyhole often bearing traces of previous hobo inhabitants: cigarette butts, water bottles and blankets, emptied 40s and liquor bottles, and perhaps if lucky you'll find a roach chance thoughtlessly or thoughtfully left in the corner, half-smoked and sticky with resin, else half a bottle of whiskey layin' in the corn dust. Similarly constructed coal hoppers don't have these first-class hobo accommodations, by the way, and are a rather dirty ride regardless. Container carriers, the type of car we'd hopped on in Cheyenne, are my second choice mounts for hobo-style transportation. If you sit behind the containers, wind and rain or snow usually blow right over, depending on the speed of the train and direction of wind, of course. Boxcars are a fine ride, except you have to concern yourself with securing the door so you don't find it slamming shut, locking you inside. More than one hobo has expired from the cold or heat or dehydration inside one of these potential death traps, seem such an accommodating ride.

When the train shortly started east, I dozed for a few hours. Upon regaining consciousness I realized the train had turned, and was now traveling north on the west bank of the Mississippi. Though my intended destination was Montreal, Canada, there was no hurry to travel deeper into the north's midwinter cold. It seemed wiser to wait till the other side of the Great Lakes before any further movement towards the pole, as the cold steel of a freight train car conducts climatic conditions straight from the air to your arse.

    We disembarked in Dubuque, found a coffee house to have breakfast, then walked across the bridge into Illinois. I recognized an obvious symbolic passage as I looked down at the Mississippi, likely at half or less it's eventual breadth, and then gazed across the bridge into Illinois. Walking between a patchy mix of clouds and clear sky above and the cold flow below whilst crossing the watery border between the "Corn State" and "Land of Lincoln," I proceeded on towards destiny, desideration, disillusionment or *deux folie*, or some odd admixture of the above.

    It seems there is a certain shift in reality when one crosses any given recognized border, if too subtle for most to notice, and something more than coincidental to the relationship between the term "state" designating a region and said word used to designate a condition of being. To cross an acknowledged border is thus to step into a realm of difference. And indeed, the Mississippi divides both bordering states and this nation on the order of no other delineation, save for the Continental Divide's heights.

    We continued along the highway just east of the mighty Mississip, and I extended left thumb to the side as I hiked to signal that I would indeed appreciate a lift, in case anyone passing couldn't tell. A lanky tie-die clad fellow with a scruffy beard took the hint and gave us a ride to the next town, sharing some herb and advice regarding the nature of the area and its people. After dark, Z-dog and I made our way into downtown Galena, Illinois. "Lead sulfide," Illinois, if read literally. Lived in Leadville for a while, a high and far from dry little town high in the Colorado mountains, a locale where it seemed from my observations that the local brand of hippies did psychedelics so they could stay up longer to drink yet more beer and whiskey . . . but I digress.

    After a half-an-hour wandering the well-kept business district of Galena, a couple pulled over and offered me a place to stay. The woman rather reminded me of Chloe's mother Julia, perhaps the first yoga instructor who taught me *asanas* (in this lifetime at least), at least from what I recall of their respective visages. They offered me some soup upon arrival at their country home. I slept a dreamless sleep on a well-cushioned couch.

Next morning, grateful for a comfortable night's rest we again hit the road. Zunaka pulled hard on his leash as we walked along the tree-lined road. Swept through Rockford, a rather sad Midwest town likely hit hard by the decline in manufacturing over recent decades, then crossed the border into Wisconsin.

Went to the library in Beloit to try to figure the layout of the railroad tracks in the area, hoping to hop another train, but according to an atlas I found on the shelves there seemed no easy boarding and no certain track to convey us in the proper direction. We wandered to a convenience store located near the intersection of highways leading to Milwaukee, Madison, and southeast towards Chicago. I penned a sign with a Sharpie—an indispensable item on the road which is found in nigh every crusty traveling kid's belongings—and Zunaka and I sat on the sidewalk holding a piece of cardboard that read simply, "Chicago, Madison or Milwaukee."

Whilst awaiting the manifestation of a ride, passers-by often offered cash and food and water and dog-treats, but no offer of conveyance toward any of the three advertised optional destinations. After a couple hours or so, a rather conservatively clad middle-aged man in jeans and a polo shirt approached and began to chat with me about various jam-bands, from The String-Cheese Incident to the Grateful Dead. He handed me a bottle of water or some dog treats or some such and returned to his pickup. Just previous to his appearance, I had contemplated potential modes of moving on: *Train? Hitchhike? Bus? I couldn't take the Greyhound, as they only allow canines aboard as service animals, unless . . .*

An acquaintance I'd known in Laramie had once told me a friend of his had feigned blindness to travel with his dog on "the Dog" on numerous occasions. *I couldn't possibly . . . I wouldn't want to take advantage . . . even if I could pull it off . . .*

The man who I'd just conversed with returned and offered some rawhide for Zunaka, and also extended his hand holding pair of sunglasses, stating that they'd be good for carpentry or some such. These shades were rather large, had side-guards and looked almost too perfect to pass as a blind-person's shades. I took this as a clear sign I ought to employ my acting skills to get myself and dog aboard "the Dog" for this next leg of the journey.

I still implicitly trusted signs at this point, not yet disillusioned with that intrinsic sense which assumes that whatever happens, it'll work out properly and fairly. I had yet to become jaded and suspicious of the subtle snares might well lie behind seeming boons and apparent miraculous manifestations. I have since learned to look a gift horse in the mouth, for my own betterment or no. I must say, I rather liked seeing the best in things the better.

I carried out my plan rather flawlessly, and without finding the least need to utter even one false word as I remained in character through three bus changes and multiple stops. That is, until arriving at the border between New York and Quebec, where my bluff was revealed.

At the time it was necessary to display both a state ID and birth certificate or a passport in order to cross the border on public transportation, whereas a driver's license was acceptable identification for drivers or passengers in private vehicles. For my identification I had only a driver's license, which for obvious reasons would not suffice as authentic identification for a purportedly blind person, with or without additional ID. The bus departed, leaving us at the border after a rather uncomfortable period during which my status was in question and whilst the bus and its passengers anxiously awaited.

As I sat in the waiting area at the Canadian border station, I couldn't help but notice that the majority of the Canadian border officers were attractive women. Upon being conveyed to the American Homeland Security run border station, I could then scarce help but notice the contrast between the paramilitary style uniforms sporting over-sized "Homeland Security" patches worn by the American officers (and the corresponding attitudes) and the more casually dressed Canadians, the differences in gender balance (only one female amongst the Americans, and a rather butch one at that), and the uncomfortable tension in the air at the U.S. border station office compared to the rather laid back Canadian officials' attitudes.

Whereas the Canadians were amicable (if not particularly humored) in spite of my potentially prosecutable offence, the American guards seemed to enjoy forcing me to wait, seemingly finding some sadistic pleasure in the power they held over me, even as they did let me go unhindered after what seemed an unnecessarily long wait. And I should also note regarding my troubles at the border: I was informed that a veterinarians certificate verifying current rabies vaccination was necessary in order to bring a dog into Canada.

As Zunaka and I began south, I looked to both east and west to ascertain the viability of a less formal or frontal entry into Canada. So far as I know, the paranoia of the Neo-con's has yet to lead to a wall or other such excessive measures on the northern border, save for some purported cameras and motion sensors along the western portions designed to impede the flow of "beasters" (mid-grade, mostly keefed marijuana grown in western Canada) between British Columbia and Washington state. And these electronic barriers are designed to keep people and smuggled goods out, and not, at this tenuous point in this nation's history, to keep people in. I decided to seek someplace to pass the night instead of attempting an illicit crossing, however, and found a 24-hour convenience store that turned out a boon for more than merely the warmth and hot coffee.

An attractive young brunette was the night clerk. I ordered a coffee and sat at one of the tables in the deli section. I ended up telling the clerk the purpose of my journey and explaining the little misadventure at the border, including the detail of missing a hydrophobia-free certificate for my canine companion. She made a phone call, and a dready kid somewhere in his teens showed up sometime towards 3 a.m. with a veterinarian's certificate certifying that one male "Saint Bernard mix" had received his shots. Zunaka was purportedly a Great Pyrenees/wolf/lab hybrid, and so could easily pass as maintaining Saint Bernard blood.

After sunrise, this sweet bestower of blessings drove us across the border and accepted my invitation for breakfast at a café a few miles down the road. We sat amongst overall-clad francophone farmers as I had my first meal in Quebec. Unimaginative and in fact cliché as this might be, I ordered crêpes.

I bade farewell to my partner in cross-border dog-smuggling, and Zunaka and I started north along the highway towards Montreal.

Hitchhiking up north is a breeze compared with the potential hours of waiting often experienced endeavoring the same in the States—indeed, as Canada is in many respects more open to travelers and gypsy sorts generally. A woman in an economy car pulled to the shoulder before I had hiked a mile. She didn't speak English, but seemed completely comfortable with offering a ride to a big, unwashed bearded man and a wolf-dog from the States. Oh, Canada! What qualities of community, hospitality and compassion you have that in this land seem oft depleted, if not sometimes almost forgotten in the face of fears forwarded by faux foes and fantastic plots presented a populace fixated on the sensational and shocking, so well trained to believe in what's presented on the screen.

After less than three weeks on the road and rails I had arrived in Montreal. Or to be precise, a rather unimpressive modern suburb across the *San Laurent*. I found the entrance to the underground rail, and attempted to negotiate the young and beautiful crowds whilst loaded down with large backpack and large white wolf-dog. Across the river (or from underneath the river, to be more accurate), we emerged into the center of Old Montreal, and as far from the cultural milieu of Middle America as one's likely to find north of Mexico, save on Native American reservations and perhaps in the backcountry Cajun swamplands of Louisiana, else deeper into French Canada.

Indeed, central Montreal is more like an old world European city than a "New World" commercial-style venture. I walked amidst stone buildings that were between or over two and three hundred years standing, strolling narrow brick-paved streets and walkways likely laid centuries in the past, and could only compare the scene to my blurry (Guinness and cider induced) recollections of a visit to London during my college years. Of course I do recognize the rather provincial purview presented by this comparison of a francophone metropolis and London, but such is the extent of my direct exposure to architecture outside of ranch-style, duplexes, macmansions, boxy condos, steel-girded skyscrapers and hometown American blasé, embellished by the occasional and intentionally-artsy experimental artifice and the increasingly rare Victorian, Art-Deco, colonial or other non-cookie-cutter style structure.

The pedestrians I encountered on this rainy, then sleeting, then snowing afternoon were notably different from the average urbanites I've encountered Stateside. Fashionably—no, *smartly* dressed hipsters (or their equivalent, rendered *en Français*) strolled the streets, along with other more seasoned residents who for the most part seemed to wear their clothes better than their counterparts to the south. Even the manner in which people on the streets carried themselves there seemed a step more graceful—or at least appeared to my eyes to express a more refined aesthetic. I will admit to having been taken a bit by the spell of novelty, and I do recognize some hyperbole in this expressed perception of mystique did coalesce as I observed these passing pedestrians' self-presentation and overheard the mostly indiscernible din of French words as these fashionable francophones carried on everyday conversations, if understandably whilst under the influence of high romantic hopes and dreamy vision in a setting so self-consciously amorously urbane.

I was amazed to discover that as I found it necessary to engage in rudimentary exchanges, I had indeed acquired enough knowledge of the French tongue from one semester studied in college to carry on moderately intelligible conversations. I soon realized, however (and to my slight disillusionment), *en Montreal* it is actually not necessary to speak the neo-native tongue (Iroquoian and like tongues being the more truly native speech, of course), as most inhabitants speak English as a second language, and many as a first. To describe the perhaps too common experience *en Montreal* of observing a conversation that begins in French and then reverts to English: there is a sudden alteration of air and mood that I would describe as not unlike the feeling of falling out of love.

I spent the first night north of the border at a hostel in Old Montreal, *La Maison du Patriot.* This place of lodging's appellation seemed an ironic reminder of the increasing police-state in the land of the *Act du Patriot* I had just left behind, as I was now enjoying what I felt were the greater freedoms of Mother

Canada. Indeed, upon crossing the 45th parallel I felt as if a heavy weight of officially and media sanctioned paranoia, prejudice, and ignorance of post-9/11 USA were lifted from my consciousness.

Even as I seemed freed from the subtle but very real oppression that in America is too often well-masked behind slogans like, "The Land of the Free" and so forth, I soon realized the grip of that particular perverse patriotism sometimes promoted in the United States of doublespeak and faux-democracy has an expansive reach, and seems want to draw back potential expatriates, perhaps for fear of being left all alone. My hiatus in Quebec was only to last three months before I once again entered a dystopia of strip-malls and fast food and suburban discontent in the midst of overabundance.

Now I must note, despite critical remarks, that I do love this land and its peoples. Though I feel contempt for a populace that is so easily swayed to follow a falsely-elected leader into an unprovoked war, and for an administration which displays such disregard for this land's own laws and for simple justice, I meet U.S. citizens nearly every day and in every sort of locale that have the sense to be incensed at the absurdity of a president that can't correctly form a sentence, livid at the loss of civil liberties supposed to be guaranteed by the Bill of Rights, and furious at the felonious fucks that hold the White House (i.e., the Bush/Cheney administration and their ilk), and who thus hold the American people and much of the world hostage to their nigh fascist whimsy.

After a bit of wandering I found a darkened coffee house that offered Internet access and which maintained the gracious policy of allowing patrons to smoke indoors. As another example of America's faltering liberty, the latter amenity has become a scarce freedom Stateside, as those who enjoy inhaling the sublime and to some sacramental smoke of the American tobacco plant are finding themselves increasingly driven to the street if they choose to imbibe.

The desperate nature of this trend is evinced by the fact that even Laramie, once rugged frontier town, has grown so gentrified (and contingently it seems, increasingly controlling) that it became the first city in the state to outlaw indoor public smoking, *even in the bars!* And this city even has a namesake brand of cigarettes featured on *The Simpsons!* and which was in fact a popular brand of smokes in the 40's and 50's. There is also, curiously, a bar and grill called Elmer Lovejoy's—think "Reverend" on the same television series—which was named after a tinkerer who once had a shop on that corner of First Street, a school called Spring Creek Elementary, and a number of "Simpsons" related to Wyoming's former Senator Alan Simpson, including a singer songwriter named Maggie. Never noticed Maggie raver-style suckin' on a pacifier, though she certainly had a similarly intimate rapport with microphones. Not mere coincidences, at some level certainly.

Now, this sort of an ordinance may be fine in those emasculated and yuppified bedroom communities back east, else in densely populated urban centers where folks don't have room to breathe in the first place. Here in the Cowboy state, however, and especially in bars like the Buckhorn—where every species of local ungulate is represented by at least a couple-of glass-eyed heads hung on the wall, and where bullet-holes embellish the mirror and ceiling—well, in such a place you oughta be able to light up your cowboy-killer whilst downing a whisky or nursing a PBR or perhaps a Fat Tire Amber Ale without harassment from the powers that be.

Back in the day, sheriff wouldn't have lasted a day trying to enforce such a law in these parts. C'mon, at least give those who *fumé* a separately ventilated section with a pool table or two, a room where cocktail waitresses or waiters are not required to serve to protect those employees from the deadly ethereal spirits of second-hand smoke roaming the room in search of a victim.

As an aside, there is convincing data that the cause of so much cancer from tobacco products is not actually anything intrinsically present in the plant. It is not necessarily the additives, either—not to say that said practice of "big tobacco" is acceptable, nor that these various added chemicals do not add to the health risks. Rather, so many cancer-related mortalities are almost certainly from radioactive fertilizers used on conventionally grown tobacco, which expose a pack a day (conventionally grown) cigarette smoker to somewhere on the order of between 300 and 22,000 chest x-rays a year. According to one source, even C. Everett Coop—one of few of this nation's Surgeon Generals to have gained significant notoriety, and in fact the fellow who put those little warning labels on packs of smokes—made a comment during a televised speech in 1990 wherein he stated that he believed ninety-percent of cancer from tobacco use was due to radioactive isotopes present in the tobacco. Regardless of the verity of this information, I've switched to organic.

    French press in hand, I made my way to an open Internet station and proceeded to seek whatever contact information I might to find Leslie. I had already sent an email through the yoga studio where she was listed as an instructor, though had not yet received a reply. I learned the times of Leslie's yoga classes from the studio's website, then sat on the patio to watch the passing pedestrians in their fur-lined parkas and trench coats and to pen various musings in my journal.

    Even insofar as it might have been a small step over the line, I decided to wait outside the yoga studio during one of Leslie's scheduled classes, hoping she would not take offense at said presumption. The studio was on the second floor of an ancient building in Old Montreal, just above a small boutique and only a few blocks from *La Maison du Patriot*. I arrived a good while before the class let out and took a seat on the steps.

    Whilst waiting on the stoop outside the studio and smoking a barely burnt Gaullouises I'd ground-scored, *une jolie juene Femme* employed at the boutique joined me for her break. She told me her name was Beth, and that she was from near Toronto. I told her of my quixotic intentions, and asked if she knew Leslie. Beth said they had met. I grew more anxious as I realized the moment of my expected encounter with this woman who was focus of long-held devotions, daydreams and romantic hopes was very near.

    As the students began to emerge, foam-rubber mats rolled and tucked between torsos and either arm, I scanned each face for a glimmer of recognition. My heart was beating fast, palms sweaty in spite of the cold, and thoughts jumbled like some high school kid just before a first date. After nearly all the practitioners had passed through the double-doors, I stopped one woman to ask if the instructor was still upstairs.

    "Oh, I am the instructor," she informed me politely.

I told her I was an old acquaintance from Leslie's home state, and asked her to pass on my email address if she happened to see her in the near future. A bit crestfallen, but able to breathe normally and think somewhat clearly again, I noticed Beth emerging from the building. She told me if I wanted to wait, she would take me to her place to smoke some grass. I was quite grateful for the offer, and of course accompanied her up the hill to *le Plateau* and her shared apartment just off *Rue Saint-Laurent.*

The three-bedroom flat was up a narrow flight of stairs, and like the yoga studio was directly above a clothing boutique. The neighborhood was about as hip as it gets, as the Plateau—and Saint-Laurent on the Plateau specifically—is *the* center of nightlife and café culture in Montreal.

As we entered her apartment we were greeted by Beth's roommate Dan, another Toronto native, his friends Arthur, a dark-locked dready with dark complexion and a generous smile, and Jordan, Arthur's housemate and Dan's coworker at a nightclub across the street. I sat on a couch in the kitchen, which also served as the living room, and we smoked some herb topped with dark brown flakes of hashish and drank some rather extraordinary chai Dan prepared from raw ginger and fresh spices. I made the usual sort of introductory exchanges with these new acquaintances and explained the premise of my trip.

Beth had offered the use of their shower on our walk, and as I hadn't bathed in a couple of days I had responded that I would very much appreciate said opportunity. Whilst we sat puffin' and chatting, Beth mentioned the offer again, only I thought I heard her say something on the order of, "*We* should take that shower, when you're ready." Did she mean "We," as in the manner royalty speaks of self in the plural? Was this some quirky Canadian use of personal pronouns?

A few minutes later, Beth stood behind me, leaned over me, and as I tipped my head back she said she was ready for a shower, and asked if I was ready—to shower *with her?!* I froze, and was struck dumb by this unusual entreaty twice offered, especially as 'twas spoken in mixed company. After she disappeared into the bathroom alone, I pondered what it was I'd just heard. *Did she really ask me to join her in the . . . Yes! What does this mean? Is such a thing customary amongst Canadians, perhaps a tradition adopted and modified from the Inuit custom I had read about, as this tribe's men were said to offer the pleasure of their wives to travelers from afar?*

Then it struck me: a friend I had known for a number of years named Dave, a California dready I knew in Laramie, once told me at the conclusion of a tale of his travels in Canada, "Jeffrey, if you're ever in Canada and a beautiful woman asks you to take a shower with her, *just do it!! Don't ask me why, just do it!*" he advised, ending his words with a hearty laugh.

Among other inconsistencies and indications of some sort of a potential alteration of time-space or mind I have noted since I have returned from said journey, the Dready-Dave I met on this side claims to have no memory of ever having offered said advice, nor any recollection as to why he might have spoken such a random-seeming imperative. Indeed, I am often left to wonder if the land I returned to is the same as the one I left, or if I might be in some other dimension or level of underworld/earth/heaven. Mayan mythology claims that something like twenty-three layers exist between lowest below and highest above. From what relatively little I've studied of the Vedic tradition's voluminous texts and sanAtana dharma's sundry teachings, the layers and *loka* ("locations," "realm"), dimensions, heavens and hells are many and rather complexly related. Oh, for an accurate map to this life (and afterlife/afterlives?) and its subtleties, a spiritual GPS or inter-dimensional chart or some such!

After her shower—I did not join her, by the way, as I had obviously come to Canada with other romantic intentions—Beth asked Dan if he'd mind if I stay in the spare bedroom. He was more than amicable to the idea, and I ended up abiding with these kindest of hosts for over a month. I was told I could occupy the bedroom until another guest, Narev, returned from a tour in South America spinning trance-dance tunes at parties and clubs in Brazil. I thought the expected guest's name a bit odd, and at first and before a bit of contemplation considered it might be merely some sort of DJ pseudonym. As I later concluded, there were indeed some odd coincidences to consider regarding the coming guest's name, and the names of my two hosts, as well.

Shorty before I had departed from Laramie, my paternal grandfather passed away. His name, as well as the names of my father and older brother, is Vern. Backwards, Vern is pronounced something like "Narev." Whilst staying at the apartment in Montreal, my paternal grandmother, Betty Lou, purportedly followed her husband's departure from Ada, Oklahoma to somewhere beyond this life. Beth's middle name is Louise, and her middle and last name correspond to the names of the streets between which sits the house where I grew up (said paralleling streets, by the way, were named to honor the first official Anglo explorers to officially cross the Western U.S., to offer a clue without betraying confidences). I later discovered that Leslie had suffered from an emotional breakup with a man named Dan, the first name of my other host. Two others amongst her most recent paramours Leslie later happened to name, Stephen and Frank, were the first and middle name of my best friend during and for a while after high school.

Certainly there is something of substance to names, and perhaps if you taught your children that the name of a rose is "the shit-stinking-raunchy-puke-smelling flower," roses might not smell so sweet to their noses. Since this time, and to a somewhat lesser degree preceding, such synchronicities and odd coincidences of names, memes, mythemes and memories have become my daily fare (as you shall read if you choose to continue), and sometimes to the point that it all feels rather like a case of 24-hour déjà vu—which sounds much cooler than it is, let me assure you.

There is no question in my mind of the verity of "synchronicity," as some (after Jung) have named these instances of vision or other sensations that seem beyond the supposed range of allowed perception and probability, given one's current and supposed time and space perspective, else as has become customary to call those coincidences too succinct to be considered "merely-." I have seen and heard too many things inexplicable by laws of statistics or other figurations of probability to deny the certain existence of some subtle mode of interconnectivity or other. I would not claim, however, to have an immediate knowledge of how all of these phenomena ought to be interpreted, though I have my theories and much corroborating evidence.

Despite whatever perils made apparent, I have maintained a want to seek and comprehend, an unquenched desire to understand these mysterious and esoteric lineages of action and effect, thought and affect, as uncanny and odd occurrences have so oft manifest in my experiences and so many seeming magical happenings continue to unfold before my eyes—all three. Indeed, impossible coincidences and virtual miracles appear too often and overt for me to deny, even if I had a wish to do so. And with a view of so much that doesn't coincide with conventional paradigms, I have a similarly unstoppable impetus to find where I might best fit myself in light of these ulterior realities revealed. Inasmuch as I might be rebel or revolutionary, I do trust in a truly good order behind, beyond, or transcendent to the official.

Similar to my certainty of synchronicity, serendipity, and subtle connectivity, I also have no doubt of the existence of many sorts of mythical creatures. I've seen bioluminescent faeries swooping through the swamp as I walked a darkened trail beneath the branches of old growth cedars and other great and aged trees, ferns and devil's clubs' thick on either side of the pathway fading from view with the sun's deeper journey below the horizon. In this particular magical section of the trail upon the onset of dark night, said little blue lights would sometimes suddenly appear and dart through the nigh pitch black marsh, to my amazement and inability to explain, save by the interpretation my friend and coworker Jonah offered—pixies.

During this same period of time spent clearing trails in the wilderness of the Sauk River drainage in Washington, we twice encountered a Sasquatch. I've seen a woman shape-shift at close range. I could have run over a skinwalker that scurried across the road one time on the Navajo (Diné) reservation in Arizona, as mentioned a few pages previous.

I KNOW by much (and much self-scrutinized) experience that there is much more to the workings of the world than meets the average eye. To sift through all the possible interpretations of what these things, and especially other hidden things less playfully made manifest might mean or portend, is a task might drive one mad if such glimpses past various veils become *de rigueur*. Nonetheless, I somewhere and sometime decided to notice and even seek out these subtle clues and cues related to the existence of those things less materially evidenced (or less *observed* or *admitted* as materially evidenced), for better or worse.

To become aware of such subtle happenings and mystical secrets generally seems to come with a contingent responsibility, by the way, an obligation to sometimes take action to assure *sattva* ("righteousness," or "order" for lack of a better translation) and *dharma* (teaching, justice, etc.) are maintained in the midst of subtle minds crossed and manifestations sometimes gone awry, and on occasion a duty to deal with demons needing to be dispatched. To see wrong or suffering is of course cause enough to confront or act as one is able and ought, at whatever level of existence, yet in certain contexts surely the more so once the veils begin to fall before your eyes. With great understanding comes great responsibility.

In spite of sometimes being subjected to taunts from passing vehicles such as "Lazy hippie!" "Get a job!" (often as not, when I've been employed, though also often as not as a playful taunt rather than a curse), etc., as it has turned out I'm not just taking "fun trips" into the forest or living care-free whilst wandering America's roads and wilderness in the company of other pot smoking, psychedelically-enhanced hippies—though I must admit I have had plenty of fun in-between occasional battles with demons and vyings with unruly demigods, intense and taxing yogic endeavors, and sometimes rather epic trials and tribulations.

Once you *know*, you become to whatever degree contingently responsible to respond to what secrets you're made privy, and likewise to act according to whatever visions you receive that meet more than the uninitiated eye, at least in relation to your given understanding. Thus the cautionary admonitions advising any who would study cabala or tantra (i.e., real tantra yoga, and not merely the enhanced Hindu style *Joy of Sex* version) or any particular mode of esoteric teachings to carefully follow a proscribed path, and thus the supposition such is to be undertaken under the supervision of a teacher or guru—though I must admit, I have approached these things as rather a dilettante and without a particular guru, and indeed at times to my personal peril.

Yes, I do recognize that certain of these beliefs certainly might allow me to figure or fit neatly into any number of psychiatrically designated categories. I know otherwise, however, from many carefully scrutinized experiences and a not insignificant mass of convincing evidences. Though science according to the "Western" model has its value, open-minded observation (a supposed cornerstone of the scientific method) has the significant potential to convince a careful witness that much cast aside by academically informed judgments as "superstition" maintains more abiding truth than many a so-called scientific maxim.

And on the lighter side of examining this supposed dichotomy between science and supernatural sight, too much belief in the reality offered by secular science and you shall likely miss the little people spying your campsite in the Cherokee National Forest, overlook the trolls peeking out from under the bridges you cross in the Schwartzwald, and ignore the wind calling your name on the seashore or in the mountains or whilst simply sitting on your back porch watching a storm blow in. You might thus miss much of life's beauty and magic, but at least they won't call you "crazy." I'm personally beyond caring what "they" think, however, and hope you too will choose the beautiful magic of life's possibilities rather than to hide behind the supposedly well known, the purportedly well analyzed and documented, those dead letter propositions prescribed by scientific dogma and official, institutionally approved and peer reviewed "truth."

Certainly meeting Beth, and the shelter and kindness she and Dan offered, and the various odd synchronicities and serendipities I experienced in their home and further on this quixotic misadventure exemplify the providential kindness and undeniable magic that comes to the good hearted and open minded traveler. For over a month I was sheltered and fed by these hosts, serendipitous kindnesses received with much gratitude despite my lack of means for any expression of material gratuity.

I seem nearly always granted at least base needs by providence, the care of friendly goddesses and gods or angels or *ganas* or everyday folks or whatever not-quite-random agents of compassion whose motives derive from a layer beyond where science has yet invented a means to describe or delineate. And of course from a merely material perspective, the generosity of my new Canadian friends was a welcomed boon. In addition to a general gratitude for shelter from Montreal's cold winter weather, I was especially grateful for this hospitality as I soon developed a toothache that might have become a serious medical condition, had I not a warm place to sleep, bathe and practice good hygiene.

    I sent another email to Leslie's place of employment, requesting that they pass on the telephone number at my temporary abode. After somewhere around one week at Beth and Dan's, she called. Her voice indeed sounded like the melodious voice I recalled from years before, yet with a note of ill-ease I had not remembered from inadvertently or otherwise overhearing her conversations at the coffeehouse, else from our terse if courteous exchanges those years before. The woman I had become enamored with at Coal Creek Coffee a decade previous was playful and vibrant. Her laughter in particular had resonated with my soul or stirred some memory within me, if one not quite understood at the time except at an instinctual level. Her tone on the phone seemed different, hinted at some distress or at least betrayed a tinge of sorrow.

    I was actually talking to Leslie! Beatific belly dancer, Divine yogini and sometimes-wrathful goddess purging me of attachments and imperfections in at least my envisioned constructions of the dilettante tantra-yoga I had practiced for the past several years. Leslie, certain object of devotion, focus of a practice of bhakti-yoga I maintained with her always at least peripherally in mind, my chivalric ideal as beloved and tantric ideal as a vision of Sakti. This is who she had been to me, and through my eyes and imaginings and interpretation of signs I yet believe her to be at least a close emanation or expression of these things (and if she ain't, may these praises raise her to a more elevated state).

    I was more than a bit giddy for the fact that I had finally made contact with this woman who had been for so long unapproachable and admired, yet a bit hesitant at noting her tone. Also, nervous and concerned and a combination of many other perhaps unnamable emotions as we made tentative plans to meet at

Café Dépôt, a block away on the corner of *St-Laurent* and *Prince-Arthur Ouest*.

She was on the other end of a telephone line, in the same city as I once again, and was quite prepared to meet me for coffee or tea. Three days, and we would meet, and I would perhaps have some answers as to what substance might explain my intractable devotion, and as importantly would be granted an audience with one of the (if not the) most amazing and beautiful of women I've ever encountered—if only a woman and not goddess or Goddess, that is.

I shared this news with my hosts, even jumping up and down a bit, yet maintained some semblance of reserve or restraint or reticence upon sensing Leslie's tone, my jubilance at this momentous occasion held in check by a recognition of this very important other's seeming sorrow. I experienced the next few days with a continued inner turmoil: excited at the prospect of a face-to-face with Leslie, yet a reluctance to maintain too much glee in the face of whatever burdens seemed to weigh upon her. And as I mentioned, off and on during this period I was suffering a rather excruciating infection from a problemed wisdom tooth, to add to the physiological-cum-psychic disharmony and the tumult comes with the prospect of true love.

I was also generally sensing an odd tension in the air I was breathing there and thereafter, a noticeable difference in the makeup of the reality I was experiencing in comparison to the reality I'd become accustomed to in a decade of wandering. A "disturbance in the force," to use the now cliché expression.

With this woman never quite not an imagined participant, I had worked up a vast wellspring of energy, *tejas* (fire, spiritual energy) stored through much practice, acts of devotion and battles with the world's ills, journeys of discovery and encounters with thousands of beautiful revelations and people and raised by *tapasia* (purifying fires) and contemplations, in and through the acts of austerities and celebrations, sitting trance and wild dance. And now all this seemed at the verge of some sort of release or resolution or transcendent fruition, yet with certain restraints brought into play, perhaps an unconscious recognition that I must not allow all my hopes to reside in these moments. *Rta kal*. Right timing.

Devi is present, yet perhaps not yet ready to reveal Herself fully. She has made Herself known at moments in my past. She is in my future as at least a true and properly manifest emanation someday to be my consort, lover, friend and companion (whether or not in this life lived), as tantra yoga doth no doubt prescribe practitioners become Siva or Shakti, or better, discover that they already are. Whether She is or ever fully has been the amazing woman I have known as Leslie, or shall be present thus in my future, I cannot say. Regardless, such devotions have at the very least proven helpful to me personally, as I have learned to be more authentic, to understand and explore ways of knowing, loving, and bettering self and this world, mostly due to such devotions to Devi, often envisioned as Leslie. Regardless of only short hours spent together in overt practice, Leslie has in this sense at least been a longstanding yoga partner to me, and I still believe for the better.

The day and time of our appointed meeting arrived, and I made my way on a snowy day down the street to grab a cappuccino and take a seat, not so patiently awaiting her arrival from the smoking section of Café Dépôt. I watched the door and more than a few beautiful women with similar dark hair and like brown eyes made their way to the counter to order whatever caffeinated libations, *en Français*. I wrote in my notebook and sipped from my cup, and nervously waited till well after the appointed hour. Disheartened, I returned to my hosts' apartment, entered the front door and was right away informed Leslie had called, hoping to reschedule.

When several days later we met, we shared moments I'll not forget. However real or dream, as life can seem and might be either or both, and whether the apparition I held in my arms was truly her or some semblance, doppel or emanation, I felt a wall between myself and Beloved crumbling, if not fully removed.

I entered the smoky café, a less gentile coffee house further up San Laurent filled mostly with older men playing chess. I sat and soon she appeared at the door, fur-lined hood framing her face, a vision of certain beauty and apparent sorrow that made my breath pause and heart skip or dance. We sat together and shared a conversation I had long anticipated.

She shared with me of her sorrows, a broken relationship and other contingent circumstances I shall not disclose. She told me it was good to see someone from home—Wyoming, I guess she meant—even if someone she said she did not specifically remember. I gently took her hands in mine and she cried on my shoulder, and in my perceptions at least these were tears of sublime property that moistened my overcoat. I felt I was receiving some sacred sacrament of a goddess's lament, and a chance to warm the hands and perhaps heart of one who had been so much inspiration to my practice and sacred devotions.

I do not here inscribe our exchanges in quotation, as it seems inappropriate to disclose not only words she would have me not repeat, but also the others that are sacred to me by my own mythology and as memories I've want to hold and not commit to print. When she finished her tea and I emptied my cup of coffee, we walked out the door and made our way down the cold Montreal street. She asked me to put my arm around hers as I accompanied her to the subway stop. She asked me to meet her again, to be her friend. I watched her walk down the stairs, her fur-lined hood pulled over lovely auburn hair. I gazed mesmerized, in an amorous and even entranced state as she descended the steps to catch her train, still somewhat in disbelief at what had just transpired.

I had held her hands, embraced this figure I had long imagined the Beloved. I had been allowed into a woman's life I'd long wondered of, admired from afar, and wished to be closer to for many moons and reveries. Yet circumstances and mixed emotions presented yet more complexities, for in my visions of our sometime meeting we were both at peak of life and health, and I'd imagined naught but blessings and an aura of celebration surrounding and in our someday manifest encounter. Perhaps some semblance of the fullness I imagined would arrive is yet to come, or else not to be fulfilled by or in this form I'd grown and have grown the more to so adore. Regardless, both because and in spite of our later times together, I maintain respect, a certain love and something not unlike reverence for Leslie, if ever or not we meet again . . .

Back at Beth and Dan's, I was still in something of a daze. I shared an account of our meeting, and it felt that the responses of my kind hosts revealed they somehow had greater knowledge of this affair than was spoken, at whatever level. Beth made a somewhat catty remark, whether at this point or later, which I took as an obvious indication she had more than a fleeting familiarity with Leslie, repeating a phrase she sometimes uttered.

"Oh m'god!" Beth said with a mild sarcasm on one occasion as I was standing in the hall talking about Leslie to Dan, and indeed with a tone that certainly seemed to indicate she knew her better than as only casual acquaintances. Beth's utterance was not so spiteful as might be imagined from the above, mind you, but rather seemed to indicate she thought I was perhaps making too much ado about the whole affair—though I might be reading wrongly.

Another very odd thing Beth said that revealed she was more intricately involved in this absurd *lila* (Sanskrit for "divine play") I have been recounting was a rather off-the-wall question she posed to me one evening,

"So pardon me for asking," she asked in a casual tone, "but, do you like chicks with dicks?" I answered "No," not meaning to imply I have some prejudice against trans-gendered folk, but to answer that insofar as my sexual preferences, women who are fully women are my choice for partners. I pondered the question, sensing such an off-the-wall query was clearly indicative of some intrigue or other afoot.

Perhaps she was just wondering why I didn't hop into the shower with her when she invited when we first met. Or *perhaps* this was an indication of some strange conspiracy of mind I had long suspected, and has been revealed (if at times revealed askew) through events and channeled information granted most succinctly over the past few years, and in bits and pieces for years before. Regarding Beth's rather odd query, by a suggestion some years previous someone planted a passing notion within my earshot that a woman who rather reminded me of Leslie in Laramie had genitalia mismatching what would normally be found upon an assumed woman.

Subtle coincidental curiosities and bizarre innuendos such as this have vexed this experiencer for quite some years. Indeed, I have often wondered if many others experience as I do, or if I am unusual in the degree to which I perceive the intentionally emplotted interconnectedness of thought and channeled information and emotions and things observed outside myself, other's words and actions too often and too succinctly fitting my immediate thoughts and certain mythemes or archetypal cycles, else not infrequently receiving channeled thoughts that too precisely meet observations of things presented to my eyes and ears to be meaningless flukes or luck of the draw.

The interconnectedness of so many thought forms and circumstances and individuals is still difficult for me to piece together concisely and neatly, and perhaps this lifetime will not reveal all the relevant subtleties of meaning and motive, or even of everyone's identities beyond facades or veiled presentations. I have even contemplated the possibility that the woman I met with in Montreal, and with whom I even shared a small studio for one month's span, might indeed not have been the same as the Leslie I only scarcely knew before, the graceful dancer and beautiful barista too beautiful and circumstantially too difficult for me to comfortably approach ten years previous. And yet at moments I did see the certain presence of that same someone shining through in the woman I befriended in Montreal who bore the same visage, if perhaps a bit altered by time and circumstance, and who claimed the same first name I remembered from before.

After some experiences to come, succeeding our later parting, I came to realize some things can make one's true self retreat inside or elsewhere hide whilst the vessel or overt form seems a shadow of the truer, and might even present the opposite of the real spirit within when certain factors assail or infiltrate. People change, as might be said, and can be likewise altered by experience or exposure to this reality's sorrows and ills, forced to show a façade that is a defensive shell, else even display in action a foreign spirit's undue influence.

We met again several times over the coming weeks, and I was granted glimpses of the spirit of the woman I had remembered and admired, laughing and insightful and graceful and even powerful. Still, some seeming fierce oppression maintained some hold of her, if somewhat decreasingly.

Leslie sometimes let it out with a scream, unapologetically uttered into the chill Montreal winter's gray and white days and nights. Once or more she rather giddily if agitatedly informed me that she was going to scream whilst walking with me down the dreamily wintery sidewalks on *Le Plateau*. Some wild energy would rise in her, fierce and frightening and beautiful and something I imagined as more than a little like Kali or some like wilder expression of Shakti. Through her dance and yoga and other healing arts, too, Leslie the yogini would transform these troublesome energies only partly understood by me, and perhaps better *felt* as mighty swells of emotion as I was made privy to her mood and momentum.

After our parting, I too became assailed by an increase of seemingly similar psychic assaults, spiritual attacks that have at moments nearly driven me to insanity. Though it seems these struggles in mind were not introduced on this journey, it also seems by braving this quest to French Canada to find and be a friend to Leslie my path had expanded, as perhaps has the scope of those ills of this world and humanity I am obliged to battle and energies I am responsible to try to transform. Regardless, these oppositions to my natural momentum, mode, mood and mind would soon challenge me to the core.

Something no doubt foreign, unless an inundation of direct opposites—inversions of my own thoughts and intentions—had somewhere acquired access to my mind and were likewise increasingly manipulated my exterior reality. I recognize in retrospect that some semblance of these infiltrations of my thoughts had begun a year or two preceding this journey, if not yet recognized as a foreign power. Such harassment and malicious psychic influences increased exponentially during the continuation and aftermath of this quest, however, regardless of the point of inception. Though I had experienced battles in "mind" and other realms previously to these past few years, something or someone had found further means to adversely affect even my internal thoughts, and to an extent greater than I had ever faced before. And it seems not unlikely that the psychic assaults I later faced were not unlike, and perhaps not unrelated to whatever energies Leslie was dealing with when we met, despite their less overt onset at an earlier and as yet unascertained moment.

I ought to note that a dream that I believe was planted in my mind by some other—dreamt perhaps eight years or more before this fateful journey—had presaged a good bit of what I've experienced over the past few years and especially after I departed from Montreal. Though thankfully much of this dream has failed to come true with precision, enough has manifest to convince me there was of certainty some degree of valid prescience (or perhaps programming?) presented therein. If I recall correctly, said dream came to me just after I had spent the night with a young woman I encountered at a party in Laramie. Can't say one way or the other whether or not she had anything in particular to do with said encyclopedic dream, save by proxy. However unlikely and insane as it might seem to the "rationally" minded, I believe dream and mind in general have a good deal more to do with reality manifest than do mere physical factors and officially sanctioned scientific notions of cause and effect.

Similarly, I have been for a long time convinced that much of what the discipline of psychology deems "mental illness" has causes that ought be traced to so called "supernatural" sources rather than to mere neurological or electrochemical factors. Many of the most spiritually insightful people I have known have spent time in psychiatric wards, and certainly many, if not most or all ailments of mind and body are indeed as easily shown to be the result of issues of "spirit" (for lack of a better English term) and not merely result of material, psychological or physiological conditions generally.

Supposedly aberrant experiences (hearing voices, having visions, observing shifts in time-space, telepathy, etc.) had first hand, carefully critiqued and skeptically surveyed, analyzed as an educated man at least relatively well versed in modern psychology and quite adept and well trained at introspective self-criticism convinces me mind and body and spirit are not aptly contemplated separately, and that at least as often as not mental illness is actually malady of the realm of "spiritual" nature—though still not disconnected to body, nor conflicting with true scientific knowledge either, mind you.

Though I do not completely reject the findings of scientific inquiry into the intricacies of human behavior, I think something important was lost when any sort of *science of spirit* (again, for lack of a better English term) was cast out along with what was dubbed "superstition." My experiences have too clearly evidenced that much more is operative in the human mind's workings and in the interactions of mind and matter than officially sanctioned scientific notions of cause and effect allow. Channeled information (for lack of a better term) has too often proven valid, visions have come too clearly true, and 'voices' heard within or without coincide with materially manifest verifications on too many occasions for me to neatly cast them as symptoms of schizophrenia. I also know myself (and Self) too well to accept many uncharacteristic thoughts I have experienced in recent times as merely self- (or Self-) generated.

Perhaps some of you might relate, recognizing there may be more verity than officially or commonly allowed to various personal experiences you have kept secreted, for fear others might deem you delusional. I am not advising that you obey the digital readout on the microwave should it suggests you should kill the President or a movie-star, mind you. Just that it is alright to believe you saw a faerie next to the lake that time when you were a child, or to admit that ghosts talk to you, or that you remember details from a past lifetime, or that God or Goddess or other celestial beings visit you sometimes.

All this said, I do not know of any one system I trust to offer a fully correct and easily accessible interpretive framework to fully decipher or facilitate a complete comprehension of the immeasurable and ethereal subtleties that create the operative rules of mind and spirit, and the interaction of these with the material world. The traditions and teachings of India have come closest to providing such a framework, though these as well as the Western scientific paradigm seem wanting in regard to certain solidly evidenced experiences I have known and scrutinized with a figurative microscope and an academically well trained skepticism (though I must admit I am not at all well versed in the Vedas). The interpretive frame I have found most useful and true is more an admixture of various religious and scientific traditions, as many paradigmatic perspectives do certainly contain clues, though not one overarching schema I have encountered has yet to prove itself to unerringly encompass or accurately explain all I have known and experienced, though I have just scratched the surface of the perennial treasures of Vedic wisdom.

Knowledges of mind and spirit and materially manifest reality I have acquired from study and experience, meditation and contemplation and intuition have likewise only granted me a modicum of certainty as I seek to comprehend "others." Even as I believe I have an open third-eye, I cannot always see clearly into the depths of who is who or what is true of many I meet in the marketplace or on the street, nor even assuredly ascertain the deeper truth of some I assume I know quite well. Mysteries and uncertainties seem to linger, both near and far.

On one certain occasion I felt assured Leslie was fully present, present as the Goddess had first captured my attention and devotion years previous, and without the distractions it seemed assailed her, moving and acting with such unearthly motions and gestures—or perhaps with the most earthly of motions, motions conveying all the beauty and seductive grace of the natural world, and the confidence of Durga Ma. At least on this one occasion I was certain I was not encountering a doppel, a dream or a mere shell of the divine young woman I had adored from afar before my pilgrimages of Self-discover.

Leslie invited me to work out with her at a health club where she taught Yoga and Pilates. Her schedule was filled with teaching these disciplines and belly dance, working at two restaurants, and performing her gracefully sublime dance at various venues. Mostly I would walk with her to and from her appointed destinations, perhaps sharing lunch or dinner on the way. On this evening, she allowed me to share with her in practice.

I met her at the corner of *Rue Rachel* and *St-Laurent*. We rode the elevator to the second floor. We performed sun salutations. *Pranam.* Reach above, bow, thrust feet back, downward dog. Flowing motions, breath observed, bodies in movement, beings becoming.

I couldn't help but notice some similarity in performing *asanas* with Leslie and having performed the same series of movements those early mornings at the Yoga Center in Laramie with Chloe. I suppose this would make sense, as both were to some degree trained by the same woman, Chloe's mother Julia. Still, certain other similarities seemed underlying.

There was a punching bag by the windows in the studio, a red and white leather cylinder dangling from chains amidst the otherwise mostly empty room. Leslie seemed to take some relief swinging at this representative of whatever or whomever her angst and sorrow might have derived. I couldn't help but find some humor in the contrast between her only moderately powerful blows and the vision I had sometimes held of her as Kali, whose fiery rage loosed levels thousands with but one swing.

Leslie turned on some Indian or Middle Eastern music, and attempted to lead me in a dance. This is the moment I felt she was again or again fully the powerful woman or Goddess I had encountered in Laramie, forever etched in my memories: rhythmic tantric motions, sublime gyrations and flowing limbs hypnotizing, face and whole form radiating an aura of otherworldly substances, the air rarefied by her very presence—only this time her hands touching mine. I was not merely audience or voyeur, but also participant with her, much more intimately involved with this beautiful being and her divine bodily movements than when I had years before been mystified by her entrancing dance. Again I felt as if a novice, a fool, naïve and unworthy, a degree of insecurity I had not experienced for quite some time.

She took hold of my hand and moved her upper body to the right upon a wave rolling from one hand's fingertips through arm and shoulders and arm to the opposite hand's reach. Her instructions were authoritative, matching the certainty of her movements, and something of her glorious aura returned else was again unveiled to my eyes as she adjusted my body's movements to her lead.

I have never been completely comfortable dancing with a partner (with the exception of a couple of times dancing salsa and meringue when I accompanied some friends in Chicago to a Latin club, my limbs loosened by a few *cerveza* or margaritas), and the awkwardness of my movement to hers made this endeavor short-lived, though I think she may not have actually intended this particular dance as partners to succeed.

This hesitance of partnered motion seemed not unlike the more general reservations I had placed upon my own *prana* (energy, vital breath) by the circumstances. We were both wary and weary. *Not fully manifest right now. Not the proper moment to perform tandava or whatever sacred dance, not appropriate timing or perhaps placement for tantra asanas or fruition of devotional mantra to manifest, and of course little if any certainty we are properly matched partners, here, now, or elsewhere, to dance this particular dance divine.*

Regardless of the seeming imperfections in this attempt at synchronous motion, I felt blessed to have seen Leslie's radiant life-energy return, face-to-face and at close proximity to view in her something of the self-assurance and graceful strength that had first attracted my attention—or perhaps more accurately, mesmerized me—as I sat sipping coffee or tea and still laboring to perfect my Master's thesis, a world in the past at Coal Creek coffeehouse in Laramie.

I am writing these words at the very coffeehouse, in fact, and perhaps yet another world away. After spiraling around the map, my movements might well have conveyed me further or at least elsewhere than whence I began this particular adventure, above or below or a dimension away from that past moment's seeming same location. After all, how can one be certain even one's hometown is the same place one knew before departing on a given journey? or even rest assured that as you get up each morning you are on the same plane or occupying the same dimension as when you went to bed the night before? that the woman (or man) you made passionate love to the night before is the same being you awaken to after the sun's rise? I suppose it is faith, or unthinking acceptance of the fiction that things remain existentially the same, when in fact they may not at all.

Detachment. The religions of what region is commonly called "the East" teach the importance of this response to the overwhelming plethora of sense stimuli proffered by this world, to the potential confusion of life experienced, the whirlwind of emotions, desire and worldly devotions that become obstacles to self-awareness. Yet is there not purpose, sometimes, for an anchor to some things of an earthly nature? A tenuous path to tread, to let go and to hold, to love and release, to have compassion and yet not be overcome by the ills of others, to maintain proper bonds whilst sundering those not appropriate or not meeting what is best or true.

Discernment. The ability to step back from the milieu of so many circumstances, emotions, and sensory inputs to see truly and clearly seems most of the time expedient. Most often it is best to allow inner strength and calm and deeper wisdom to guide action, rather than to act in the midst of the tangles of attachments or in the heat of the moment. And yet there are certainly those times to hold on and reach out with fierce determination, irrational devotion and absurd romanticism.

Bandha. IndriyasaGga. Moksa. Bonds/bondage versus freedom and liberation. Attachment and nonattachment. Paradoxically both true and good, at least circumstantially. Too much or the wrong application of the former and you might be dragged to whatever hell-realm by what you won't surrender. Too much of the later, and you might just float away or at least face the danger of losing those connections that make life the beautiful and worthwhile and fulfilling experience it was meant to be. A *"razor's edge,"* this endeavor might be called, a term coined in the Himalayas that derives from the practice of following paths from place to place upon the steepest of ridges, where one misstep can be fatal (or at the least make for a nasty fall).

Treading the razor's edge in my interactions with Leslie was a tenuous task, as she was in a rather fragile state, and I, desiring to offer devotion and friendship unbounded, had good reason to maintain some detachment from this seeming culmination of long held feelings. Had I poured more into this endeavor of devotion than circumstances allowed, I might not have recovered from the intensity of what this journey would bring. Struggling with a toothache I had no ready means to pay to cure, and simultaneously recovering from a trying journey in the midst of winter, I was physically drained from the start. Beyond these immediate factors, the emotional investment I had made over years —wittingly, wisely or by conscious intention or no—and would increasingly offer over the next three months, would later prove to bare a rather disheartening return, and a rather trying (semblance of a) denouement.

    For the span of the next month I would often meet Leslie and walk with her to and from her classes and work. I was at her beck and call, and she did not behave unworthily of my devotion during this time (with one or two slight exceptions). She was almost always immediately and by all accounts genuinely grateful and courteous. I was quite happy to be friend and support to Leslie, even perhaps overeager to play the role of a smitten errant-knight, archetypal love-crazed god, and perhaps even, from an outside perspective, a fool rather pitifully desperate to display his mad devotion. As I had somehow presciently sensed her distress months before my arrival, I had at least hints that the role of helper or healer might be my lot in Leslie's life, though again and in all honesty I had expected little more to actualize than a nice chat over coffee or tea.

    One of few instances where I felt that Leslie was less than gracious and kind during our friendship in Montreal was an occasion when she was in the presence of a certain coworker at a cafe where she worked as a server. On this occasion, perhaps to try to impress her handsome fellow employee at *Soupe Café* else to make some sort of statement, Leslie rather callously greeted me as I entered the small restaurant, doing the favor of delivering some item or other of which she had need. She then very intentionally kissed her suave Quebecois coworker on both cheeks whilst I sat nearby, an intimacy she did not share with me—though I have more than slight inclination to believe there may have been other, subtler reasons.

    This was perhaps reminiscent of instances of less than generous words I had thought were subversively directed towards me whilst she was employed at Coal Creek years before, words which through my perception at the time had seemed in fact some brand of wisdom disguised as sass rather than words truly meant as harsh or unkind or crass. I have considered that this kiss in this café in Montreal may have been to kindly if pointedly reinforce her expressed intentions to maintain a platonic relationship with me— again, if not to effect some subtler factors—as I likewise interpreted what I perceived as slights meant for my ears years before as hints to be overheard, intended as a compassionate means of telling me to shape-up.

Amongst my most pleasant memories of this short period were of sharing walks with Leslie upon *Mont Royal* when chance we encountered one of the few less frigid days of the Montreal winter. I was only slightly jealous when she would speak fondly of experiences hiking this large hill with her former lover, Dan, a man she said could call the birds to land upon his hand at the mere motion of his hand or *mudra*. I was glad to be her confidant, and in fact felt privileged to play this role even when it meant hearing of Leslie's past lovers—a title that would not come to apply to me during these months shared as her companion.

At this time, my proclivities toward a nonjudgmental and generally neutral empathy had yet to be forced into the recesses of my inner-self, as would become a necessary defensive measure after a series of traumatic experiences, psychic assaults, and seemingly someone's intentional use or abuse of *AvaraNazakti* (powers of illusion) that would increasingly vex this mystic adventurer after we had parted company. I had yet to become jaded, a state I have since been forced to fight and am continuing to be forced to resist, to whatever degree, to this day. Not jaded by excess, mind you, save excess of clues, signs and supposedly substantive symbols that often since have shown themselves mere smoke and mirrors.

Mont-Royal is the central geographic feature of this grand old city, perhaps aside from the *St-Laurent* River. It rises above *le Plateau*, and is a draw for cross-country skiers during the winter, and joggers, walkers, sunbathers and hippies gathering for the popular drum circles during the summer, a weekly event quaintly and colloquially called "Tam-Tam." Leslie and I walked the spiraling trail to the top on a few occasions, and aside from her somewhat mournful reveries about lost love and other woes she seemed happy upon this high hill, elevated above the sadness of Montreal's long winter hibernation.

I think I may have made a mistake smoking a cigarette after waiting for Leslie outside a public restroom on *Mont-Royal*, as smoking seemed somehow to bear some undisclosed significance to her. "I can't believe you just did that!" she said without explaining her protestation as she watched me smoke a bummed cigarette. I think I may have made a mistake by not slapping her once when she requested of me, "Hit me. Don't knock my teeth out, just hit me hard," she said, tensing her face as if she were expecting me to do as she asked. Instead I gently but firmly placed my hands on either side of her head and drew her to me for an embrace. Actually, I think I should have kissed Leslie on that occasion, and perhaps ought not to have smoked that cigarette upon that mountain above the streets of Montreal. What man can know the deepest intricacies of cause and effect, right action in the right moment to effect the desired results? And perhaps more to the point, what man can comprehend the intricacies and complexities of a woman?

    In between our appointed meetings, I tried to be attentive to my kind hosts, though I was quite preoccupied with the unfolding of my role in Leslie's life and with her wellbeing. Dan and I developed a fairly sound friendship, and he claimed to gain some sort of inspiration from tales of my wandering ways and explications of the largely Hindu-inspired spirituality I've developed over the years. I ought to offer in return that I was inspired by his kindness as a host to a stranger, as I have encountered only few who have shown the sort of beneficence that I myself endeavor to maintain. He was indeed very generous, sharing food and herb quite freely, as well as warm shelter and conversation. After my departure he traveled to India, and from his most recent communique told me he was spending his time caring for an ailing *sadhu* who lives on the banks of the Ganges.

    Beth and I did not grow much closer than when we met, and considering the intimacy of that first evening's proposition, we in fact moved further from said state. Since I departed from Canada, however, and thanks to the virtual miracle of email we have maintained something of a friendship. In fact, she is nigh the only person I met on the whole of this journey—nearly three years from initial departure to return—with whom I have maintained some degree of continued contact, at least at the time I write these words.

Beth and Dan were constantly receiving guests, most of them beautiful and interesting and bearing names and faces that seemed to show yet more subtle and oddly coincidental connections to others I had know in times past. Not so unlike my experiences at hippie-houses in the States in terms of comings and goings, save that these were a more overtly sophisticated brand of bohemians—though I should add, not at all presenting the pretentious air one might expect from beautiful cosmopolitan francophones. I was hardly outgoing during this time, however, and was quite preoccupied, as I have made clear. Perhaps this was to my loss, though I would not devalue the time and devotion I spent upon attending to Leslie, at least no more than I have in the few pages previous.

When Narev (the other and overtly expected house guest) arrived to claim the spare bedroom, I was offered lodging at Arthur and Jordan's place, east of the plateau towards Old Montreal and a short distance from McGill University. Canadians are pretty fuckin' cool.

Dan also thoughtfully offered space on his bedroom floor, but I mostly declined, as his girlfriend who had herself recently returned from India was often his overnight guest. Her name was Adi (Addi?), which though bestowed on her by her Jewish parents has significance in Hindu lore. Adi is a name of Shakti, and means "Ancient-One," but is also a name associated with a demon who attempts to munch Siva's *linga* by that most terrifying of mythic means (to a man, at least), the vagina-al-dentis (I *cringe* merely typing the words). Of course the Hebrew meaning, whatever that might be, would likely be the more pertinent of the three options in terms of her parents' choice of name.

On the eighth of March Leslie and I attended a Sivaratri celebration at a Murugan temple at the outskirts of the city. It was not nearly so lively as the version of said celebration I have experienced at the Hanuman temple in Taos, but was pleasant nonetheless. We drank chai and sat in front of *murtis* of Siva and Parvati whilst singing *kirtan*.

Again, this was rather a mellow celebration compared to the sorta rock-and-roll Taos version—think Ravi Shankar at the Monterey Pops Festival performing just before Jimi Hendrix:

reportedly, Jimi humbly said something to the effect of admitting Ravi's sitar licks would be "a hard act to follow." At the Taos temple celebration, perhaps one in ten of the attendants are of Indian descent. At the Montreal temple most of the devotees were actually immigrants from India. In India, I should note, Sivaratri is a hash-smoke hazy holiday night, with celebrations till dawn, parades and parties and plenty of puffing black chunks of *charas* by the faithful as *pujaris* bathe the linga and yoni.

    We also attended an Easter Celebration at a Cambodian (or was it Vietnamese?) Catholic church just down the street from our shared apartment, and a few other events of religious significance. Leslie was at the time most inclined towards a mix of yoga and Buddhist philosophy, and various forms of other healing arts. Though I'm certainly a bit less fond of Buddhism, we shared many similar perspectives and practices. One certain difference in our approach to the so called "spiritual" was that she was less inclined to deconstruct the subtle synchronicities and mythic meanings surrounding the everyday than I, and grew a bit annoyed if I went on too much with such esoteric musings (perhaps for having dealt with such issues more than she was want to in recent times).

    I had received a promise of on-line employment previous to my departure cataloging a private library's holdings which, seemingly as a matter of course, had fallen through. I was thus left with little alternative than to request minimal fiduciary assistance from my father. A search for other temporary employment in Montreal bore no fruit, and so when Leslie was asked to vacate her friend's flat, I requested the means to rent a small studio apartment to share with her for a month or so and till she and I both might make other plans. Leslie had intentions to apply for employment as a staff member at the Omega Institute, an interfaith retreat center in the hills of upstate New York, but needed shelter until at least the beginning of May.

    I searched the classifieds for an affordable place, and found that for a city of its caliber (and due to favorable exchange rates), Montreal offered a fair number of options within the areas surrounding *Rue St-Laurent*. We rented a not unpleasant little place on *Rue Berri*, located quite near the metro and a short walk to most of Leslie's classes and to her job at *Café Soupe*. The building superintendent, a gaunt and hollow eyed Eastern European fellow whom Leslie nicknamed "Vlad" showed us to our chosen studio. She was not thrilled by the tiny apartment, though it did have new hardwood flooring and paint, and was thus at least a step above some of the alternate choices. She moved in a day or two after I, and upon doing a bit of decorating was more pleased with these temporary accommodations. For around one month Leslie was my roommate in this o'er cozy abode.

    This was far more, and far different, than I had ever expected of this impetuous and foolishly romantic endeavor. It was all more like a dream than even the scarcely grounded reality I had known as a wandering hippie cruising the highways and dirt roads of the Rocky Mountains and western states over the previous several years. This might be read as ironic, as during those previous journeys psychedelics were a regular part of my routine, and on this journey I scarcely even smoked herb, or at least compared to my customary inclinations.

    Perhaps the endorphins and serotonin released during intensive devotion are comparable in certain respects to the effects of mushrooms or LSD or dream. Perhaps my presumptions to pursue the possibility of true love, to endeavor a quixotic quest across the country under the influence of a wild and fanciful notion that a woman I'd scarcely known nearly a decade before might be more than an imagined beloved or a hopeless daydream possibility; perhaps these motives put in motion altered the very fabric of my realm of experiential reality in an age when romance takes second-place to finance, and chivalric, foolish and impetuous romanticism is more the stuff of film or fiction than of life lived. Or at least in that corner of reality I seemed to inhabit during those days of an at least partially realized dream come true, with certain unexpected hardships notwithstanding. And these things said, how can I be sure anything experienced is not in fact a dream, or at least as well described by this as any other metaphor?

    Leslie and I shared her inflatable mattress for the first few nights until she found a futon mattress on a nearby curb. Being bedfellows was both a delight and a mild torment, as she had expressed the wish that we not become lovers.

On one of these long and rather dreary late winter Montreal nocturnes, snow and gray sky and bitter cold reigning outside our small yet warm abode, I dreamt a dream in which I was walking along a bleak city street and feeling a sense of despair the likes of which I had not known, save perhaps on the most mournful occasions or in similar nightmares. The street seemed quite like Montreal's streets, though I believed that, via this dream persona, I was in something not unlike a hell realm. I awoke, quite relieved to find these feelings did not return with me to wakefulness. A few hours later, I awoke to Leslie talking in her sleep.

"There are ten models . . . no, they're soldiers," she uttered, mumbling indiscernibly in between, then quite clearly exclaimed, "Persephone!"

I later considered the obvious allusion: I had become much better acquainted with Chloe, Leslie's friend from years before, just previous to this quest. Chloe is another name for Demeter. Demeter's daughter, Persephone, is kidnapped by Hades and taken to the underworld in the well-known myth. I dream of a hell-realm, and then Leslie unconsciously(?) utters this captured maiden goddess's name. Had Chloe sent me to retrieve Persephone? Was someone trying to figure me as Hermes, who according to Demeter's wish travels to the underworld, to retrieve this lovely figure playing Persephone in some absurdly scripted play?

In spite of shrouds of mystery or uncertainty that would not quite be removed from between us, even in such close quarters, I relished my time spent with Leslie in this tiny home. Once or twice we wildly and playfully wrestled around the small room, releasing tensions held on both sides. To become physically entangled and entwined with this lithe and loveliest woman I have known was an intimacy I had only scarcely dared dream. I should note, however, that as we wrestled I was by no means seeking some subversive sort of personal gratification, but in each moment held in mind an intention to provide whatever catharsis I might to seeing to it Leslie might be restored to the glory I knew (or at least powerfully envisioned) as herself. I thought of myths of Siva and Parvati vying, archetypes I knew of that might naturally apply, and considered what flows of *prana* might be appropriate to make this playful vying horizontal dance most transformative for us both.

Regardless of attempts to make this a "healing experience," I did thoroughly enjoy this delightful closeness, both of us straining to gain playful advantage as we rolled around on the floor and mattresses. Though her breasts often pressed against me, and her legs sometimes wrapped round mine as we wrestled, I was not *exactly* sexually aroused—contrary to what might be expected—though this was as close to making love (at least in any physical sense) as we would share in these times together. Yet, in simple playful wrestling, principles of *tantra-yoga* were manifest. To my surprise, her Buddhist-inclined counselor—who I had to some degree mistrusted—advised Leslie to wrestle with me often. She thought it would be cathartic, as I had indeed imagined was a good part of the purpose of our rolling round upon mattress and floor, as well as just plain having fun.

Tantra is a dance, movements of energy, as well as emanation or expression of the abiding romance of Mahadeva and Mahadevi. It is the manifestation of a "sexual" vibration,[15] yes, yet as a tuning in to the pure and eternal love of the Divine Feminine and Masculine (in truth Advaita, "not two"), and not with base sexual gratification as the goal. *Tantra* might also be understood as manifest in story lines in life lived, *lila*, that reflects or transforms by these archetypal expressions of gender-perfectly-balanced, informed by the eternal dance of male and female, *tandava*, and expressed in variegated expressions in human relationships of many sorts, and in the very expansions and contractions of the Universe, Siva-Shakti, breath-out breath-in.

Tantra is prana flowing to heal and to transform, vibrations created by whatever particular practice to properly order practitioners in relation to this basic binary (that is sometimes/somehow still *advaita*, "not-two") in harmony with the ideal, with that most primal romance, Siva-Sakti. Tantra is imagining and manifesting transformation in certain subtle forms of relationship, with Deva-Devi in mind and practice. *Tantra-yoga*

---

15   "Vibration" (*anunAda, prana, sphUrti*) or "vibe" isn't merely some silly made-up hippie thing, but a concept from *Ayurvedic* science that relates rather succinctly to particle and quantum physics, psychology, instinct and a well thought out science of interpersonal interactions—not divided by some taxonomy as Western science would have them.

proposes that a balance and elevation might be met in sometimes conflicting vibrations and actions (*karma*) and mind, set in motion by means of properly channeling *prana*. Basically, tantra is practice utilizing (sometimes/the roots of) sexual energies to heal and grant transcendence and offer healthy "union" (yoga) to practitioners of this most ancient religious form, is tauted the swiftest path to *moksha*, and by the way does not necessarily entail coital activities.

Of other physical intimacies, Leslie showed me some pressure points and we thus practiced acupressure on each other, as well as employing various other methods of bodywork on occasion, and did sun salutations together sometimes. I was only once granted a glimpse of her uncovered body's beauty, except for what was afforded by her more revealing belly-dancing costumes. One morning as I started towards the bathroom for a shower, she lifted her shirt to reveal her extraordinarily well formed breasts, then making pretense she had not intended this indiscretion, she swiftly lowered her shirt to cover her lovely chest, yet again veiling her beautiful bosoms' form.

"Oops!" she said coyly.

I tirelessly devoted myself to Leslie's service, always considering ways I might make her happy, sooth her mostly unnamed sorrows, and encourage her to be the empowered woman I knew lay underneath or somewhere in the cosmic stuff that is Leslie, divine belly-dancer, yogini, mystic beatific friend, focus of deserved devotions.

On one occasion, she left for some undisclosed destination rather late in the evening. I had a few dollars, and thought of how much she liked Montreal's rather sweet version of the normally blasé sesame seed bagel. There are small storefront bagel bakeries throughout the city where one can procure these mouthwatering delights fresh from the oven. I decided to run (quite literally) to attain some for breakfast, imagining my swift errand as somehow an apt mostly personal symbolic expression of my still fiery devotion. I took a direct route that led me to leap and scramble over various barriers in the dark Montreal night to arrive at the bagel makers before closing time. In my absurd knight-errant's errand I scaled an eight foot or better chain-link fence, slicing a nice gash in my leg which I hardly noticed as the adrenaline wrought of crazy devotion flowed through my heart and veins. I was so wanton to please, so desirous to satisfy this woman who had long been beloved and was now friend I made up austerities to express my madman's devotion, even if she would not see. Crazy *bhakti*.

I underwent mild *tapasia* (purifying-fire) sitting in practice in the cold on the slopes of *Mont Royal*, imagining my exposure to the elements and the intensity of certain meditative states might offer up the fire that would end whatever ills assailed her, and might remove whatever obstacles prevented the *prana* of the divine couple, Shiva-Shakti, from healing and granting elevated states of yoga in my relationship with Leslie as well as in a broader context. These heartfelt and sometimes silly symbolic and absurdly expressed devotions might prove over the top for even the archetypal romantic fool, Don Quixote.

Leslie soon received a much-anticipated call informing her that she had been accepted to work for the summer at the Omega Institute. Among other perks, she would be able to enroll in various classes, take peaceful walks along the shore of the picturesque lake and meditate in various places designed to be conducive to peace-of-mind, keep company with other like-minded practitioners and seekers, and enroll in one seminar of her choice. She had attended a belly-dancing seminar at the Institute a summer or more previous, and felt this environment would be conducive to whatever respite she might require. At her suggestion, I also applied and was accepted to work in the kitchen.

As the date of our departure approached and the cold and brutal Montreal winter began to dissipate, it seemed as if the whole city was lifted from some figurative underworld and back into the light of the sun. And indeed, there is some literal truth to this metaphor, for during the long and frigid winter much of the populace disappears to beneath the streets to spend much of their time in the vast underground city. Shops and restaurants and nearly any service you might imagine are located in the miles of tunnels, a subterranean labyrinth that allows many to never don a coat or even a sweater from apartment to work to shop and back home, though the surface air may reside well below zero, Celsius and Fahrenheit. Come the spring, Montreal's troglodytes emerge as so many groundhogs.

Though I hadn't been much below during my sojourn in this many layered metropolis, I felt as if I too had risen into a kinder realm as the snow melted and temperatures sometimes soared to well above freezing. Leslie likewise seemed to feel better as the buds began to thrust out their green to absorb the renewed life giving rays, and as the sun climbed higher and lingered longer each day.

The change of season signaled our approaching departure to the south, an inverse migration I've done often. We boarded the train, and I once again wore sunglasses to obtain passage for my "service animal," but this time had a new passport to allow easier passage. Leslie grasped my arm as we made our way to a seat, and Zunaka curled at our feet.

We arrived in Rhinecliff, New York, and stepped off the train, once again in the United States of America. Leslie called for a cab, and we walked up the hill to wait beside a restaurant. I decided not to ride with Leslie, largely as I had to figure out some sort of lodging for Zunaka, who was not allowed on Omega's grounds. There were two fellows in their late teens or early twenties hanging out by the restaurant, and they seemed quite eager to greet me. I said goodbye to Leslie, then watched her step into the cab. I believe I may have made a mistake by not accompanying her.

On the next few occasions we met, she did not seem the same woman I had spent the previous few months with. She was no longer so eager for my company, and in fact began to treat me with something not entirely unakin to disdain. I wondered if yet again something like a bait-and-switch or shell-game tactic had been employed by whatever presiding deities or other beings had sway. Else I might more optimistically imagine portions of a dance or acts of a play not always carried through to completion or finale in one particular set of figures or another, nor even necessarily played out in full upon one particular stage.

I suppose I understand this in relation to familiar patterns of devotion to Devi, as I envision her manifesting to whatever degree in women I chance to know and love in order to complete some particular phase or other of what I suppose might be termed *kleem-karma-dharma* (teaching in action in relationship). As one cycle of this divinely directed relationship ends, one act of the play closes or one stage of a dance finds completion, it seems to follow that another then begins, another lesson scripted and choreographed ensues, the next dharmic/didactic screenplay plays out in one's life lived.   Thus, to remain too attached to one particular form or player at a given moment in the process may be a mistake, as She may have other plans for forthcoming *lila* and romance, love play and divine dance, *nata*.

    I believe I smoked a bowl with the two Mainers after Leslie rode away in the taxi. There was something I found questionable of these two, perhaps mostly their prompt appearance upon first stepping back onto American soil—too staged, but I had not yet been pressed from within and without to become so skeptical of the everyday as later experiences would make me. Zunaka I walked to the next town, Rhinebeck, and spanged up some money for food ("spanging" is a hippie/gutterpunk neologism equivalent to "panhandling"). A day or so later, or perhaps that same day, I hiked towards the Omega Institute. I think I had Leslie's sleeping bag or some such, though I don't recall the precise details. I was not scheduled to begin at the institute for another week or so. I shortly found Leslie, and she showed me to her room.

    Painted on the wall behind her bed, a large eye gazed into the room with an eerie glassy stare. I thought of other symbols analogous and related to "The Eye" I had seen in recent times. Leslie had either a pendant or ring or some such article of jewelry that bore a *hamsa*, or alternately termed, "hand of Fatima" or "hand of Miriam." She said shared Muslim and Hebrew artifact is worn to ward off "the evil eye." "*Hamsa*" is also Sanskrit for swan, and is associated with Brahma, and is purportedly a pet name Neem Karoli Baba gave to Bhagavan Das, the seventeen year old American-born *sadhu* who introduced Richard Alpert (later Ram Dass) to his guru. Rapidly repeating this word as a mantra is said to render it as "*soaham,*" meaning "that I am."

    I believed the ominous apparition of the eye on the wall rather an ill omen, and felt Leslie had changed rather drastically in a matter of however many hours. Maybe her *hamsa* wasn't properly tuned or needed batteries or a recharge. From holding tight to my arm as we sat on the train, to expressing what seemed a scarcely veiled contempt, I wondered right away if the woman I had accompanied from Canada had been stolen away by the taxi, and now a *doppelgänger* stood-in (or perhaps even a *doppel-doppelgänger*). On the occasion of this or another visit, Leslie and I sat on her bed when another staff-member knocked on the door. He was a rather handsome if short man somewhere in our age range (early to mid-thirties). I cannot recall what he had to say whilst at the entrance to her abode, but I distinctly heard him say, "Just leave!" after he had shut the door. I immediately commented on this to Leslie, and she claimed I was imagining things.

Though as I mentioned, I could have interpreted at this very moment that the woman who now bore the face of the woman I had come to know in Canada was not the same person—perhaps even quite literally, I still had a wish to maintain the myth of a virtuous and intact beloved. I would not even deny the possibility that the friend I had known in Montreal was indeed not even present in or as this woman I now encountered at the Omega Institute in the hills above the Hudson Valley, regardless of appearance, in addition to the possibility the barista encountered years before was a different than the being or being(s) encountered as "Leslie" in Montreal and New York. Definitely a disorienting perspective and one I'd generally rather not consider, and yet one perhaps unavoidable after so many of the strange things I have seen and experienced, such as sex with a shape-shifter and so forth. Regardless of the details, my friendship with this woman oft imagined as a goddess had seemingly suddenly changed.

I later discovered that the name "Leslie" means "garden of hollies" or "garden by a lake" according to a catalog delineating the meanings and origins of alphabetized appellations. This definition definitely described the place she lived and worked, as a picturesque lake resides in the middle of the property, though I can't say I saw any holly bushes. Holly, as mentioned, is my former wife's name. Now indeed, what might a man suppose of such synchronicities and coincidences?

A number of possibilities seem to exist, various modes and means to interpret obvious signs to reckon relationships of souls in these obviously interwoven experiences, names, denotations, people, times and places. Perhaps definitions somehow reform to meet expectations or imaginings, manifest alterations of reality slipped in while I wasn't looking—truly revisionist history. This could be a sort of if "a tree falls" type question: have my own associations created these so-called synchronicities retroactively? Is it that someone with some degree of powers of illusion (*AvaraNazakti*) has been paying o'er much attention to my thoughts manifest and life-happenings? thus perhaps attempting to prescribe or proscribe my path, to plant "clues" and obviously contrived obstacles and to arrange so called *chance meetings* and other such evidences of extraordinary measures made however transparent, and sometimes quite succinctly presented to my thoughts and manifest in my daily experiences as indubitable intrusions of factors outside mere coincidence? a hand divine? of some trickster or genie? or perhaps . . . of both? Or are these experiences to be fitted within the Jungian concept of synchronicity, i.e., that once you start looking for something you are likely to encounter said something more often than is statistically likely (and indeed without any word on why or how expectations held in mind made manifest might defy probability).

  To offer another example of the sort of alterations of reality which give me more than cause to pause and wonder, just before I departed from Laramie to endeavor this mad adventure around four years previous to this penning, a rather inexplicable series of events began whilst I was employed at a bistro that bears the same name as my forename in an old building in downtown Laramie. One evening when I was working washing dirty dishes, a small fire began in a wall next to an outside door frame. The LFD showed up and tore open the antique door frame and extinguished said minor conflagration.

  Shortly before I left Laramie to travel to Montreal, this side-door's frame was already replaced with new pine boards. Upon returning to Laramie after this journey, I happened by this side-door that was the site of the flames and was quite startled as I noticed what appeared to be the original door frame in place, with neither damage from fire nor ax! I have yet to investigate fully the possible "logical explanations," but the door frame that is currently in place is warped, splintering, and is covered in layers of paint that do not seem to have been altered anytime in the past ten to twenty years.

Is the Laramie I have returned to a different *loka* (Sanskrit root of the English word "location") than the one I left? is there a more "logical" explanation? or would the explanation offered serve as but yet another veil or layer of intrigue? At this time I have not investigated this anomaly thoroughly—i.e., haven't asked the business's owner of the supposed sequence of events—though with a view of current facts, the change evidenced by what I know of this particular green door frame before and after this journey rather well exemplifies the sort of odd alterations of the assumed continuity of time-space I seem to experience with a rather excessive frequently these days. And though likely some of these discrepancies have a 'rational' explanation, that does not necessarily mean that some collusion of illusion or manipulation of *maya* is not involved.

In order to properly respond to such mischief or confusion I generally try to intend and manifest and even sometimes scream out, *"Rta-dharma,"* may it be that action reaps appropriate teachings and due consequence, as is good and true and just. Usually I try to remember to add a nice *"bhutadaya"* or *"karuna"* in the same breath ("compassion"), and maybe some other ancient intonations thrown in for flavor or further effect. If I am playing the plaything of some transcendent or pseudo-transcendent other(s) as some twisted *dharma*, may he, she or they receive their due *dharma*, too, with all due wrath and of course with all due compassion, too.

I spent several days in Rhinebeck, a couple of miles from the train stop in Rhinecliff on the Hudson and a few miles shy of the location of the Omega Institute. Picturesque and expensive, this town might be compared to a Hollywood set of the "hometown" America busy city dwellers less than an hour away dream when they long for that mythical place so enshrined in Americana (that rarely ever and for most never seems to match with reality's version).

Numerous aged whitewashed churches are interspersed between large colonial homes with well-manicured lawns, and various picturesque creeks with well-shored banks flow in and around the quaint Colonial era village. The downtown streets are lined with all the appropriate shops and restaurants, an ice cream parlor and New York style pizza by the slice, a hardware store, a department store and a few rather gentrified bars—none the least bit seedy. I often ate at a diner called Pete's Famous, where they had all-day breakfast affordable on my spangin' budget.

    I might explain here my philosophy regarding begging. Throughout recorded history (i.e., the past few thousand years), many if not most of the prophets and spiritual teachers who have impacted society for more than the span of popular whim acquired their sustenance by this means, not to mention so many millions of unknown extreme practitioners from the Himalayas to the Andes, renunciates sitting or standing in whatever pose with outstretched hands or an empty bowl. In much of this world there is an honored place afforded the seeker or renunciate who lives for those ideals the householder has generally accorded at best second place to material goals, and it is considered a blessing to bestow alms upon these who represent more overtly the spiritual longings of community and humanity generally.

    For years in my travels I would not resort to outright begging and would always seek work or means of trade to sustain my humble needs, as is the case with most the hippies and other American-gypsy types. Generally the trade amongst these circles is in some special or magical plant or fungi, in addition to hemp jewelry, patchy pants and padded pipe bags and crystals and other pretty rocks picked up in the desert or mountains, didgeridoos and drums. Sage smudges and semiprecious stones fueled my ride a number of times round, circling through the Western states clockwise or counter, as well making means by trade in weed and other botanicals, and by many odd jobs here and there. At some point, however, as need and circumstance required, I learned to swallow my pride and accept more fully the assumed role as *sadhu*, and consented to sit on some curb somewhere with a sign or a solicitation and a smile. I still prefer to pay my own way by at least finding goods in the wilderness to trade in town, else by my recognized labors either above or below the table, as is the way with most wandering hippie types.

I believe that, as it turns out, everyone eventually always pays their own way, at whatever level, regardless of whether you receive a paycheck from a "legitimate business enterprise," or by sitting with a human skullcap as a begging bowl. Even the guy who purportedly "paid for the sins" of all those groveling evangelicals and various other flocks of sheep said they gotta take up his burden, and gotta carry that rude soldier's shit for an extra fucking mile if they want a part of his heaven. And said purported avatar, Jeshua ben Joseph (aka, "Jesus"), affirmed the very basic principle of karma-dharma in a statement he is reported to have uttered, "You shall reap what you sow."

The renouncer makes his or her way by reminding the rest of higher goals and possibilities for humanity, and sometimes by willingly bearing the burdens of others, as well as by intense devotions to the divine. In the traditions of India, a yogi might even sometimes elect to absorb the physical or karmic ills of his or her devotees. Jeshua ben Joseph, as I already mentioned, is believed by his devotees to have taken on their sins. Shamanistic healers often heal their patrons by ritual modes involving vicariously receiving and endeavoring to transform a patient or devotee's problem sickness or demon, and sin eaters might yet be encountered as they work their circuits in isolated parts of Appalachia or the Welsh countryside. These are services and legitimate occupations recognized in many, if not most traditional societies, from the Himalayas to the Andes, the shores of the Bosporus to the islands of the Pacific, the deserts of Mexico to the depths of the Dead Sea's shores, and throughout the course of history and from the earliest of records and time immemorial. In the *Rig Veda,* the most ancient of books, mendicant forest dwelling renunciates are described as partaking of a psychedelic brew and dancing 'round like a bunch of trippin' hippies. Indeed, nigh certainly these first recorded *sadhu* or *brahmachari* made their way by begging. It might be posited there are in fact unbroken lineages of these sacred beggar types stretching from the most antique all the way through time and even to the post-postmodern reality of the streets of present day America.

In this land these days such figures are less overtly recognized, though I would say some of my many and varied benefactors seemed to recognize I was *not* taking the easy road by living off the largess of passersby. Indeed, in moments of agony as well as spiritual ecstasy I spoke an intention and willingness to serve what role I might in helping to heal this world's ills, and indeed I feel I have at times had some of these heaped upon my shoulders or head or heart (or whatever *chakra* or *bandha* or other *loka*) to transform or destroy or otherwise deal with.

    I have placed certain limits upon what burdens I will accept as appropriate need to endeavor to transform, however, i.e., that I can and shall prove able to handle the task at hand without irreparable damage to my own mind or life or path, and without causing unacceptable or unjust or uncompassionate peripheral damage to any other by such an effort. I do recognize my own certain and potential limitations within given temporal, spacial and situational contexts—as should any serious practitioner, and also that in some cases taking on another's burden might not be doing any favors.

    As a contrary or related corollary, for those of you calling yourselves disciples of "Jesus" who will likely contend it's already all done, "paid in full" and all, I can perhaps best respond by handing you a newspaper with headlines telling of sufferings and wars and violences of whatever form that yet plague humans and animals and the rest of creation—and many atrocities in fact carried out by some claiming to "follow Jesus"—to state quite simply, "No it ain't." We all gotta pay our way and do our share, and there's still much to be done. We shall reap what we sow, indeed. *Karma-dharma.*

    This might all appear further quixotic insanity to the modern Western mind, at least by the standards of officially and scientifically informed (and formed) intellects and discourse, but most of the world's peoples recognize the value of ascetics for a functional and integrative society and a healthy community, as well as to maintain good relations with whatever given understanding of spirit or divinity or other subtle realms of being that connect people and other life and the eternal and what is transcendently and otherwise good. I mention these things not only to help the reader better understand the character in this tale that is also narrator and author, but also to perhaps prod you to consider the random hobo, bum, hippie or even rude-ass gutterpunk begging for some change as likely more than meets the eye.

As a tradition best known to many of my likely readers has admonished, be careful with strangers, for you might be entertaining angels unaware. Or as I might phrase it, a holy man in the clothes of an alcoholic, God or Goddess or *gaNa* (Mahadeva's minions and a term which may actually be the root of the word "angel") in the guise of a madman or woman, or at least quite likely a pilgrim on a path towards something "higher," better, healed and beautiful.

Leslie had a hard time recognizing this of my sometimes mendicant ways and means, at least in what she spoke to me in the contexts of our personal interactions, and specifically after we had left Montreal and first parted company. I don't deny the likely possibility that she understands otherwise, or at least that the teacher and goddess that I believe I have seen in her or with higher sight envisioned of her—unfettered by illusion and perhaps necessary veils—and in truth has respect for these paths. She nonetheless admonished me in an email after our initial parting that she thought my life as a beggar was not good for my health, and that I ought to go home and get work, else I should consider going to "be with your people" in India—meaning some band of *sadhu* I suppose, adding that "they probably miss you."

Now please don't mistake, even in moments of seeming harshness Leslie never quite reached the point (to my conscious knowledge, opinion or observation) where she would deservedly be granted the appellation or expletive "bitch," excepting perhaps the two aforementioned incidents, at *Soupe Café* and in her cabin at the Omega Institute. For the most part, and even in the few moments when she was being other than kind, I found her delightful or at least inadvertent teacher, whether or not she was even always the same being or expressing the same spirit or vibe from one encounter to the next, and indeed sometimes harshings or slights are the best thing for a friendship, especially between two friends of the opposite sex.

I do recognize that intense belief in someone or something can indeed alter one's perception, and love can manifest rose colored glasses. Yet even if what you view with faith is only a *murti,* a metal or clay statue or two-dimensional representation, the truth of your higher vision can gain a glimpse of what is intended in said representation. Regardless of when or whether Leslie was fully an *"Avatar"* at any given moment, in at least some glimpses or instances of observing her beautiful form and actions and words and movements I know I viewed something at least very close to transcendent, and thus perhaps had eyes to perceive the Divine in and about her even when she was perhaps unaware or unwilling to acknowledge this of herself. She is one of very few I have known who I believe at the least might be or might have at one time been an *Avatar* in the fullest meaning of that term.

I suppose, regardless of emphasis, this is not unrelated to the substance of the greeting *"Namaste,"* which basically means, "the Divine in me bows to the Divine in you." Likewise related is a decision I made several years ago regarding intimacies with women in general, which was that if I go so far as to make love, I resolved to act towards my lover as if she *is* an Avatar or at least emanation or expression of some version of the Feminine Divine. Even if this might be far from the "truth" about this or that lover (save as all are vessels of the Divine manifest as *Atman* and as Great Goddess Mama is in all the ladies, however much self-realized), by projecting such a vision you cannot help but elevate her, draw blessings and good teachings and so forth to her life, and also to yourself.

Indeed, the utterance of *"Namaste"* more than implies this transformative tendency of devotion to and reverence for an "other," and of course I do apply this recognition of the ever-present divine elsewhere and to others other than those I've known as lovers, though the potency and intimate nature of sexual interaction requires the more that one maintain the highest degree of devotion and respect. These things said, *lila* (divine play) doth manifest strange scenarios, and courting one's lover or beloved as a goddess may manifest scenarios as strange or intense as any I've mentioned.

One of numerous visitations or experiences of *lila* that I observed after parting company with Leslie was an encounter I had in Rhinebeck with a high school girl who told me her name was "Jasmine"—a flower which is quite succinctly associated with Siva and Consorts. I had been studying about various goddesses (mostly Hindu at this point), and had come to wonder about the relationship of the Hindu goddess "Lalitha" to "Lilith," a figure variously portrayed in Jewish and Gypsy lore as well as in modern pagan and feminist mythologies, and these to Lolita of Nabokov's famous work (which was actually penned here in Wyoming).

As I sat on a bench, a block or two from the Starr Bar, this girl and a couple of her peers approached the strange bearded man with backpack and wolf-dog, asking the sort of questions often posed to seeming eccentric transient figures who don't quite fit the scene. She presented herself as an outcast, and attempted to cozy right up to me as I showed encouragement and understanding in the few words I spoke. Though she was certainly flirting, I have a very clear and concise line drawn at around twenty-something that would only drop a smidge below that limit for a fully revealed and proper and effulgent avatar of Devi Durga Herself. Despite this standard, I read a certain *lila* in this plot from the start, regardless of whoever it was actually lay behind this façade of a Lolita.

At one chance meeting as I sat upon the same park bench, she nigh forced me to receive a rather fierce-looking necklace with metallic or stone teeth and red and black cylindrical beads. I later read that Lalitha is said to have decided upon a husband between the three male Gods of the Trimurti, Brahma, Vishnu and Shiva, by flinging her wreath into the air, resolving She would marry the one over whose head and neck it fell. As the tales tell it, t'was Siva's neck the ring of flowers fell around.

A bit wary of this gift, I nonetheless placed it around my neck. Later this seemingly symbolically loaded item of apparel became a focus in an exchange with a rather confrontational liquor-breathed bald man I later realized was very likely Dave Atell, the comedian whose show (at least at the time) was airing on Comedy Central. No, really!

This episode occurred outside The Starr, a historic restaurant and bar along the main drag in Rhinebeck. The fellow who looked very much like Dave Atell seemed to be with at least one companion (co-conspirator), and I am not certain whether or not they were filming (i.e., if indeed I am correct in my later reconstructed identification of the bald provocateur), though it seems by the presentation of the show the cameras aren't hidden. He was certainly playing well the proverbial devil's advocate as he tried to intimidate me and press my already rather taxed mind with the brand of conflict and head-games that sell well as entertainment, but are otherwise likely received as rude and unnecessarily provocative.

    I will admit, despite my general belief in *ahimsa* (nonviolence), I had my right hand clenched and ready to swing, if the need arose. I was not certain, as his face and cue-ball cranium began to turn bright red, his face only inches from . . . my chin, that he was not preparing to strike me—or for all I knew pull a knife or gun, and my body instinctively prepared to react. As things cooled down in the exchange, he asked for the necklace I wore, and I started to give it to him, not that attached to the necklace as I had not consciously considered the Lalitha connection, then thought the better of the exchange. I later left this necklace in the forest on the edge of town.

    This is far from my only odd encounter with apparent media celebrities, but those stories for another time. Suffice it to say, if you choose to live your given span of years large, tread the path less traveled, a life less ordinary and so forth, you likely shall, and shall likely be noticed despite any intentions to maintain a low profile, and likely encounter others who are likewise living large by whatever given medium or guise.

    I soon concluded I should leave New York, and decided not to work at the Omega Institute. Actually I don't recall precisely whether this determination was made before or after the aforementioned seeming slight in Leslie's cabin, and thus whether or not this incident was a factor in my reasoning at this juncture. Come to think of it, I am even somewhat uncertain whether it was at this point or upon the occasion of my next visit, on my (presumed) thirty-third birthday, that I decided the Omega Institute was not the proper place for me, or at least not at that time.

    Things were a bit muddled at this point, perhaps as a result of having returned to the states after having somewhat acclimated to Canada, and certainly as hopes for further time shared and possibilities for romance had faltered. I was weary and discerned that I ought allow myself some time to recover health and hopefully clarity of mind by retreating to the home of my sister Lisa and her husband Marc in Maryland. Once again I donned sunglasses and boarded a passenger train with my "helper animal."

Though I regained some physical strength during this respite enjoying my sibling's hospitality, I had not escaped whatever was assailing my psychic and dream life, not to mention someone's seeming abuse of powers of *cidacit*—mind and matter—that was increasingly effecting as well as affecting my reality and sanity (that was never, I should add, lost to the point I became any physical threat to anyone's life or limb. I'd have to know with no margin of uncertainty that I was slaying a demon or other evil being deserving destruction before swinging my *Trishul* blades or bringing like deadly force to bear).

Lisa and Marc were hospitable hosts, as always, and tolerant of my uncharacteristic funk, though without going into detail neither of them seemed quite their respective selves, either. I never quite fully emerged from my protective cloak except when left alone in the house to veg-out to the television, eat myself back to proper health, and smoke whatever herb they might leave for me to enjoy.

In times past I've shared great fun with Lisa and Marc. Among other fond memories, we have on a number of occasions conspired with various others to wander around forest or field, amidst the granite canyons and promontories of Vedawoo or to the mountains west or south, consuming various quantities of psychedelic mushrooms and playing much more amicably than were many childhood interactions with said sister. For the duration of this occasion the pair were good hosts, but a weight (and perhaps not only the one(s) that arrived with me) made this visit not so intimate as past fun times with these friends who happen to be relatives.

In continued contact with Leslie, mostly via email, she consented to spend the day with me on my (purported) birthday, May 1. I rode the train to Rhinecliff once again, Zunaka again posing as my guide-dog. When I arrived at Omega, Leslie and I walked together by the small lake on the institute's grounds, and I couldn't help but be reminded of the picturesque *bardo*-realm lake featured in the movie *What Dreams May Come*, a film I watched with former girlfriend Meghan a year or so previous, and which she had noted was her favorite flick. Indeed, there have been more than moments I have wondered exactly where I am, between or outside of the purported parameters of those states dubbed "life" and "death." Leslie expressed to me that she had no small discomfort with *What Dreams May Come*.

There is unquestionably a strong similarity between these two bodies of water. Come to think of it, I believe the lake at the Omega Institute may very well have been the inspiration for the painted-(sorta) come-to-life lake in the film. I seem to recall, in fact, that Robin Williams has visited or taught a seminar or two at this interfaith retreat center, and Leslie may have even mentioned that she understood this to be the case, else I noticed his name slated on the Omega schedule or came across some other corroborating evidence.

Leslie seemed again different upon this visit, certainly having benefited from living in a peaceful place to practice where others are also overtly seeking to heal and be healed, to explore higher truth and transform the earthly shell into some greater semblance of divine or transcendent perfection. She again behaved a bit more like the Leslie I had come to know in Montreal, save that she seemed more at peace.

I shall not contend that I perceived this former Jewish turned interfaith compound/yoga retreat center with a name evokes Christian symbolism as entirely without unseen subtleties and potential intrigues, nor devoid of any shadows, though any such sensed may have been merely my personal perceptions during tenuous times, else sorrows projected. Regardless of my experiences or impressions one way or another, this place has certainly been a haven and healing center for many.

I should make note again that I am not so detailed in descriptions of all my interactions with Leslie out of due respect for her. I have no want to exploit what she shared of herself and her time, nor breach any confidences she granted me, though would share of the glories of romance and *bhakti*. Certain such consideration accompanying candor ought be *de rigueur* for telling true tales involving identifiable others, unless someone deserves or needs to be exposed for some important and justifiable reason.

Though I would also grant the reader all due respect, and want whomever might have stayed with me to this point in the text, well into this story, to have the benefit of adequate description, fullness of factuality, accurate quotation, and appropriate insights into each character and the 'what happened,' I would rather maintain the good faith of friends (and even the remnants of this with former friends) over telling damning or embarrassing or too intimate of truths for my own gain or to make for a better story. And even in telling whatever scene in fine detail, I often omit the most subtle and perhaps esoteric features I recognize, similarly out of respect for certain secrets or persons, and sometimes to avoid exposing the reader unawares to knowledges that might be hazardous to his or her health—figuratively or otherwise.

In spite of the decreasing intimacy, I was still very pleased to share Leslie's company on this day, anniversary of my purported birth, day of celebration and display of solidarity for world laborers, and pre-Christian European fertility festival (though a celebration not at all entirely faded in the wake of said religious conquests, and might be said a day again gaining popularity in a traditional guise). In many respects this day celebrated is aptly analogized as a European version of *Sivaratri*, though celebrated a bit later in the year due to differences in climate and latitude. Where the European holiday represents the phallus with a pine pole and feminine as ribbons woven 'round the stick, *Sivaratri* recognizes stone *linga* and *yoni* (phallus and vulva) adorned as emblematic of the perfect union of male and female.

Leslie and I walked by the lake, and sat not far from the water's edge. She told me she was still experiencing ups-and-downs, but that she was generally benefiting from her routine of work and meditation, dance and yoga. She went to the kitchen and brought me an apple. We talked a bit more. We embraced and I departed.

To this day, I cannot say I have let go of my longstanding devotion to Leslie, though certainly my perception of her has changed and some of the associations I once held are unquestionably transformed, as indeed I have been by our time together and by the peripheral circumstances and the continued sequence of events that followed. I have changed for better and worse, and as stated, my perceptions of her are inexorably altered, though not detrimentally to any significant degree. Be she Divine, she showed she is also human, and that is not a bad thing.

It is also not a bad thing to return to a less specifically manifest vision of Devi, to return to the romance wherein my lover is always present, at the verge of the moment, on the cusp between now and eternity, wherein She reminds me of her presence at least in the least reference to one or another of many names I've known her by, in a particular quality of sentiment observed in a woman's eyes that reminds of a vision I've of Devi, else in the sway of a shapely woman's hips as she walks past, or in whatever other random little reminders of the other in the cosmic love between male and female, Deva and Devi, a love that has something to do with me, and with you too, if how I've envisioned love is true.

This mode of romance would compare, archetypally or metaphorically at the least, to how Siva is consort to Maha Maya, and thus engaged with the Goddess of Illusion in a subtle dance of synchronistic romance, Shiva and Shakti manifest in day-to-day occurrences in *maya* (i.e., field of worldly illusion, and not precisely referring directly to Goddess Maha Maya Herself). Though according to some traditions Siva and Devi as Maha Maya have only had sex three times, their subtle love story permeates reality and is manifest in a more domestic mode in the romance of Siva and Parvati. Indeed I'm cool with that less tangible mode—I suppose. Yet I still anticipate the appropriate manifestation of a divine yogini as my lasting lover and more, whilst still delighting in the little reminders of love She leaves as the least serendipities and slight glimpses behind or beneath her shimmering veils, graciously granted in the meantime.

This love dance and unmanifest romance has sustained me between and to whatever degree upon the occasions of time spent with however many lovers. I suppose I can as need be thus still continue to abide or at least survive with Her more as possibility than present with me, as my partner in a dance broader in scale than just here and now, whilst I yet sit still seemingly alone.

I have found that place where I believe Shiva-Shakti balanced within and outside of my person and spheres of influence, in body and mind and in relationship, and have delighted in granted glimpses of the grandeur of our mutual devotions in the love notes writ or painted in the clouds, a breeze answering my thoughts, else in whatever other pleasing synchronicities manifest on this stage of *maya*. That stuff's quite cool, yet also having an appropriately embodied lover as suitable expression and proper manifestation or emanation of Devi is even cooler—whilst desire and romance are still a thrill, and a yogini as partner is necessary in certain tantric rituals. Sounds rather 'convenient' as means to justify license, yet keep in mind that Mahadeva, Great God, is a Seducer and is sometimes seduced by the Great Mother, and by some accounts has a record as a sex offender, as it's quite illegal most places to walk down the street with an erection fully displayed.

  Moments in which I sit, now returning to revise and sight check these words typed over—over a year sitting in Laramie, again and again revisiting this text which grows and is refined each time I peruse its pages . . . whilst meditating upon and reconsidering words writ and attending to other random tasks, I sometimes and randomly see flashing before my internal sight visions of so many women divine who I've known in whatever capacity, as lovers or friends or someones I chanced to glance who somehow stayed within my memories as significant, and who all figure as at least likenesses of Her through my intentioned lens. With no little tension felt inside and even displayed outside my form by actors and actresses in what seem skits performed and choreographed to meet my thoughts and memories—perhaps unaware they are characters in an at least somewhat preordained or preconceived play that's at least somewhat scripted and makes some coherent sense as such, a fractal tantric dance of these visions flows before my mind and other senses, and I sometimes must stand from my seat and dance frenzied to appropriately symbolically and empathically order these factors and figments and faces and myself and physical form and various other energies, subtle and sublime to the tunes that play on my laptop, in relation to Self to keep from going mad, though bystanders who happen to see me in the throes of wild *nata* in the parking lot by the patio likely think me already quite insane, if my moves generally meet a fine reception at festivals or music shows. My devotion to Her is indeed not ashamed of displays unusually manifest, as is generally the way with true *bhakti*.

Whilst compelled to consider where it was or might possibly have been that I already-already knew Her—if not as Leslie—yet absent-mindedly passed Her by . . . I utter random Sanskrit phrases and subtly and sometimes not so subtly make intuitive and learned *mudras* and movements to correct or respond to felt imbalanced flows of our relationship (and of others contingent) which come flying at my thoughts like arrows or bullets or thunderstorms, and chant praises to Her most sacred names to assure Her of my continued devotion and to ask Her help in healing loves and other vibrations of experience, and intone other ancient potent words to bring about purity in relationships and energies generally—locally, globally and beyond.

'Twas perhaps easier to do this yoga when the envisioned highest and likeliest "Her" was known but unknown, corporeally certain yet inaccessible, named and encountered yet not bodily present—not unlike a *murti*. Though since I came to some semblance of awareness I've made a practice of envisioning every lover I've held as object of or conduit to my certain devotion to Devi (at least whilst we were romantically involved), with each relationship faltered I found comfort in the possibility of Leslie (or at least of some like emanation of Divine Feminine perfection—perhaps another *Avatar* of Her or the person of Goddess She showed me in Her transcendent movements and sublime subtleties) crossing paths with me somewhere in the future. And now with that question at least half-answered, seems what once were delightful reveries on lovers past and possible have now grown fiercer, storms of thought forms flowing and questions rushing past and through me as my passion for Devi reforms to altered conditions of devotion, and as I sense more resistance than before from contending forces or jealousies or perhaps from some reservations or other immediate intentions of Devi Herself as I approach the hem of her gown—or perhaps draw near somewhere a bit further towards the waistline.

Soon after this mostly quiet and rather reserved encounter by the lake, I resolved that it was time to return to the high mountains, return to some semblance of stable practice, and return to a more conventional mode of employment. Though I bounced around the Hudson Valley for a while before attaining escape velocity, including spending a very interesting stint in New Paltz, the home of a once very (and still rather) hippie-saturated SUNY school and a strong local Green Party, I did eventually get out of the Hudson River drainage and on to Syracuse, then to Buffalo to visit a friend I'd known from Laramie, and then a little further west . . .

New Paltz is not entirely unlike Rhinebeck. Both are quaint colonial era villages with old homes and churches and particularly cool old graveyards, urban populations of deer and a nice assortment of locally owned restaurants and other businesses. Being a university town, however, New Paltz was much livelier, and had a history that included regular and sometimes unscheduled appearances of the likes of Janis Joplin and The Grateful Dead at a place on campus known as "the Tripping Fields."

I was first conveyed to New Paltz by a young woman I met in Kingston, across the river from Rhinecliff and north of NP. She and I met at an uptown Kingston coffeehouse, and I felt a quick resonance develop as she told me of having recent experiences that were quite like mine, i.e., in the psychic-weirdness sort of way. Her eyes were an amazing mixture of blue and green and brown and various other shades, and were more than mildly reminiscent of an exterior view of the earth. She convinced me I ought to come to New Paltz where she attended the SUNY school, and I readily agreed. We arrived at her parent's home, and I soon met her two sisters, who were also interesting women, each in her own manner.

I must say, my suspicions were raised by the apparition of "three sisters," a partnering more than occasionally present in myth and story. As soon as this lovely new friend offered me temporary lodging, assuming her parents agreed, a vision came to my mind, and of a sort I had been increasingly experiencing that arrive with a feeling not unlike déjà vu and that had been proving startlingly accurate, if not unalterable. I saw my form laying awake and aroused upon the couch, then climbing the stairs in the darkened house and cavorting with one or more than one of the sisters in her/their respective bedrooms.

Not that the thought of sex with any of the three was in itself the least unpleasant. Rather, it was the potential implications of a possible union with a member (or especially more than one member) of a potent threesome of unknown identity—goddesses? fates? witches?—that caused my reticence. One of the three I later encountered at a show at a club on Main Street (a Green Party benefit, if I'm not mistaken), and if I recall she greeted me with a warm embrace, and definitely and most memorably bore the strong scent of yoni—in a pleasant and potent and possibly even sacred way, mind you, evocative of an elevated or concentrated feminine sexuality, and not of a lack of hygiene. Too much potential intrigue to expose myself to at the time—i.e., to sleep just downstairs from this intriguing and enticing trio, as tempting as the offer might have been. I slept in the patches of forest in and around town, and my only bedfellow (at least for the duration of *this* visit to New Paltz . . .) was a large furry dog who kept my feet warm.

In addition to other attractive features of this quaint college town, there was an active group of Green Party activists allied with local and transient hippies in a cooperative located on the main drag in downtown New Paltz that was combined art-space and coffeehouse (which only served the drip-brewed sort) and site for music and activist sorta stuff. I was impressed with the community in general, and was treated quite kindly by nearly all the citizens I happened to meet.

Zunaka and I would join the hippie kids, gutterpunks and hipsters who would sit in front of the co-op building on "the stoop," smoking cigarettes and drinking whatever was in various paper bags and talking shit about the cops or other happenings, and occasionally forming a contingent to march to the edge of the 'haunted woods' to puff a bowl or a joint. I encountered various figures amongst these and others I met elsewhere in this town (as elsewhere is oft the case) who later seemed to remanifest in like forms—or like spirits at least—in various others in various other places over the course of travels to come.

Indeed, on numerous occasions over the duration of the continuation of this journey others with similar appearance as distant friends or other figures from the past, if not near *doppelgänger's* and sometimes even bearing the same names, began to appear more regularly than I was already accustomed, often after a mere thought of someone I have known from elsewhere. I have experienced this to some degree for quite some time, and have considered or envisioned that perhaps some invisible or psychic chord reaches out far beyond one's physical presence to find an analogous person who has the like "receptors" to the remembered faraway friend or significant figure from elsewhere, drawing this other with familiar visage or energy to answer said subtle psychic call, else drawing one to said other (an analogy borrowed from Carlos Castaneda). On this trip such phenomena increased exponentially beyond the scale to which I was accustomed.

To frame this phenomenon from a slightly different perspective, imagine the popular figure or metaphor of the mysterious person or likeness presenting him-, her- or itself just visible in the background in precisely the proper scenes to create a sense of intrigue. Is this multiplicity of a shadow-veiled figure sign of a friend or a foe working behind the scenes? Do the repeated glimpses of an archetypal form manifest from one far-flung site to another, a fleetingly familiar yet not fully known someone often seen just out of the foreground—does this "other" perhaps portend "a friend on the inside," a friendly spirit, else perhaps the figuration or manifestation of an actual assassin, even? Is this a "good-guy" or "bad-guy" (or –girl, respectively) in the trench-coat with the derby pulled low over brow and dark sunglasses waiting to hand off a briefcase or attaché of secret documents or an ancient scroll or to offer some secret advise, else sitting in the corner trying to appear nonchalant whilst watching the scene (and possibly watching you) whilst half-obscured in the shadows? What exactly is one to make of the recurrence of a number of like figures accompanying or randomly appearing on one's journey, people popping up sometimes phantom-like with only slightly different faces in a series of places coinciding with contextual precision, as if on cue? These sorts of things feel natural when watching a film, yet rather strange when living what most folks like to call "reality."

This practice of vision, recognitions of the Divine and various archetypes writ in myth and meme and popular culture and past experiences manifesting particular memories or spirits or energies of various traditions new and old, these collections of consciousness revealed or constructed as gods and goddesses and echoes of ancient and recent heroic figures and so forth can and do indeed animate life lived and experienced, whether noticed or no amidst the purportedly mundane, and even in these days of the prominence of so many technological wonders and the attempted segregation of magic to books of fiction, movies and TV and tabloids. Those figures lauded as pinnacle of things good and true (as well as their supposed opposite), Gods and Goddesses in mythic arrays and portrayals indeed do present figurations of every-person's reality, leastwise if those persons are willing to meet any semblance of their personal potentials. Third eye vision shows, among other views, that each figure in any given scene is at least a partially realized expression of forever stories, if generally without an immediate awareness of the particular myth or story's plot foretells the play being lived. Each is a dancer in the Universal song and dance, however poorly- or well-practiced; all are players in the eternal theater, if not always playing a starring role.

    Thus a stranger passed on the sidewalk or on the bus might be the fulfillment of the proverbial pop-music question, "What if God was one of us?" And indeed this is true, and of Goddess, too, at least from the one most important venue of vision to keep in mind. *Namaste, namaskar,* or however best pronounced to convey this eternal truth, also roughly expressed or translated or transliterated through whatever means of transmission by the phrase, "Love thy neighbor as thyself (or better, *Self*)"—for *Atman* is there, too. We are all living *lila*. Whether consciously or no, we are the Divine at play.

    I should mention that in mentioning certain individuals I remember from this or that place I may not make note of various others present on the given stage, and indeed may not mention some who might in fact play a more pertinent role than those who do make these pages, had I either a more complete purview to appropriately recognize an unmentioned figure's importance, else the inclination to reveal something more than I deem appropriate in this moment as my fingers press the keys. Some keys to the plot of this narrative (told from a perspective admittedly not immediately omniscient) are thus left out quite intentionally, and others likely omitted by some other's wish, consciously or unconsciously registered and respected.

    I do hope to write with utmost sensitivity to those others who are involved in this story in whatever guise, with like due respect to whatever other narratives exist interwoven with what storylines I have been made privy to or experienced directly, and have no intention of penning any semblance of a slanderous script. I would hope, however, to be excused if some friend present at whatever point in this history being told goes unmentioned, lest someone I love is left feeling slighted, else if I miss another important parallel or intersecting narrative by some sort of subtle vision myopia. To chronicle each event with such exacting detail would tax my patience and yours, dear reader, and would make for a work far too voluminous to carry in your pocket or purse.

    A tributary to the Hudson flowed gently through one edge of New Paltz, and I often camped by its shores. Never really established a set campsite, here or elsewhere on this trip, but regularly shifted both where and in what direction I slept, with careful attention to all available senses. I had a rather dark and disturbing dream life during much of this journey, and felt as if some other or others were accessing my REM experiencings, as well as other portions of my mind at times, and thus I quite thoughtfully selected my site to bed down each night.

    On numerous occasions while sleeping under the open sky, especially whilst in New York, I would awaken from a strange dream, roll a smoke then roll onto my back to gaze up to the starscape immediately above to ponder what I had dreamt, and then notice that one of the "stars" would suddenly dart away, from stationary to faster than the speed of sound in an instant. As absurd as this might seem, I believe these were someone or thing from "above" invading/interacting with my personal dream space—whether actually of extraterrestrial origin or no. Once you open your eyes to see, you will see. Not that what you see will necessarily always make sense.

    In New Paltz is one of the oldest still extant roads in the United States, with equally aged tombstones residing and subsiding on a hill on one side, and on the other a field with a community garden and nearby aged stands of trees alongside the river's banks. There was a large fallen tree in the midst of one of these groves that often served as a seat for smoke sessions. Beyond this was a grouping of trees that bore rather grotesque faces sculpted in burly knots upon twisted trunks. This part of the forest was thus called "haunted"—though there might have been other reasons. I never camped here, not desirous of any further supernatural weirdness than was already a constant.

  As example of said weirdness, on one occasion as I sat on a bench near the bakery in downtown New Paltz I observed a man with dark curly hair wearing a striped jogging suit walk past, and then up some stairs suspended on the side of what I believe was a toy store, then entering the second floor apartment. A couple of minute later another figure that appeared identical—same hair and face and same mafia-style leisurewear—followed the same path past my seat and up the stairs and into the door above the toy shop. A third time the seeming same man walked past, this time turning to offer a rather creepy grin before proceeding up the same (and only) set of stairs into said abode.

  Now either this fellow was going to a great deal of trouble to startle me, jumping out a second story window on the other side of the building, then rounding through the alley or some such to pass my vantage thrice, was a set of triplets, else this was some sort of bend in time-space or what in the movie *The Matrix* is dubbed "déjà vu"—i.e., when the black cat twice saunters past and twice utters the same "meow" whilst the film's heroes are climbing some stairs.

  These sorts of experiences experienced too frequently can add up and tax one's mind's ability to maintain a grasp on what (nearly) everyone else pretends reality to be, making it difficult to keep a figurative foot in the door between some semblance of third-eye vision or extra-sensory awareness, and the realm of consumer-fixated media-mesmerized zombies and 9-to-5, the seeming state of many folks' consciousness these days.

  To the defense of the latter, however, I must admit I have sometimes found solace from the confusion of other sensory inputs by viewing mindless media, vegging to the tube and so forth, as evidenced by various movie references interspersed throughout this narrative, and must confess I've sometimes found comfort in the stability of regular employment. When meditation is not practical, trite entertainment can sometimes expediently empty the mind of unwanted chaff (though perhaps merely by replacing it temporarily with other chaff), and offer an otherwise pleasant distraction, and the workaday can become mindful practice.

There is at least one other odd occurrence of note I might mention of my time in New Paltz, as it related to a string of coincidences to come. An o'er friendly and rather effeminate fellow of Asian descent I often encountered in New Paltz would generally greet me and others with a high five, followed by the proclamation, "You're It." I would have only taken this as a quirky habit, were it not for the very darkly tanned woman I soon met at a pool party in Ohio who very seriously stared into my eyes as she, too, tagged me as "It." A few months later I would discover that the weekly paper in Fredericksburg, Virginia is *It*, too. Said sometimes surreptitiously ambiguous and overtly androgynous personal pronoun has indeed been haunting me since, though I've faith I shall recover.

After this initial stay in New Paltz, I caught a ride north and west with a woman named Margaret I had met early on in this sojourn. She had a friend named Meredith who was a startling *doppel* to a friend of mine named Mary (who is sometimes Miriam —or the other way around). She was staying at the hostel (Margaret, that is), a three story colonial house with a statue of Poseidon posted in the garden perched above a fountain and small pool.

Greek and Roman mythological figures were showing up rather too frequently for my taste (please pardon the possibly politically incorrect assertion). Though I recognize the various mythologies of the world as unquestionably interconnected, often harboring tales in texts and traditions that are chapters in the greater story or at least fragments containing clues, I have both an instinctual and aesthetic dislike of the aforementioned paradigm, and to some degree lament the extent to which this tradition has been employed in the construction of the "Western tradition"—a construction that is designed by its very geographic designation to selectively exclude the mention of other influences, to mistakenly categorically deny those strands of the narrative which are "Eastern," despite however important those influences actually are to an accurate history of European peoples.

Those who've adopted said traditions as representing some sort of ideal would have done better to venture further east for insights on ancient truths, closer to the most ancient extant sources of our history, rather than lazily settling for the handiest dissemination and distortion of the earlier wisdoms, slothfully unearthing or "rediscovering" the near-east near-ancient mere-emanations of the depths of India's wisdoms, accepting a third- or fourth-hand telling buried just under the surface of Europe's only briefly forgotten past issuing from Rome and Greece rather than admitting it was dark-skinned peoples in India who first developed those strands of civilization much later manifest in the so-called "West." As an example, Mohenjo-Daro in the Indus Valley had running water and sewers nigh two-thousand years before Rome, and regionally variant versions of the Indus Valley Seal have been found at least as far away as Northern Europe.

Having already seemingly settled for these "sources" of civilization only half-way traced to the truer sources of those traces of past thought, Western culture then granted comparably scant attention to the very oldest extant versions of the oldest tales and philosophies yet available whilst the British held colonies in India. The racist mindset of the colonialists could scarcely see the light of Vedic lore, apparently deeming the dark skinned people and apparent polytheism of India more "primitive" or damning to those earlier strands of thought that are in fact closer to the roots and closer to the truth of the beginnings and wisdoms of civilization's most recent stories (i.e., last 10,000 years or so).

With many Greek and Roman and Egyptian appellations appearing as place-names in the United States, Sanskrit words are surprisingly more often and more closely echoed in Native American place names than in those granted by the narrowly schooled and shallowly rooted newcomers' geographic vocabularies. This, despite widely admitted Sanskrit/"Indo-European" roots of European languages generally, as well as said tongue leaving imprints upon various native languages of the

Americas (which is not widely admitted), lands colonized by *real* Indians—i.e., from the Indian subcontinent—long before Europeans decided to invade.[16] The Vedic timescale posits the Earth's inception at around or just under four-an-a-half billion years old, by the way, surprisingly close to the figure posited by modern astrophysics.

    Only in recent years have America and Europe begun to grant due recognition to the most intact ancient tradition in the world as worthy of sincere attention, mostly arriving as yoga and meditation practices, though also by influencing a departure from o'er simple binary thinking to a more integrated recognition of the greater spectrum of what is, artifacts redeemed from the closet of the "Western mind," and reintroduced from over the Pacific and on the Hippie Trail. And yet, consider what Columbus was purportedly looking for when he set sail towards the setting sun: none other than India.

    All this said, I found I was being rather bombarded with specifically Greek and Roman mythical references, both in names and effigies encountered, and in various experiences where these figures seemed to whatever degree manifest in the expressions of illusion presented in the *lila* of my life experience in the Eastern US. If you look at a map of New York, for example, you will note numerous appellations of Greek and Roman (and Carthaginian) origin as place names, from Ithaca to Utica, Rome and Carthage, Medusa, etc. (though I should note, there is a Delhi, NY). As a rather more fleshed out instance of the *lila* that matched these themes, soon after leaving New Paltz I met "Fortuna" at a gas station on the south end of Syracuse. Fortuna is the Roman goddess of fortune. She was hitchhiking to Chicago to see some jam band festival or somethin.' I should note, said encounter was not at all displeasing to my aesthetic sensibilities.

    Margaret took me to her "parents" house in the farmland southeast of Syracuse. We arrived and entered the old farmhouse and Margaret introduced me to her parents, who she then told me she had just met . . . weird. She made a bed for us in the living room, as most of the rest of the house was being renovated. I shall

---

16   see footnote 2.

just say that our night was odd. No, we didn't fuck. That's all I'm saying, out of respect or due to remaining confusions on my part. Margaret and her parents(?) dropped me off at the edge of Syracuse near a convenience store with a McDonald's grafted to the side on their way to the airport. I sat with Zunaka at a picnic table flying a sign requesting conveyance to Buffalo. I called my friend Sarah who had recently moved to Buffalo to tell her I was on the way, then waited . . . and waited.

    I wandered around to the front of the McDonalds, and immediately noticed a beautiful woman with a very short dress sitting by an open portfolio of her artworks. She was attending to a small black cat, and hoping to make a few sales of her fantastic sketches of naked faeries and goddesses and other buxom nudes done in colored pencil, paint, and various other mediums. She introduced herself as Fortuna. We immediately took to each other's company, and I rather immediately noticed she wore not a shred of cloth under her very short dress, and was not ashamed to grant a rather full view of what loveliness did lie between her thighs. I will not lie: I rather immediately entertained hopes of more than a casual acquaintance with this fellow wanderer.

    As the sun began to set, we made our way through a nearby field to a small clearing next to a channel of water and under a twisted tree with large low branches extending every which way. I laid out my tarp and blankets, and we proceeded to puff a bowl of some kindbuds Fortuna presented. Her little black cat climbed into the tree, and Fortuna and I talked at some level I cannot easily represent. One comment she made I will report, however: "It's nice to meet someone who is my equal," stated she after we had had a mild bout or dance with words and subtleties beyond the normal exchanges of mere mortals.

    The greatest oddity of this interaction with Fortuna was that when we several times began to raise desire's fire, kissing and otherwise exploring intimacies, else finding strong resonance in intense conversation, or some combination of these modes of raising heat to kindle flames in both mind and body, she would stop and place more layers of clothes over her sensuous form. As soon as the heat dissipated, she would again remove layers. I concluded that she had some particular "key" or "button" or other such something that would reverse her inverse response to desire and almost certainly set her off into an unbounded passionate frenzy, but only realized what I believe were "the magic words" as she loaded up into a ride the next morning (of course!!), leaving me to wait for Sarah to pick me up.

    As I bade Fortuna farewell, I made a complement of sorts to an otherwise unmentioned feature of her accouterments. Offering an *adieu* to her sweet pussy . . . cat, I immediately noticed a fire ignite in her eyes, just as the van's door was shut from the outside and she was conveyed away. As the light blue caravan conveyed her away and towards the highway Fortuna's gaze was fixed on me like a lion or a leopard about to pounce, or as a hungry tiger wantonly staring at people as easy prey from inside a cage at the zoo. Of course! I would untangle the riddle guarding her chastity *as she was leaving!* Oh well, who knows what would happen if a Roman goddess and a *sadhu* got it on. Almost certain troubles, I'm sure. Nonetheless, she would've undoubtedly been a great lover, and my concerns about inter-pantheonic sex would've certainly lost out had her desire been loosed to meet mine. Regardless, I do recognize this as an oddly auspicious meeting that ought not be the least depreciated just cuz' I didn't get any (much).

    On past and less trialsome adventures, I lived harmoniously with the understanding that my encounters with serendipity and synchronicity were almost wholly encounters with Devi and her entourage. Durga was the playful lover and teacher, and in whatever series of beautifully strange events or encounters with a new lover, it was but some facet of Maha Maya I understood stood behind the scenes of whatever *lila*, or was somehow manifest in whatever woman with whom I was engaged in love play. These are certainly aspects of *tantra*, a less physically expressed manifestation of the typical images of a curvy devi-yogini sitting on the lap of her lotus-seated lover, linga deep in yoni.

    Among other things, I suppose embarking upon this journey was making a statement to whatever powers that be, whatever aspects of Divine being might have sway, etc., that I was ready for a woman who'd remain with me as a steady partner in practice, a *tantrica* with whom I might share in mantra and asana and bhakti, a lover with whom this practitioner might find resonance in practice, and who'd likewise find me good teacher and student and lover and friend. Though I left Laramie with in mind a particular person as envisioned manifestation of said possibility, I would neither confine Leslie nor myself unduly to a particular storyline or writ role. Stories about Deities are meant to empower, and myth is meant to guide, not to confine either the deity represented nor those "mere mortals" who contemplate, revere, and sometimes imitate depictions of the Divine delivered through whatever temple or sacred text, tradition or mythology or iconography.

Among other challenges subtly posed on this journey was the introduction or interjection of other mythologies presuming to take space in my perceptual reality and conceptual constructions, as if to confuse (else to force some mode of synthesis with) my already well-formed practices. This is *yoga*, too: the integration of global history into the grand and beautiful love story it really is. Regardless of my distaste for certain mythologies, there are bits and pieces, or at least emanations or vestiges of this grand (if sometimes twisted) tale to be gleaned in myths and collective memories from every corner of the globe.

Sarah arrived in a small sedan. We cruised west to Buffalo. Sarah was an avowed skeptic—she even worked for an institution that overtly promoted said state of being in the title of its primary publication. Annie DiFranco owns an old church building in Buffalo, as I have been given to understand. Ani is a skeptic of another sort, or at the least has expressed a fierce rage against the status quo, patriarchal abuse, and ills in the relationships of men and women and gender power relations generally. Obviously Ani is an optimist too, 'cuz she tries to get people to listen, become aware and assumedly to change for the better.

Sarah lived in an apartment north of the downtown Buffalo. Ani's church is in downtown Buffalo. Sarah is fairly tall and quite hot. Ani D. is sorta short and of a certainty both lovely and sexy, despite her claims that she's "not a pretty girl." Sarah and I went to a coffee house downtown on the first morning of my stay with her. I was sorta hoping to happen to run into Ani D., as I am given to understand she frequents such establishments. I had questions to answer about a mystery that had unfolded mostly on the West coast over the course of several years that may or may not directly involve said female singer/songwriter. I didn't see Ani at the coffeehouse, though I did meet some construction workers who were coworkers with the son of a friend of mine from Laramie named Mike who's a dead ringer for Wild Bill Hickok (the friend, not the son that is), works at a tattoo shop and pierced my ears, though said son of said Wild Bill lookalike from Laramie was not with his coworkers at the coffee house.

    Sarah and I went to the falls one sunny day, my second time to view these grand tumbling cataracts. I stayed with Sarah for a few more days, then departed to the south then west once her boyfriend from NYC came for a visit.

    After a depressing meandering jaunt through the barren neighborhoods in the southern part of Buffalo, an experience that rather reminded me of my underworld dream in Montreal, I found my way to a highway that led into Ohio. I caught a ride with a couple who told me they were conveying the ashes of a man named Jeffrey to Columbus. The purportedly incinerated was brother to the male occupant of the soft-topped Jeep, and lover (husband?) to the woman (widow?) in the driver's seat. I immediately recalled having met a man who was driving out from a hot springs that sits east and over the ridge from Santa Barbara who had just spread his friend Jeffrey's ashes somewhere around the springs and the creek that flows by said steaming, scorching geothermal pools. We smoked a bowl (I instinctively knew he was carrying), then I drove the rest of the road and went for a soak.

    The couple in the Jeep driving from New York to Ohio handed me some herb to roll up into a joint as Zunaka and I sat in the back of their Jeep CJ (come to think of it, the guy near the hot springs was also driving an old Jeep or some similar vehicle). The couple dropped me off at the edge of Cleveland. I headed towards the heart of the city, recalling that I knew a couple from Laramie and thereabouts that I'd heard was now living somewhere in this metropolitan area.

    I walked into a bar that I soon realized was of the sort that mostly catered to gay men. I glanced at the phone book, which bore no trace of the names I was looking for, and then hastily made my way back onto the near empty streets, not quite comfortable with the fellows donning leather biker caps and sleeveless T-shirts seated at the bar checking me out a little too much. Now mind you, I don't take offence at a gay man finding me attractive, just not so hot about being looked at as a piece of meat for the skewering.

Zunaka and I began to hike south. As we stopped to rest under a road sign by an intersection a couple of girls just over or under twenty stopped to chat with me, and ended up giving me a lift to an all-night coffee house. The place was filled with the sort of patrons expected to inhabit a smoke-filled late-night caffeine-pushing hangout in an urban setting. The ratio of black to other hair colors was far too high considering the ethnicities represented, and eyeliner was employed liberally all the way around. Tattoos were amply displayed, and skinny black-clad teens with glasses played chess in the corner. I sipped some coffee, wrote a bit, then shortly hit the trail again and within a day arrived in one of the purportedly more enlightened centers in Ohio, Oberlin.

As I approached this liberal college town, riding late at night with a fellow who'd stopped for my extended thumb, some strange musing or channeled information told me a tale that involved Adolph Hitler and Eva Braun (obviously triggered by the place name, minus the "O") and reincarnation or a *bardo* journey, all whilst the driver went on about the town and region. Granted, sometimes such thoughts are self-generated, but other strands that have presented storylines or other information directly into my thoughts are so foreign to my own consciousness that I am quite certain they derive from some other sources, vis-á-vis a muse or dead people or something of the sort. Again (and rather eerily) these sound-bytes with an internal feed sometimes tell startlingly accurate truths.

My stay in Oberlin was short, but not particularly unpleasant, if surreal in a way I can't easily describe. I liked the park in the center of town. Someone in this central park asked to take my picture, and oddly my form came out quite blurry, though I had not moved and another in the picture appeared quite clear. This phenomenon repeated on a few other occasions hereafter as random strangers wanted to photograph me and Zunaka (I suppose some folks haven't seen a hippie with a dog before, er something . .

.). Perhaps I was experiencing some bizarre passage in space-time or inter-dimensional flux, the lack of clear outlines seeming evincing that I was truly in transit.

From Oberlin, Zunaka and I wandered north to the nearest of the Great Lakes, Eerie. We walked west along the shore, or alternately along the shoulders of roadways paralleling where beaches were posted "private." Upon arriving in the city of Sandusky, I was almost immediately met by an outgoing hippie chick in a short dress who burst out of a downtown bar to greet me and to lavish abundant affections upon Zunaka. She invited me into the bar where she and her boyfriend were drinking it up with the locals. Cara (Kara?) and Paulie were from Chicago, and were moving into a trailer house just a hundred yards or so from Erie's shore in a smaller town just to the west of Sandusky and next to the lake's shore. They immediately invited us to move into the vacant back room.

I stayed in Port Clinton for the next few months, occasionally attempting to hitchhike out from either there or Sandusky, but each time I tried to leave I ended up running around in circles or hitching rides that did no more than return me to Port Clinton from Sandusky. Biding my time between attempts to move on, I did enjoy being near a large body of water and mostly slept on the beach, though I sought other places to bed down during the intermittent periods of deluge or drizzle.

Rather randomly met a rather attractive woman at the bar in Sandusky who took me home with her, hoping I could cure her headache (ehem), which turned out unnecessary by the time we got to her place, though she let me sleep on the couch anyway. Met another pretty woman in Sandusky who offered me couch space, and informed me she had been stabbed seventeen times by her x-boyfriend and was fighting cancer. Interesting town.

On one occasion I took the ferry to South Bass Island, and spent a while wandering amongst golf cart-driving drunken vacationers. Bought a coffee and sat outside a bar where a band played oldies. Rather randomly a bachelorette fell at my feet, as her celebrations had led her to expire just there. I helped her friends help her back to her feet. I recall that some exchanges that went along with this incident were particularly ironic if not literarily clever, but as I lost my notes and journals a few times between there and here I cannot currently report anything more of this incident.

I met another woman at another bar on this odd little island where a pretty decent band led by a rather attractive female vocalist was playing. This woman was a few years older than I and quite sauced, clad in a mid-length skirt, white frilled blouse and a suede cowboy hat, and after the bar closed she told me she was lost and couldn't find her way to where she was supposed to stay with her friends. She ended up accompanying me to a patch of forest to spend the night. We didn't quite fuck, by the way. In fact the extent of our sexual encounter was quite similar to my night in bed with Margaret, minus one or two quirks. We smoked some herb, and maybe rolled around a bit before the sun rose. I think I stayed on South Bass another day or two, and one night drank myself to a slight puking drunk. I should note, my tolerance was far from those peaks maintained in my past, which I had developed to a very respectable level by much exercising of my liver and stomach's limits in the high altitude and thin air of the Rocky Mountains.

Oh yeah, I also met a fellow named Dan at that same bar that night who wore a striped black suit, and if I recall correctly wore a red button-up shirt and slicked back hair. He sat next to me at the bar and asked me if I knew "what this was," as if he were asking some sort of existential question. In my immediate and contextually informed perception, this figure, bearing the name Dan, seemed supposed to be interpreted as in some guise connected to the Dan I had stayed with in Montreal, and the Dan who was Leslie's former lover, and a Dan I knew in Laramie who, according to a mutual acquaintance, had once taken a meaningful journey to Montreal, and perhaps another Dan or two who have played roles in other plots further back in time and who may or may not tie directly (in an esoteric sense, that is) into this story. Names are often cues, or at least offer clues.

For some reason I felt my life was in danger on this island, and later followed a premonition to keep my distance from a stage where a guitarist who bore a striking resemblance to Jeff Bridges was playing rock & roll ballads for a crowd sipping beers and soaking in whatever sunshine might show through the layer of dull gray clouds. As I listened and watched from a distance, I had a picture flash in my mind that the singer pulled a pistol as I approached the stage, said something, then shot me. I realize the likelihood of such an absurd vision coming true would seem beyond calculation, but I've experienced many visions coming very true to the represented "internal screen," and many events as odd, if not so public. And I believe I have in fact been shot on various other occasions, though did not return to consciousness with the resultant wounds on any of said occasions, so who knows?

One particularly succinct and poignant instance of a prescient vision manifesting very overtly before my eyes occurred at the edge of the mountains in my home state as I was driving the Miraculous-Beast-Shanti-Mama on a dirt road on the south side of Elk Mountain. The Snowy Range was in front of me to the east. As a bright orange-yellow October moon rose above the peaks to the fore, framed to my vision by a cracked windshield, I thought of the "medicine" that sat on the shelf on the door of the icebox in the camper on the back of the pickup truck I drove. I thought this might be an auspicious time to take some of this medicine, which consisted of a few feet of San Pedro cactus skins sliced off with just a thin layer of flesh included to ensure the majority of the mescaline contained therein would make it into the brew, then boiled down to a concentrated fluorescent green tea.

I decided such a decision ought to be ceded to divine deliberation, and thus to some sign to say it was the proper time to take this essence into my body. I knew I had to work the next day, though I also knew my employer would hardly mind if I was a little under the weather for having partaken of said medicine. I was setting up a drip irrigation system for a medicinal herb company, and my employers were, of course, all about the botanicals. As I continued to cruise around the mountain I contemplated what sign to ask, and immediately concluded it must be an animal.

Not a deer nor an elk nor a pronghorn, too common. Not a coyote, not quite appropriate. Not a cougar—I think I saw one a week before sprinting away from my headlights late in the night. Two cougar sightings in as many weeks would be too much to ask.

A bird? Yes, but not one of those tiny little roadside fluttering night flyers, darting out across the beams of light preceding the potential threat of the fast moving and large projectile of an oncoming vehicle.

Then I saw it in my mind's eye, this sign of certainty, assurance from whatever transcendent something had sway over psychedelic journeys, and specifically mescaline—perhaps "Mescalito," as the appropriate presiding deity is called by some Native American tribes whose rites include the use of said psychedelic substance.

That's it! A great predatory bird, with wings three or more feet in breadth, whose flight brings him or her from the left side of the truck, accelerating and then veering to directly in front of the windshield, about 15-20 feet ahead, then after leaning one way, then the other, the large owl or hawk cuts off to the right and out of view, thought I as said apparition proceeded before my inner eye.

I forgot about my deliberations and this vision and rolled a smoke with a pinch of herb mixed in, enjoying my still relaxed body, freshly soaked in the Saratoga Hobo Pool, a healing hot springs that bubbles out of the ground at somewhere between 110° and 120° Fahrenheit. I was savoring a drag from my mixed-cigarette when suddenly from the left, precisely as in my vision, a large bird with white and brown feathers flashing in the beams of the headlights soared to pass the pickup truck, then slid upon the air to directly ahead, maintaining the lead for a moment or two more, leaned to the left, then turned off to the right to disappear again into the night.

I am fairly certain this was an owl, and likely a great horned one, though from my venue I couldn't tell for sure. Regardless, this manifestation was a perfect copy of what I envisioned several minutes before. No clearer sign than that could I have asked. After I returned to the ranch where I was working on an experimental osha root garden, I sipped a few swallows of the bitter green brew, built a fire and watched a mild show of colors and fractals and visions reformed, yet felt that the sign was indeed the greater teaching of this trip.

I occasionally sought shelter with my two friends from Chicago whilst I lingered on the shores of Lake Eerie, but found their frequent late-night parties not befitting my tastes in light of my mood at the time. And besides, the female of the two had a habit of dressing not unlike Fortuna, sans underwear, and in short skirts. Not that I don't like . . . just a little much to be constantly and sometimes rather provocatively exposed to such a view of something and someone so lovely I oughtn't touch, out of respect for her partner and so forth. Mostly I slept on the beach and tried from time to time to roll-on.

When finally I resolved to head to a rail hub east and a bit south of the circles I'd spun in for the past few months, I walked along the highway towards the east to find a train going west. As I trod the four-lane's shoulder, a white work-van pulled over ahead. As I approached, waddling with heavily loaded backpack whilst I ran to catch-up, I noticed Oregon plates and Green Party stickers, and felt a sense of relief at the sight of these signs of the familiar and endeared. I loaded packs and dog aboard, then climbed in.

The driver was an Oregon-style anarchist, earth-protecting, migrant farm-worker type. His comrade in the back of the van was a card carrying Athabascan Communist from Minnesota. They were on their way to Maine to pick blueberries. In spite of my resolve to get back to the west I decided to ride with this odd couple on to Rochester, where the driver's brother and his family lived, and then on to somewhere near Herkimer. I had considered a trip to seek out some of the high quality quartz crystals to be found around said town when I was in New York previously, and decided I might as well while I had a ride goin' thataway.

From where this interesting pair let me out I caught one short ride then hiked the remaining 15 or 20 miles to where I ended up camping, just outside the small town of Middleville at a nice site by the river. I quite savored this respite from cities and concrete, and managed to find a couple-dozen respectable Herkimer "diamonds," as these super-hard quartz crystals are called. Had I demanded market rate for these finds, I might've made a grand or two. Instead I mostly gifted and traded these shiny stones once I arrived in Ithaca and then at the regional Rainbow Gathering in the forest to the north and saving a few to send to friends, after the tradition of the tribes respecting the earth's gifts.

I won't be too specific about where I searched for the shiny clear crystals, but suffice it to say I found a spot where layers of rock and dirt were often disturbed to reveal quartz crystals up to three inches in length. I walked to the peaks of large piles of rock and rubble to scan one-hundred feet or more in a swath of ground between my vantage and the sun. Reflections from clean surfaces of these "diamonds" would sparkle brilliantly, showing me the location of stones from a centimeter to a couple inches in length. I quite enjoyed this treasure hunt, yet felt it was not the pleasure it would have been if I'd had companions likewise experiencing the joys of chasing sparkly treasures in the intermittent beams of sunlight.

I thought a good deal about Meghan Ann during this endeavor of seeking sacred stones. My traveling partner and lover for eight-moons or more, Meghan was quite enamored with shiny pretty supernaturally endowed healing gems from Mother Earth. I would've done good to come in a distant second to her love of colorful and sparkly rocks. She did natural stone beadwork, had some silversmithing skills, and could tell you the metaphysical potencies of whatever semiprecious or precious stone you might name.

I imagined the giddy joy Meghan would certainly have felt upon finding these most precious of clear quartz crystals to be found. I looked around me at the barren red dirt, dusty red cliffs, and pale blue sky, and recognized my displeasure with the brand of solitude I'd been offered. I do often seek to be alone in wild places, and yet I've never quite found more than a semblance of a full-blown hermit in myself. Now mind you, if I had the right tantrica with me, a beautiful yogini-devi appropriately matched to me who wanted to practice for long hours on a rug in some dark cave, I s'pose I might give up the city's thrall and cadres of comrades once and for all. In the meantime, I do favor the company of friends at least part-time, and especially when there's good fun to be had.

After I had gathered a sufficient quantity of Herkimer diamonds, I returned to my campsite. There was a car in the parking lot at the end of the short dirt road, a Subaru wagon embellished with peace signs and Rasta colors and the likes. A short while later, after I had started a small fire, a company approached crossing the river barefoot, and I could just make out careful twistings or carelessness knottings of follicular growth protruding from at least two of four heads, and a tie-died shirt or two. "Family."

The group was heading to a Rainbow Gathering in the small patch of National Forest north of Ithaca after a hunt for some of the Herkimer area's gems. I told them how to find the location where I'd had good luck, a spot to which I had been directed by a kindly local, though decided not to join their foray as I felt I'd gathered my share. After a successful search, this crew gave Zunaka and myself conveyance to Ithaca.

Before endeavoring to get to the Gathering, I decided to explore this beautiful and progressive bastion of freethinking and traveling hippie/anarchist-hub, set amongst gorges that drain to one of the watery gashes (or scratch-marks made by some ancient god or goddess) that are called the Finger Lakes. Cornell University sits on a plateau above one side of downtown Ithaca, and Ithaca College resides on a hill on another.

I had applied to grad school at Cornell years previous, and was summarily rejected. Instead I ended up at the University of Chicago, where I enrolled in an interdisciplinary Master's program. Never quite finished the thesis part of things, which was titled, "Non-Essentially Occidental: Heteroglossia in the European Discourses on Islam," and have nothing to show for my graduate studies save for an obscenely defaulted college loan debt. Think I might've fared better at Ithaca, as I am no city-boy, and there's hippies there, a very strong progressive community, and beautiful natural places quite nearby.

I met quite a number of interesting and significant persons in Ithaca and at the regional gathering. I cannot recall with certainty which of those I met in Ithaca and thereabouts were first encountered before, at, or after the gathering, so I'll begin with the gathering. Sarah, aka "Soulo," first arrived into my realm of experiences when I was sitting at my campsite, which was just off the path to main circle, only a couple dozen yards away under a tree. We chatted for a few and she ended up camping with me for the rest of the gathering.

We didn't quite end up lovers, which was fine. It was nice to share tarp and bedroll with a beautiful woman regardless of degrees of further intimacy. She was twenty-two or twenty-three, if I recall correctly, had short auburn hair and a well curved-form. We shared a camp and bed for a while in Ithaca as well, and had plans to travel west together but got separated just before our planned departure.

"Soulo" was rather composed considering some of the trauma she had encountered in the previous year, including viewing the murder of her x-boyfriend Charles, who she told me was dealt a blast from a shotgun in the chest in Chesterfield. She'd sit with me and spange up means for a meal or coffee with a calm and repose that reminded me of a Buddhist nun I met during a march for besieged elders on the Diné (Navajo) Reservation. Said nun could split apples into several well-proportioned wedges with her bare hands, then distributed these sections of red delicious to her impressed audience.

Speaking of the Diné, I encountered a very unusual Diné woman in Ithaca with whom I shared some rather unusual exchanges. She had black hair highlighted with some tint or other, red or purple I think, and she told me she was a practitioner of "skunk-magic." Her name was Sylvia and her nickname was "Skunk." She was smokin' hot, and as sincere an educated anarchist-activist as I've met. She told me she was in a heavy metal band, which was inactive, with her brother and some others.

One night whilst sleeping up one of the gorges that proceed outward from the center of town, I awoke to a small black and white animal to one side of the foot of my bedroll casually strolling towards Zunaka. Zunaka backed up to the length of his leash, but the three to five pound beast kept coming. In a behavior I have never before heard-tell nor seen in all my time in the hills regardin' said species of critter ('cept'n f'r one had the hydrophobia), that polecat leapt on that seventy-pound dog like it wanted to brawl. Well now, that hound didn't want nothin' to do with fightin' one of these feisty fellas, maybe havin' met the wrong end of one once or twice in his days. Soon as 'n I figured out what was a' happnin' I hopped up likewise, and started lookin' f'r stuff ta' fling at this likely rabid critter. After nearly bustin' that skunk with a thrown stick, it high-tailed it for the creek. Stayed up all night frettin', then strolled on down to the Health Department next day, and they almost put 'ol Zunaka (formerly known as Zeus) down.

Well, I don't remember if'n it was the day before or the day after, but I happened to run into that Diné princess-rocker one-or-the-other of them days. Three other nights, if I recall correctly, I had brushes with skunks either directly proceeding or the day after I met Sylvia/Skunk at the coffee shop or, on one occasion, as I happened to encounter her struggling with her van's passenger door. I ended up holding her door closed while she drove her van home on that particular day, then that night had a striped (not stripped) caller well after bedtime. On one night my black-and-white visitor flirtatiously woke me by brushing her (assuming . . .) tail against me face. I rolled over to watch her saunter away, swishing her tail, and I swear said skunk had sway to her hips. Gotta say, I would've much rather "Sylvia" had come for a midnight visit than "Skunk."

KC (or Casie?) was a spike-haired punk-ass girl I would often encounter at one of the coffee houses in town. She was a sassy and precocious, if sometimes coming-on-too-strong kinda chick, though in a rather endearing sort of way. Just mentioning her because she seemed to often pop-up at various and sundry places I happened to habit in Ithaca.

And then there are the "Twelve Tribes" folks, a cult of sorts that draws in a lot of hippies, and which is supposedly run by some former carnie who decided women should wear dresses and be subservient—and somehow free-spirited hippie-types get drawn in? Weird world. They own a large mansion in near downtown Ithaca where they live communally. By some accounts I heard that breaking company with this group is a rather hazardous affair . . . though at least I haven't heard of forced marriages to kin amongst this odd manifestation of religion Americana, and hearsay's just that. Did attend a free dinner there, where stories about the backwardly subjugated place of women were indeed evidenced to my eye. Not my kinda scene. I left before dessert.

Anica or Anika or Anaka (?) of Ithaca was another notable woman I often encountered whilst wandering between downtown, Cornell's hilltop environs and various coffeehouses and cafes, the lake at Stewart Park and the creeks in the gorges. We rarely stopped to chat for long when we met, usually walking in different directions, yet she seemed familiar. She rather reminded me of Chloe, for one, except she had nearly black hair instead of blond. She was tall, delightfully curvy, and was a student at one or another of the universities there at one time or another, and that's all I can really speak of her. Our not infrequent encounters seemed notable, nonetheless.

There was a fellow with a white kitten who also seemed a figure of note (mainly for the obvious contrasts: a blue-eyed blond hippie with a white cat to a brown-haired and eyed hippie with a white dog) who'd often show up for the feeding at "Loaves and Fishes." This is the local feed-spot ("soup kitchen") where carnivores, vegetarians and omnivores and even vegans can get a free meal several days a week. A broad variety of folks usually show up, from dirty hippies to well groomed hippies, gutter-punks and hobos, unemployed or unsuccessful hipsters, anarchists and activists, the lonely looking for fellowship and various other generally less-than-wealthy figures from the community. During good weather, the lawn is littered with hippies and other random freaks and dogs and cats sharing a picnic and rolling smokes and so forth.

A number from amongst those I met on the lawn at Loaves-and-Fishes would hang out at a site just up one of the gorges where a small circle of seats was arranged in a small clearing. I'd occasionally approach whatever gang was hangin' here, sharing some smoke but generally not lingering long amongst this conglomeration of gutterpunks and younger hippies, where 40's and bottles of liquor were more common than bongs and bowls smoked. The only figure who immediately comes to mind of those often encountered amongst these circles was a young woman called "Honey." She was a wild-girl in her late-teens who would wander with these wilder Ithaca residents, and I think she said she was from California. She camped up one of the gorges with her boyfriend, and she reminded me of a line of others I've known elsewhere.

Oh yeah, and one night I ended up having a pretty cool conversation with a rather voluptuous woman named Jade who took me to her house, along with some seemingly gay fellow, to swim in a private pool. I don't recall if I swam at all, but I did get a shower, had a beer or two, and ended up in bed with Jade.

From Ithaca, I traveled again east, with intentions of turning south. As I noted, plans to journey with Soulo didn't come to fruition, so I hitched and hiked with Zunaka to New Paltz, where I remained until mid-December. I camped again amidst the forests at the edge of town, except for on the coldest nights when I would find some shelter or other, and on the one night I spent with Emily. *Lila, lila, kama.*

Emily was perhaps the most beautiful woman I came to know on the streets of New Paltz, and was quite intelligent. She engaged me in deep conversation one night as rain was beginning to turn into ice. I was eating a slice of pizza at the pizza place on the corner of Main and Chestnut. We conversed rather intensely and intentioned, and she told me about a book she was reading that was about "Snakes" and "Spiders" fighting an inter-dimensional war, an absurdly if interestingly symbolic something she later gave me to read entitled *The Big Time*. Emily let me stay at her apartment that night, which was in the basement of a house that was above a lake as I recall, or at least above an open field or river. The rain became a sheet of translucent ice then snow. I showered and ended up in bed with Emily.

A few days later, Emily told me she decided she wanted to see someone else, even apologetically. She said she liked this guy who sort of ran the co-op. I had, of course, made no presumptions that our night together meant she wanted to permanently shack-up with a hippie-cum-hobo passin' through town, though I'd likely not have been at all disagreeable if she had decided she wanted to see more of me. Yet what more might a sometimes smelly hippie-cum-hobo hope for, save even one night in the bed of the most beautiful young woman in town (after a shower, of course)? Such is the life of a rambler, I suppose. Emily gave me her phone number and family's address (which I've since lost), which was in some New England town I can't recall, and on a street called *Leslie Lane*.

From New Paltz (or perhaps just before, as I can't recall the precise sequence of these visits), I decided to stop by the Omega Institute, as I was indeed inadvertently in the neighborhood. I had not received any responses to recent emails sent to Leslie, and so felt obliged to check-up on her. Perhaps a bit of presumption on my part. She wasn't particularly happy to see me, explaining that she was attempting to sever many ties (detachment . . .?) and wasn't really communicating with anyone except for close family and one or two others. We've communicated only little since, unless by some means other than material. I admit I've "Googled" her name since she last sent an email, and even searched for her current whereabouts on a people-finder site or two, though with no intention of further seeking her out beyond such minimal and non-invasive means, unless she beckons me. I hope she is happy and healthy.

I hopped a train in Kingston, NY, to get south and to where it wasn't so cold. I awoke from a dream on the back of a container carrier to a dreamlike rhythmic melody vibing through the night. I awoke to what sounded like a rave, or whatever they call them these days, going on in a warehouse district just off the track. The music carried in the otherwise quiet of night sounded exactly like a DJ my Montreal hosts would often spin on the house stereo. I was too tired and too ready to get south to follow this queue or call, however. Didn't really feel like getting stalled in the industrial labyrinth I could make out while standing tall on the train-car and gazing into the orange-yellow glow of floodlights and gray shadows, assorted neutral colored warehouses and soot-stained factories' smokestacks not quite inviting me to adventure despite the call of familiar trance tunes.[17]

The freight train stopped again and I disembarked at the north edge of Philadelphia. Rode a commuter train to the other side of town, and kept going till Media. I immediately found a coffeehouse, and there met a beautiful young woman who had nearly black hair that reminded me of Leslie's at the time I first encountered her, wearing the sort of straight-cut bangs Uma Thurman wore in Pulp Fiction (Leslie used to play the soundtrack a

---

17   I am referring to said spun, electronic dance music as "trance," though I am not at all clear on the differentiations of the various genres of what these DJs spin. "House," "trance," "jungle," etc., though perhaps not all the same to my ears, are not designations I've learned to assign according to genre or sub-genre at this particular point in my career.

lot when she was a barista at Coal Creek). The woman in Media had a long Arabian sword at her side, and whilst contemplating the length and edge of blade I imagined the seemingly sharp scimitar applied to my flesh, for whatever odd reason. She gave a belly dance performance at the coffee shop, and she asked me if I knew or was "Hamsa." I told her that I am not any such person, and that I didn't personally know anyone by that name. Leslie, by the way, had a similarly shaped implement of dance—a scimitar, though I think the woman in Media had a sharper blade. I've already mentioned the thing with "hamsas." The woman in Media was with a fellow, if that's important to tell.

    I called Lisa and Marc's home, and Marc agreed to pick me up in Media. Oh, yeah . . . also might mention that one night on the path to Media from Philly, if I recall correctly the location, I had a strange dream as I slept next to a creek and not far from a populated crossroad. The sky was threatening to rain, an intermittent light drizzle inclining me to draw the tarp over my bedroll as Zunaka curled at my feet.

    Whilst I slept I dreamt a dream in which I was hangin' out in some hall and adjoining kitchen with Prince Charles (the British royal, ya' know) and seemingly others—perhaps one or another or both of his sons. I went out into the large dining hall, then attempted to re-enter the kitchen with Zunaka through a different door. As I opened the heavy hardwood door, a large white wolf-hybrid in the kitchen started to snarl viciously, held back by one of the heir-apparent's sons. I think there was another dog or two there, both smaller and less intimidating. Of course Zunaka started to snarl and strain at my restraint, ready to leap upon the other seemingly unneutered male wolf-dog. Zunaka was a very intelligent being, but not one to keep his cool when it comes to fighting—if the other dog had balls, that is. Anyhow, at that moment someone grabbed my arm from behind and stuck a syringe-needle into my flesh.

    As I immediately started to wake from this dream, *perhaps* into another "dream," I recall someone grabbing my arm through the tarp which covered me, and had the distinct impression said person assaulting me whilst half-sleeping and covered by a tarp stuck a needle into the arm I raised to fend off the assault—just as someone had injected me with something or other through a hypodermic needle in the previous dream, upon which I fell into a dreamless sleep. Indeed, it seems if one chooses to live to fullest potential and to challenge the status quo, you shall not fail to attract the attention of others who maintain pretensions of right and might, even in the dreams of night.

    I've since tried to locate photos on the internet of kitchens and dining halls at the Prince of Wales' various residences to see if any match the location in my dream, but have yet to locate any. I have had dreams that occurred in locations I'd not yet been, then later found said locations corresponding quite astonishingly to what I'd seen in the earlier dream, thus I shant be surprised if I find a photo of the kitchens at Birkhall or Highgrove to match the scene of the near dogfight in my dream.

    I might add here that I had much considered (whether of my own accord or by suggestion) the myths of Camelot at times in my musings upon the first train or two going east, and then the more as related signs began to appear. Beth and Dan lived in a second floor apartment on *Rue Prince-Arthur Ouest*. I stayed with *Arthur* and Jordan for a short while before moving into the studio with Leslie. The river surrounding Montréal is named for a man who was purportedly a keeper of the so-called Holy Grail, a central story in the myths of Camelot. Other assorted signs and suggestions related to said mythic tales appeared in other places and instances in addition to these through the course of this journey, though I shall leave the topic at what's writ above.

    Questions of royalty tend to surface in one's spiritual quest when, accomplished in practice, intentions are drawn towards bettering this world, towards taking authority over those ills one wishes to see healed, and to confront those ailments needing destruction. Yogis often bare titles pertaining to kingship, such as "Maharaja," which means "Great King." Whatever these passages pertaining to monarchs might mean in relation to some broader plot revealed (or obfuscated) within this self-told narrative, I cannot fully represent. Am I somehow a perceived threat to the House of Windsor? Just in my mind's meeting with some muse or other?

    Mind is complex, and the differences between dreams and waking and life and death are sometimes more arbitrarily defined than most would want to maintain, as even the division of "self" and "other" can be. These lines can become blurred, especially as one seeks to press the paradigms and common sense realities we're trained to believe.

As amply noted, I have seen veritable and verifiable examples of the existence of much cannot be as well fitted into a modern western-scientific paradigm as fits well a mystical, fantastic, and mythical worldview. Indeed, I believe one ought to live life heroically, beautifully and true, and ought strive to better the experience of life for all, to heal unjust injuries and vanquish evils, and to strive for justice, regardless of whose toes get stepped on. Even if living life as a householder, family man or woman, I believe each of us has the responsibility to respond to the gift of life with intrepidness, strength and a passion for justice and truth.

Most presumptions of "Western science" do not allow for these sort of factors to fit an equation. Life longs for such aspirations, for the least childhood dreamer to aspire and to become a great hero or heroine. Science, or at least the immature variety (spiritually) that has gained prominence in the past few centuries, does not allow "love" or "heroism" to be considered in an equation related to Unified Theory (save perhaps in the theorizing of individuals on the razor's edges of this science). Yet it may prove that these sorts of words come quite close to describing what holds it all together.

Just to clarify, I am not so deluded to claim that I had some "real" encounter with these British royals, though I did also see a nigh exact doppel to Prince Charles in a three-piece blue suit walking the opposite direction to me on the sidewalk in Ithaca whilst quite awake, as well as having the odd experience of this (these) dream(s). This figure gave me a rather cursory if rather loaded once over as we passed each other on the sidewalk as I likewise considered said odd apparition with a curious glance. It may be I shoulda let Zunaka battle that rather scruffy-looking canine in the royal's kitchen, in that dream. I rather think he woulda kicked that mangy mutts royally pretentious arse!

Stayed with Lisa and Marc for month or so, rested and once again gratefully gained back a few pounds, watched TV and smoked herb and sat on the back porch rolling and smoking cigarettes and attempting to provoke Zunaka to play with Kaya, Lisa's coy-dog she found stray on a rez when caravanning with me near Chaco Canyon. I didn't make it much further south than DC on the next leg of this journey. Ended up staying in Fredericksburg, Virginia, for several months.

Met some kind local hippie kids all around twenty to twenty-five or so in Fredericksburg whose names I shall not mention due to the presence of certain substances in some of their lives. A number of them liked to poke holes in their veins (speaking of needles), something the cops take much more seriously than weed—and also, by the way, not my kind of poison.

Cannabis is one thing, an herb humans have had an intimate relationship with since time immemorial. Opium, though not a good thing to do habitually, is still right from the plant and not, in-and-of-itself and only smoked once in a while, an unmanageable or generally life or health threatening spirit/substance.

Once you start poking holes in your body to get a headchange, else take a substance too far away from its natural context and content by chemical processes, you've stepped over a line across which there isn't generally anything good to be found. Sorta sums up my sentiments regarding much of what comes with the title "pharmaceutical," too. Closer to nature is nigh always closer to health and happiness.

LSD might be the one exception I'd make to the "pharmie"/overly refined guideline, and possibly DMT, as well (i.e., when used with exceeding respect and ritual appropriate to this more potent plant-derived psychedelic which I don't quite even consider pharmaceutical). Heroin (not the feminine version of the term "hero" with an "in" and an "e" at the end), however, is something I've never seen better a life. Not so noxious in my book as meth or the likes, but still a thing that drags down the lives of too many people I could otherwise trust unequivocally with, say, a $50 or a CD collection when there's a nearby place to pawn them for a few bucks a piece, and who might otherwise live happy and healthy and productive lives. Never met anyone who'd be more likely to do you wrong after they smoked a joint than if stone cold sober.

I ought to report, however, that I had no experiences of the loss of property or trust whilst sometimes staying at the Fredericksburg hippie hovel (where heroin was sometimes used by some of the occupants). Yet I must wonder how much cooler and more fun these kind friends might have been if junk had no place in any of their lives. Somewhat inversely, I might add, I have often considered how much more fun I might have had with so many people from my past, had the mellowing medicine of marijuana been a part of these people's lives.

Mountain climbers and cyclists and professional basketball players smoke marijuana. The "founding fathers" of the United states seem likely to have smoked the "India hemp" the likes of George Washington grew.[18] A large portion of functional professionals have smoked or still do smoke herb. I've puffed with lawyers, professors, accountants and even a law enforcement officer or two in all of the smoke-circles I've been party to over the years. Heroin pretty much just brings people down, with the exception of a few notable authors and artists of the last century, perhaps.

There is a coffee house in Fredericksburg called Hyperion. Here is, yet again, a place named after Roman deity, who was in fact derivative of an Egyptian. Hyperion, analogous to Seth in Egyptian lore and almost certainly traceable to the Hindu Surya, guides the sun across the sky in Roman mythology. During spells sitting at this coffeehouse I seemed to attract the attention of more than a few attractive and young women, especially considering my rather shoddy appearance, having mostly spent my nights in a bedroll on whatever suitable patch of ground and rotating through but a few changes of clothing. I was hardly trying to get laid, though likely could have found my way into a few young women's beds whilst hanging out in this Virginia college town. Young being a key word.

I have lived three-and-a-half decades this time around, and have decided from experience and otherwise that somewhere around twenty-three is about minimum age for a lover considering

---

18   In a letter I have seen represented, Washington imported "hemp" seeds from India, which unlike the North American version contains plenty of THC, as well as wonderful qualities when used to make textiles.

my years of life lived, though I could imagine myself going so far as to accidentally fall into bed with a twenty-one year old that drags me home from a bar after I'd had a few to drink. Below that, she'd have to be pretty damn close to an avatar, else a genuine incarnation of a goddess to get me to drop my pants—and even then, still there are obvious bounds to what's appropriate or acceptable. Still, rather puzzled me that I was such a magnet in spite of feeling quite unattractive during those rather rough days on the road.

Whilst wandering 'round the country on this occasion, I was more stressed and scrawny than I'd ever been, underweight by upwards of twenty to thirty pounds at certain points. I was living off spanging, and was fighting psychic battles more intense than any I had faced before. Though I had a tad of gray in my hair and beard previous to this journey, the count of white hairs on my head had increased significantly since my departure from Wyoming. And to be quite honest, with only minimal access to a place to bathe (the hippie-house was a good ways outside of town), I often stunk. Nonetheless, for whatever reason I seemed to attract even more positive attention from random college women than I am generally accustomed to (with the exception of not getting laid so much as usual). Goes to show the nigh impossibly complicated task of understanding women.

Suppose I was a pleasant and amusing distraction in some cases—an unusual sight in those parts, and perhaps in other cases an object of some sort of psychologically complex patterns of desire, though I must note I've often experienced times as a younger man, well dressed and healthier, when I seemed less prone to draw the company of beautiful young women. Perhaps there is simply some sort of mystique to the wild and weathered traveling sort in the imaginations of young women just beginning their explorations of the world. I suppose not even the most in depth of scientific or psychological inquiry shall ever unlock the subtler mysteries of attraction and desire.

To be honest, had I been a bit less burdened with subtle and esoteric riddles, dharmic burdens and karmic responsibilities, and less hobbled (traveler-speak for poor and without wheels), I might have pursued one or another of these romantic possibilities proffered by whatever deity or saint, benevolent spirit or phenomenal excretion, as a few of the attractive women I met were college seniors. Did spend one night on the couch at the apartment of a couple of college girls, Joanna and another whose name eludes, after a night at the bar. Nothing happened, however, other than a warm night's sleep on a cushiony couch.

Though I took advantage of offered floor and couch-space from time-to-time whilst in Fredericksburg, I also often slept upon the banks of the river, sight of significant bloodbaths in both the Revolutionary and Civil Wars. I awoke from a dream one night whilst seeking shelter underneath a concrete embankment a bit above the Rappahannock's flow that left me a bit stunned. This dream in fact transpired at the precise location where I slept, making said nocturne the more disturbing and leaving me to wonder whether what I had just dreamt was still going on in a dimension only slightly out of phase with my waking reality.

In this dream, grayish phantoms in tattered antique military uniforms attacked me in the darkness. One after another they charged, faces scarcely discernible between collars of threadbare and torn uniforms and bills of dusty caps. My defense against these assailants was grasping them around the throat and rather effortlessly popping their heads off. As one figure approached, apparently noticing my dismay at the violence, he looked at me and stated rather matter-of-fact, "What do you expect? It's a battlefield." I believe I then popped his head off as he proceeded to attack, then awoke.

As I lay in the darkness I pondered that perhaps my response to the assaults in this dream may have been related to something my younger sister had once told me regarding a tactic our father's father had employed as a recon and intelligence soldier behind the lines in the Pacific during WWII: piano wire. Also came to mind, a former girlfriend telling a tale of having been abusively choked by her father when she was a teen. Odd how suggestion and odd and random memories might affect the unconscious mind and the formation of the future, how waking words might manifest in dream and how dreams sometimes bear fruit in life later lived.

Finally departing Fredericksburg, I caught a ride with some of the Rappahannock River-rat hippie-crew to Virginia Beach. We were supposed to catch a Reggae show, which we were unable to locate. I was happy to see the ocean, to sleep on the beach and breath the salt-spray saturated air (pollution from nearby centers of industry and military, notwithstanding). Despite my relief and gratitude to see the open ocean, I ought to be honest and note that Virginia Beach is far from my ideal of an oceanfront paradise. Hotels line the beachfront, and storefronts selling plastic beach baubles and sunglasses and oversized towels, arcades, restaurants and bars dominate the next street up.

Cheap commercialization and commodification of life dominate what was certainly once a beautiful stretch of oceanfront. In addition to this, the military has a significant presence in the area, and fighter-planes constantly fly over the otherwise pleasant sandy beach. The one most redeeming quality of the city, as far as places of business go, was the one coffee house I could find: Bad Ass Coffee. And I must also admit, I did appreciate that a couple of the hotel restaurants along the beach had fairly reasonably priced breakfasts.

A statue of Poseidon stood at the center of the beachfront, and as I had been continually barraged with images and names of Greek and Roman deities over the course of my journey, I took this as something of an ill omen. The trident which this figure carries is, after all, derivative (a bastardization) of the much more ancient and authentic *trishul*, sign of the presence of Siva. This symbol's misrepresented use in Western mythology, from Poseidon's trident to the pitchfork held by the devil, indicate yet again the rather myopic perspective Western culture has so often taken on the earlier themes and symbols, still faithfully represented in the traditions of India known as *sanAtana dharma*, that are in fact our collective global heritage. Indeed, these metaphors matter in the construction of those subtle collective consciousnesses that help direct the balance of human life—and every society has it's sacred or sacrosanct and vilified icons, most often designed to direct thoughts and inspire culturally appropriate behavior if sometimes proffering accurate information historically and spiritually. Often enough these symbols hold secrets—if oft to be read between the lines—that afford clues to the real stories of world history, true accounts and histories not generally sanctioned by the academy that make conspiracy theories such as is depicted in *The Da Vinci Code*'s plot seem but anecdotal, and secret societies such as the Illuminati and Free-Masonry, mere social clubs.

Though I'll not go too deep into my theories regarding the subtleties of the story I perceive as underlying the transmission and twists of culture and symbols and the stories that began with migrations (expulsions?) and emanations out of India towards the west, suffice it to say Abraham and Sarah and Hagar, who according to the Torah came from a place on the perimeters of Indus Valley Civilization, were preceded by and likely representative of the Indian figures Brahma and Saraswati and Ghaggar,[19] Christ by Krishna, and Islam by Siva and His consorts, all maintaining respective analogies to degrees that cannot be denied, except by dishonest scholars bent on making "the West" look better or more rooted in antiquity in comparison to their truer forbearers. Likewise, ancient Greece derived much of the framework for their culture, if second- or third-hand, from India, and as noted elsewhere Native American Indians are actually descendants of colonists from the Indian subcontinent.

Similarly, the term "devil" seems likely to have been derived from a Persian language alteration else desecration of the Sanskrit word for God or Goddess—*Deva* and *Devi*. Quite interesting and amusing to note, the English word "God" is derived

---

19   Interesting to note, Brahma is not much worshiped in India as, according to one popular myth, he is understood as guilty of incest, or at least incestuous desire. He created a beautiful maiden named Shatarupa, then proceeded to lust after her. When Shatarupa sought to evade his gaze, Brahma grew a fifth head so he might continue to view her. Siva responded to Brahma's transgression by cutting off Brahma's fifth head, as directly creating another implies a parental relationship. Basically Brahma, the Creator, got bored in the process of creatin' stuff, and decided to make a hottie. Siva comes along and says, "Yo, Brahma! Here's the skinny: you directly created this sexy mama, therefore she's your daughter, therefore you can't fuck her." Then with pinky fingernail Siva severs Brahma's fifth head. Thus, another curious and should-be obvious connection between these two strands of belief (i.e., Judaism and "Hinduism") is that the primary rite of Judaism, male circumcision, credited to Abraham, is very much analogous to Brahma's head being severed. If read thus the Hebrew rite of circumcision is in essence an incest taboo rite.

from the Sanskrit word *go*, which translates directly as the English word "cow."

By the way, the Aryan invasion theory—i.e., that much of the sophisticated culture of India derived from pale-skinned-blue-eyed invaders—is being proven quite errant by modern scholarship and archaeology. These revelations generated by academically sanctioned methods are being accepted only reluctantly by many "Western" scholars, some in fact fighting tooth and nail to save their faltering myths. European scholars of the nineteenth and into the twentieth century who studied the more ancient and sophisticated cultures and arguably greater wisdoms of "the East" were often quite intent upon proving "Western" superiority and propping up various racist theories. Some noted "Orientalist" scholars have been shown (by scholarly scrutiny) to have even intentionally lied regarding the antiquity and sophistication of early civilizations in India and other regions of eastern Asia in order to bolster their case, claiming later dates for the Vedas and Indian epics than these works internally proclaim of their own dates of origin. Thus my contempt for the fascination and reverence Europe and America have held for the relatively young and derivative cultures of Greece and Rome, or at least for the European and American fixations on these relatively recent cultures to the detriment of attending to roots to those more ancient and sophisticated cultures of Asia. More than a little revision is indeed due.

Upon deciding to depart from Virginia Beach, I considered a hike down the beach to the Outer Banks of North Carolina, but was dissuaded by the fact that a significant installation of military-controlled property was in the way. Instead I headed inland to a fairly hip neighborhood in Norfolk, where I found a very cool coffeehouse called Fair Grounds, a two-story hippie hangout where I felt much more at home than anywhere else in the Hampton Roads metropolitan area. From the Seven Cities I hiked the majority of the way to Petersburg, then hitched a ride to the southern border, where I hopped a train that only carried me a bit further south, disembarking in Greensborough, North Carolina.

The main problem I discovered with hopping trains out East is that due to the proliferation of lines—a complex web of tracks and yards that densely covers the better portion of the eastern states—a train you hop in one town may only take you fifty miles before it is broken down and switched around. Out West where the cities are spread thin, a train is likely to take you hundreds of miles before you need disembark.

Greensborough is a university town, and I found a nice population of hippies and punks and others I could relate to a bit better than those young people I generally encountered in Virginia Beach, who were mostly the sort that sport sweatshirts with school or popular-brand logos and blue-jeans. Not to stereotype, mind you, but what one chooses to wear is generally meant to convey something about the personality and social intensions of the wearer (though of course inversely, to immediately judge an individual based upon such indicators is clearly and likewise an error, as books are only sometimes to be judged by covers).

I spent a good portion of my time in Greensborough hanging out outside Tate Street Coffee House by a large planter where the hippies and punks and other freaks young and old would often congregate to smoke and sip their cups of black brew, and 12 Steppers would likewise get their nic and caffeine fix. Also often sat to write and sip my dark drink of choice at the Green Bean downtown and at another little bakery/coffee house closer to the tracks. I often laid out my bedroll in a little stretch of forested land on one edge of UNC property in the undergrowth next to a lazy little rivulet that flowed through that part of the campus.

I made a few friends, or at least became relatively well acquainted with a number of the regulars on Tate Street. The further I wandered south, however, the more alienated I began to feel. Perhaps a significant factor was that I was sleeping outside when most of the people I encountered were insulated from nature by right angles, brick and shingles. Perhaps it was the harassment I regularly received from the police. Perhaps it was that begging was my only means of income, where whatever peers I might meet were working or supported by trust funds or college moneys from moms and dads or the government. Maybe it was the preponderance of psychic battles I found myself forced to fight, as well as the dark and foreboding dreams channeled to my mind by whatever malevolent entities or fearful realities of this world.

Perhaps it was that I had been endeavoring, to no avail, to find some way back to the Rocky Mountains and my regular stomping grounds out West ever since shortly after I had decided not to work at the Omega Institute and had parted company with Leslie.

Nothing overtly extraordinary occurred during my sojourn in Greensborough, though one instance comes to mind that might have some poetic meaning in relation to the broader aesthetic of my journeys. One day on Tate Street I encountered a fellow trying to avoid the cops who was ranting on about a woman named "Coreena." As I sat and smoked a cig with said lamenting fellow on the lamb, he continued to rant rather randomly and abstractly, ending his convoluted soliloquy with his oft repeated refrain, "You know, *Coreena*! Everybody's got their *Coreena*."

After a couple of months or so in Greensborough, I hopped a train that seemed to be heading west, but then ducked south and ended up in Atlanta. Big cities are not my thing, except for brief visits and when I have cash to spend. Nonetheless, I decided to venture into the urban jungle to see what I might find, as I'd never been to the Big Peach before.

In Atlanta I discovered a fairly hip coffee house not too far from the railyard called Octane Coffee Bar & Lounge, which I found served as quite a decent spot to sit and write and smoke and sip. I made my way deep into the city only twice. Once to an area called "Little Five," a pretty cool hippie/Rasta district where I was able to acquire a small bag of herb—the first I'd had in some time, and a second time to try to find some footwear to replace the pair that were rapidly disintegrating from my road-weary feet.

One phenomenon which has rather vexed me for quite a number of years but was particularly taxing to my already stressed psyche by this point in my travels and travails is randomly overhearing what seem clear references to myself, and even noticing my name spoken in sentences that seem clearly to indicate personal knowledge about my person. This may seem a bit egocentric (if not further fitted to other, more narrowly definitive psychiatric designations). Nonetheless, after much self-critical analysis of my perceptions pertaining to these particular instances of audible synchronicity, I could not deny such occurrences if I wanted to, and indeed I would often prefer to believe such things are figments of my imagination for the startling implications they might imply.

As I sat on the patio at Octane Coffee, three complete strangers were conversing whilst I was writing and thinking out loud, but without my audible voice being engaged. I overheard a comment which, as I recall, seemed to indicate some direct reference to my immediate thoughts, and which was followed by the response, "Oh, that's just Jeffrey," spoken by one of the three as she looked my way. The speaker was a rather short and sexy young African American woman with patterns shaved and died upon closely shorn hair who worked the counter at this coffeehouse. She reminded me rather startlingly of a once upon a time friend and lover, Jessica/Star, and I sat and pondered the meaning of this "coincidence" for some time thereafter.

As sort of an aside, one of the last times I spent time with Star we were at Trinity Coffeehouse in Laramie. As I stood at the counter, a beautiful barista from Montana named Tara handed me my cup, and she commented on how beautiful Star appeared, six or seven months pregnant and sitting at a nearby table (not with mine, mind you). It suddenly occurred to me how the two looked very much alike—both wearing mid-length dark auburn hair and summer dresses and both quite gorgeous—except that Star stood at somewhere around five-feet tall and was pregnant, and Tara only a few inches shy of six-fit tall and quite slender. I have since discovered that the name Tara, Hindu Goddess and consort to Siva, translates simply as "Star." Tara wore a gold bracelet around her wrist that bore the Devanagari letters spelling "AUM Namah Shivia."

After a week or two or so in Atlanta, I attempted to hop a train out. Already once caught by a "yard-bull" (hobo-speak for railroad security guards) and cuffed and escorted out of the yard, I was especially cautious as I attempted to board a hopper, first with intentions of Florida, though that train only took me to another yard south of town, where a worker then directed me back to a boxcar that returned me to Atlanta. Second time I got as far as Nashville, where I boarded another train I was told was heading north to Indiana, where I figured I could catch the main line towards the west, but awoke to find I had instead been railroaded back southeast to Atlanta. Third attempt got me only as far as Chattanooga, where I was held seeming captive for over one year by fears channeled from some as yet unascertained source, weariness of the road and rail and general malaise, and because of the fact that the small city was fairly welcoming despite a few unpleasantries.

     A number of months before arriving in Chattanooga I had a rather dread-filled dream wherein Zunaka and I rode a train that ascended an exceedingly steep incline. Shortly after unexpectedly arriving in Chattanooga I discovered there is an incline railroad that leads from the valley to the top of Lookout Mountain. I didn't try out this steep train ride whilst I was in Tennessee, in spite of the curiosity to discover how the dream and the corresponding reality might coincide and the temptation to determine what wonder or terror might await at the top-end-of-the-line.

     I should note that I have never felt so much "not myself" as during much of this journey and since, and the more so the further I progressed. Indeed it felt as if some other consciousness or consciousnesses were constantly attempting to psychically influence or usurp my thoughts and dreams and intentions. As already noted, I do not subscribe to the notions of secular psychology that attempt to describe all instances of "hearing voices" or certain other seeming indices of "insanity" to merely physiological factors—nor did I accept APA dictated guidelines as aptly applicable for defining human experience even before such "aberrant" experiences were made personal, mind you.

     Even at those moments where I felt most influenced by another and least in control of my immediate thoughts and actions, however, I have nigh always maintained a keen awareness of self, and of Self (Atman), and the ability to discern potentially self-generated delusion from illusions manifest by an entity exterior to my person, and thus to maintain mostly reasonable judgment. And indeed, hearing voices and seeing visions of the ordinarily unbelievable has been a trait of saints, gurus, purported avatars, seers and mystics generally throughout the span of world history. If Jesus or Mohammed or Moses or Mahatma or Yogananda or Joan of Arc can hear voices and have visions, should you not be also given leave to hear voices and have visions? Not that these should always be believed or obeyed, of course.

I am convinced that scientific-rationalism has made a mistake, or at least has omitted veritable factors worthy of consideration by denying what has in recent centuries been delineated, separated/segregated from supposedly rationally discernible, dissectible, and quantifiable "reality" by the term "supernatural." These attempts to minimalize and cast contempt upon what cannot be controlled in a laboratory setting are in fact clear evidence to the insecurities of much of what has been propped up as "pure science."

Though I do have respect for much of what has been accomplished by these relatively recent ways of knowing and categorizing or managing knowledge, said attempt to divorce spirit/mind and matter is unmistakably incomplete and wanting, as indeed, too many so called "supernatural" phenomena remain outside the ability of at least the generally assumed premises of "modern science" to explain. Life-lived cannot be reduced to scientific maxims, as this world is too great and variegated to fit entirely into mathematical equations or chemical formulae.

Scientific explorations have failed, for example, to explain the Tibetan Buddhist practice of *tumo*, wherein the practitioner can raise surface body temperature to upwards of 117° Fahrenheit by means of a particular meditation. Similarly, many yogic feats of "mind-over-matter," such as the ability of some *sadhu* to munch enough cyanide to kill an elephant or meditatively manifest other states of seeming superhuman tolerance to extremes of heat or cold or pain have yet to be explained away by so called modern science.

I do understand the want of early modern scientists to escape the often-stultifying nature of what they deemed "superstition." And yet, has not that science which intended to replace such beliefs become equally stultifying by its endeavor to reduce the variegated experiences of human life to electrical impulses and chemical reactions, thus seemingly devoid of meaning? Indeed it seems, as is so often the case, revolutionaries fall prey to the same faults as that which they sought to replace. Too often the oppressed have become the oppressors.

In America's colonial history, the Puritan pilgrims seeking religious liberty soon set about persecuting Baptists and Quakers. Many Baptist groups, one of the most persecuted religious sects from the sixteenth to eighteenth centuries in Europe and New England and in fact early proponents of religious liberty, have in the last century or so endeavored to attack nigh any other sect they came across, and often as not in recent times have sought to restrict freedom of religion and speech. The French Revolution ousted one oligarchy only to become more violent and bloody than the oligarchy they ousted. The Bolsheviks likewise matched the severity of their predecessors.

And across much of the world and especially in Europe and America, the scientific revolution has largely replaced diverse mystical worldviews with materialist dogmas that can become as confining to freethinking as any set of religious maxims. Proselytization by both religion and culturally-loaded education and the rigid methodologies and dogmas of modern science have undoubtedly depleted the plentitude of viable and valid ways of knowing, sustainably maintained over eons by so many indigenous peoples. Perhaps before we conclude "science-takes-all," we should take some time to remember and meditate upon the beauty of our ancestors varied ways, to recall the lore that held true through many, many tellings, and grant a respected voice to *others* not so much a part of the money driven, materialistically-minded mega-culture and its presumptions and purportedly refined opinions about the nature of things, conveniently called "modern science."

Where might we find a shift of consciousness and society that matches compassion with transformation? change with mercy and a just integration or at least acknowledgement of what was good from the past? science that recognizes spirit? a state of revolution that welcomes challenges from previous paradigms, acknowledging that these may maintain certain valuable features lacking in the succeeding? This might be described as attending to the oscillations of the socio-cultural vibration manifest in the interactions between those supposed binaries of said dialectic, culturally, economically, socially and ideationally, then responding to tune the vibes through many modes of experiencing, from music to dance to romance, meditation, contemplation and honest discourse scientific and otherwise. "Herein is Yoga: Yoga is the alteration of the range of sense vibration, that therein pure consciousness might abide" (Patanjali's Yoga Sutra).

I did feel mostly welcome in Chattanooga, with the most notable exception being the treatment I received from the local police. I had grown somewhat accustomed to be randomly asked for my ID, in spite of the unconstitutional nature of such an action. On one particular occasion during this sojourn in Chattanooga, however, I decided I had had enough.

I had just left a coffee house downtown in rather a rage, as I had read an article in the New York Times telling of yet another unconstitutional violation of civil liberties made law by the current criminal regime. As I walked down the sidewalk, a fellow I had met at another of Chattanooga's quite decent selection of coffeehouses stopped me and asked if I could bum him a buck. I had just been given a twenty, and so gladly obliged. As this transaction transpired, one of Chattanooga's stocky bald-headed pigs[20] stopped his squad car beside the curb, rolled down his window and yelled at the fellow I was handing a dollar.

"You don't have to give him that! You don't have to give him that!" he hollered, his face and shiny skull turning bright red.

"No, I asked *him* for a dollar!" said the fellow I'd handed the green piece of paper with a picture of a pyramid and a dead president who reportedly was want to smoke "Indian Hemp."

Ignoring this explanation, the cop got out of his car and swiftly approached me, demanding to see my identification. My acquaintance once again extolled my innocence of any crime, but as I was the one with the backpack and unshaven face, he continued with his illegal course of action. At first I tried to explain to the enraged officer that my passport and license had been stolen and lost, respectively. As he continued his rant, I decided I had had enough, briefly explaining to *Herr Gestapo* that he had no reason to see my ID, and that his actions were

---

20 Please do not misunderstand, I do not maintain a disrespect for police persons generally, despite the absurdity of some of the laws they are obliged to enforce. I only employ such derogatory terms for those who are deserving, by merit of their bad behavior. Those who truly serve and protect, I respect.

unconstitutional. I then turned and started to swiftly walk away through a small passage lined with shops and restaurants that is called "Jack's Alley."

As I reached the end of this alleyway, I decided the wisdom of my actions was questionable, and thus thought I might try to reason with this unreasonable man. As I turned and started back down the alley, the approaching officer yelled out, "Tie up your dog, I'm gonna taze you! Tie up your dog! I'm gonna shoot you with my tazer!"

Now of course I did what was instinctual when faced with such an imperative and threatened with a potentially deadly projectile with no means of defense or retaliation: I turned and I ran. Across the busy downtown street I ran, and as luck would have it, a female city cop followed by a sheriff's deputy were rolling down the hill from the direction of the courthouse. At first thinking to evade, I instead turned to speak with the female officer as she stepped out of her car, hoping for a just exchange. I assumed that she might be a bit more reasonable, as female law enforcement officers often are, and that the added presence of the deputy might afford me a better chance at fair-dealings. In Chattanooga, it is the city cops who are most often the perpetrators of unjust practices, or so I had been told by a number of locals.

After briefly explaining my stance, the skinheaded pig showed up (an epithet I do not use to describe the cops generally, mind you. So long as they are protecting and serving and not harassing or violating I got no problem with the police). Shaking with a scarcely controlled rage, he proceeded to handcuff me, barely refraining from slamming my face into the hood of his car as he pushed me down to place shackles on my wrists. I continued with my correct assertions that this action was illegal and unconstitutional, and I suppose he may have realized the truth of my statements as I was soon released without charge.

On two or three other instances I was unconstitutionally harassed by the police in Chattanooga, who were probably the least civil cadre of cops I have encountered in all of my travels. Indeed, I was told that said department is among few in the nation that, at least at the time, had no external oversight.

In addition to these instances with the police I had one other overtly negative experience with some semblance of "authorities" during my stay in Chattanooga that I want to mention. Whilst walking through a parking lot on the North Shore side of the river, I was interviewed by a television reporter regarding the issue of homelessness in Chattanooga. I proceeded to offer an intelligent critique of the socio-economic factors that leave people homeless, and then explained that many who have no home are indeed living closer to the example of the man who a majority in the southeastern United States claim as their teacher and god. When the interview aired, every bit of this social critique was cut, and the remaining interview framed myself and the homeless in general as nothing but a bunch of worthless social undesirables and dangerous criminals. Oh yeah, and the mayor was rather a creep when once we met in the same parking lot.

I ought to also mention that I awoke early one morning, whilst sleeping face down on a hill, to what felt quite like a shotgun or high-powered rifle blast in the upper-middle portion of my back. Not the first time I have been murdered—if that's the correct term to use when I seem to yet live—so I decided, based on experience, that the best thing to do would be to go back to sleep, thinking that chances were I'd have no injuries upon reawakening. Sure enough, I awoke a few hours later, not necessarily feeling so great, but alive(?) and with no gaping hole blown in my back.

Think me insane if you will, but at least take the time to read the account of my initial realization of having been murdered before you think me worthy of institutionalization.[21] Incidentally, I later concluded that this incident probably relates rather directly (or backwardly) to the account Sarah ("Soulo") in Ithaca told me of her boyfriend Charles having been murdered by a shotgun blast to his chest. Synchronicities such as these leave me longing for the (at least seemingly) innocent magic of my earlier journeys.

I could continue on about my captivity in Chattanooga, but I have tired of telling this tale, so I will merely say that I found the riverfront area and its coffee houses and cafes and parks pleasant, that I met some nice kids at one of the coffeehouses, and had a very

---

21   Chapter 2, "An Account of a Murder: From Another Side."

difficult time leaving. I was forced to leave Zunaka in the care of some kind women I met at a coffeehouse there, as his hind-quarters had become paralyzed, apparently due to eating macadamia nuts from the sprouted fruit and nut bread I would eat almost daily. It was later reported to me they put ol' Zunaka (formerly known as Zeus) down. May he find rest and peace and happiness in whatever doggy afterlife or rebirth.

Despite what some folks back west might contend, the experiences I had in over two-and-a-half years out east left me with a decent impression of most easterners. Though my psychic life became increasingly characterized by constant battles with subtleties of *samsara*, mixed-up *maya*, twisted *karma-dharma* and psychic crap from who knows what ill source, my experiences with people were generally pleasant. I suppose there were a few overtly unpleasant instances involving embodied humans—mostly with the police in Tennessee.

I certainly presented rather a poor and pitiful sight, most the time not dressed like a hippie so much as a hobo, and was thus without the benefit of even that layer of partial respectability—depending upon who you ask, of course. And yet most folks were still kind, and even generous. A 6'2" big-bearded un-bathed "hobo" (if that term properly applies to all who hop trains) wearing a well-worn backpack with bedroll attached and accompanied by a large wolf-dog is going to draw some sort of attention in all but a few locales—perhaps excepting certain mountain towns and the northern-half of the West Coast—and the majority of the consideration I received was overtly positive.

I never quite fully got used to being arbitrarily asked for my ID by the cops, despite the fact this seems to have become a customary greeting granted many who arrive to any given town on their own two feet, and who are then seen wandering the streets without an apparent home or hotel room. This despite the purported "freedom" of this land. The Fourth Amendment is still law, if any of you weren't sure, and even applies to homeless vagabonds, to tie-die clad freaks who almost certainly have some weed amongst their effects, to black leather jacket wearing punks or protesters with anarchy symbols freshly spray-painted in black on their hoodies, and even (gasp) to folks of obvious Middle-Eastern or Arab descent, regardless of religion.

Just a few closing statements about my experiences east of the Mississippi. This might be called an "overview" of personal signification, both literally and figuratively.

I realize that despite my explication towards the beginning of this tale regarding geography and sacred (or at least symbolic) significances, I have scarcely touched on said subject since. So just to catch you up to the particular point where I am now narrating, allow me to offer a few interesting observations that came to my attention whilst wandering about in the eastern states, whether you find these worthy of pondering or no.

The Adirondacks and Appalachians were the only significant mountain ranges I encountered during this journey, and of these elevated places I've only a few limited observations to make. First, the names given these two aged and worn gatherings of peaks, promontories and weathered hills among the oldest on earth, seem to hold clues that at least in the context of this journey seem to make some sense, if only by some rather odd associations.

The Adirondacks and the name "Adi" is the first association that stands out to my personally opined esoteric analysis. "Adi" in Sanskrit means "ancient one," and refers in myth, as previously mentioned, to either Sakti, the feminine source of life energy and consort to Siva, or else is found in reference to the story of the penis munching demoness with sharp teeth where one would expect soft labia. Though the actual mountains of the Adirondacks are relatively young, the rocks recently made to rise to make these mountains are indeed quite ancient. As to which of the metaphoric analogies I might surmise the Adi-rondacks might aptly be poetically or metaphorically associated, I shant decide within this writ work. Recall also that Dan, one of my hosts in Montreal, had a girlfriend named Adi.

The actual name comes from the Mohawk word *ratirontaks*, a derogatory name said tribe used to refer to the Algonquin tribes which means "they eat trees," referring to the practice of eating buds and bark in times of hunger. Though I've some personal and complicated if not nigh inexplicable esoteric associations which might meet with the meaning of the native term, I shall leave those unwritten.

The Appalachians, obviously not a far step or leap etymologically from "appellations"—*names*. Indeed, many names I learned or encountered as signs during this journey seemed to hold no small significance in the mixtures of meanings informing my appraisals, and as clues to the confused constructions of this "play." Though indeed I've yet to draw any succinct conclusions even with the sum of so many coincidences of names and faces and places—sometimes even lining up perfectly on a map when plotting people I've known to the places I knew them in an endeavor to make sense of the greater story's plot—I have noted that some strange order or other often underlies the arrayals of people, names and places.

Also of note regarding said mountain range, I noticed from a satellite photograph that the "leg" of the southern Appalachians which extends to the edge of Chattanooga seems to end in what suspiciously—even startlingly—resembles a foot. The other leg, rather swollen and misshapen, extends through the Carolinas and into north Georgia. I couldn't really make out any succinct torso, arms or a head above the waist of this behemoth body, but the foot is unmistakable. The Shawangunk Formation which sits just east of New Paltz is a northern extension of this aged mountain chain.

Of inland waters I encountered, the most obviously significant in a general sense and perhaps in my personal associations regarding this journey is the Mississippi. This river is the largest and longest in North America, and as already mentioned, divides this land on the order of no other geographic feature, except for the Continental Divide. I crossed this great river (which bears a name which actually means "Great River," from the Ojibwa words *misi-ziibi*) twice on this journey, once traveling east and once upon returning west, once on foot and once in a Greyhound bus.

This crossing is a well noted symbolic passage, and indeed seems the most significant geographic demarcation noting the transition from my usual stomping grounds to an "other side" and back again. The source of the Mighty Mississippi is a body of water named Lake Itasca in Clearwater County, Minnesota. This starting place for the mighty Mississippi purportedly derives its appellation from the last four letters of the Latin word for "truth," *veritas*, and the first two letters of the Latin word for "head," *caput*. Though perhaps a spurious etymology, in many respects this journey to the other side of this nation-dividing waterway proved a trial of the truths in my own head, as well as heart, as both beliefs and devotions were tested as I embarked on adventures beyond its eastern banks. Indeed, the relative clarity of my intensions at the first crossing, from Iowa to Illinois, had given way to a sullied mind and wearied heart by the second crossing, far downriver and after both the Mississippi River and myself had become rather more polluted than was the case just after I'd hit the rails and road, and as I walked over the waters from Dubuque to East Dubuque.

    The Saint Laurence River (or perhaps more properly, *le fleuve Saint-Laurent*; or more proper still, *Kaniatarowanenneh*, Mohawk for "big waterway") encompasses *Île de Montréal*. Indeed, I was an island dweller for the duration of my stay in Canada, and whilst I was with Leslie on this isle very little on the mainland mattered to me at all.

    St. Laurence was one of seven deacons of Rome martyred during the reign of Emperor Valerian, and was purportedly a custodian of the Holy Grail. Once again, myths of King Arthur are referenced. Indeed, my quest was to find something not unlike a holy grail as I sought source of life and wellspring of feminine perfection, like unto the yoni chalice of Devi worshipped (along with linga-stones) on Sivaratri, wedding anniversary of the Divine Couple in Hindu myth. I sought nothing less in this quest than the company of the Feminine Divine source of beauty and love and bliss, in and as the beatified Leslie—even if only to share her company for a cup of coffee or tea—and on the North American continent few places would seem more fitting by at least one mythological lens than this island amidst a river named for a caretaker of a sacred chalice.

    The Hudson River, *Muh-he-kun-ne-tuk* (Iroquois), River Mauritius ("River of Mountains"), the North River. This river and its valley was central to my stay in New York upon departing Montréal, and correspondingly it's crossing might be seen as symbolic of the dissolution of my relationship with Leslie. The Hudson's source is a lake in the Adirondacks called Lake Tear of the Clouds, and the waterway leading from this lake to the Hudson River proper is the Opalescent River.

    The next river that comes to mind on this journey is the Wallkill, named the Palse River by early European settlers (after the town of New Paltz through which it flows), and known to Native Americans as *Twischsawkin,* which means "the land where plums abound." This river idiosyncratically flows to the north, where it idiosyncratically flows into a creek, called Rondout, before meeting with the waters of the Hudson. Oddly to an English speaker, quite a few place names in New York have "kill" as suffix. "-kill" is a Dutch suffix for creek, and does not designate homicide. Of not quite random associations I might make, whilst often sleeping on the shores of the Wallkill in New Paltz I felt as if my heart, rather broken upon my parting with Leslie, was starting to beat once again. In actuality Paltz is derived from the German word for place and not pulse, though the proper denotation does imply new beginnings. Indeed, in the midst of seeming loss, finding meaning, however spurious, is often vital for getting one's bearings and back on one's feet.

    Lake Erie—well, the name speaks for itself, except that in the case of my experiences, it mostly did not. Erie is the fourth largest and fourth in sequence of drainage of five Great Lakes, is the tenth largest freshwater lake globally, and is named for the Erie tribe. The conglomeration of these five massive lakes is unique in the world, and my time spent with Erie gave me a bit of time for reflection whilst gazing over its waters. My summer along this Great Lake's shore was a time of pleasant respite, a time of healing before once again—if not according to plans—resuming a clockwise journey 'round the eastern United States. I should note, Buffalo and Sandusky were both a tad "eerie," but Port Clinton was a very pleasant and welcoming place, and my slumber and dreams on Erie's beaches were quite peaceful.

    Though I stayed in Maryland not far from the Potomac for a few months, I saw this capital river only fleetingly. The Rappahannock was next in a series of flows upon whose shores I lingered. In Fredericksburg whilst sleeping by this now tranquil river's banks, I dreamt of the soldiers of two wars whose blood had in fact fallen and flowed so heavy as to turn the waters of this river red. The Rappahannock was more or less a boundary between North and South during the Civil War, and similarly served as something of a dividing line between my wanderings North and South. The hippie crew I came to know in this colonial town sometimes called themselves the Rappahannock River Rats, and it was here I first considered constructing a bamboo boat to drift down to the big waters, to float away from cares and sorrows and to the Ocean's healing waves crashing, though sailing away was not yet to be.

My first and thus far only encounter with the open Atlantic's waters was a bit of a disappointment, as a statue of Poseidon—misappropriator of three-pronged spears and Greek deity generally represented as amongst the meanest—and kitschy commercialism characterized my experience of Virginia Beach, Virginia. Though the Ocean is beautiful from almost any venue, military jets and tourism did more than moderately detract from my first ever encounter with this Ocean named for a lost Mediterranean civilization. Virginia Beach was rather different than the idyllic visions of the Atlantic's shores I'd held of quaint New England coastal villages or of those grand and flowered Southern cities that survived the civil war intact.

The Tennessee River, once known as the Cherokee River, was the last great river of the east I was to see on this adventure (I don't recall noticing crossing the Mississippi on my way back west whilst on the bus), and I spent more time with these waters than any other on this journey. The name possibly translates as "meeting place" or "the bends"—as in bends of the river. Both banks of this broad river in Chattanooga are beautifully arrayed with monuments both natural and manmade. High above the flow on the south shore is Chattanooga's Bluff View Art District, where modern, Victorian and classical structures sit atop a cliff, and on the other side of the river is the North Shore District, where large parks and a strip of coffeehouses and cafes and boutiques offered pleasant distractions and places to sit during my stay. Some of my ancestors, both Cherokee and Choctaw, lived in this region before force marched to Oklahoma on the Trail of Tears, and I feel as if my long sojourn here was somehow related to my long deceased relatives, some ancestral homing beacon that held me along the banks of these waters longer than anywhere else during my wanderings out east.

Insofar as any esoteric significances related to this place, the only myth or story or construct that comes to mind is reading a tale of a waterfall not far from Chattanooga where a Cherokee princess purportedly leapt off the falls to follow her Choctaw lover, who her family had summarily thrown off to perish on the rocks below. Whilst visiting Niagara Falls with Sarah when I was in Buffalo, I similarly considered the lovers' leap theme (though I should note, Sarah and I never attained any such intimacy).

Waters are both life and death, love and loathing. Without water, we perish. Too much and we drown. Goddess Ganga is the Goddess of Rivers, and Her love with Siva is a source of conflict with Parvati in various myths. In perhaps the most well-known Hindu myth regarding the mighty waters of the Ganges, and thus of the whole world, fall upon the *jata* (dreadlocks) of Mahadeva so that the planet is not destroyed by such an unimaginable deluge. With so much time spent along so many rivers during this epic journey, I have to ponder whether devotions to both of these Devis may have led to some of my angst and internal discord whilst endeavoring this quixotic quest for love,[22] else that I am both part Cherokee and part Choctaw.

One last note on waters, few are aware that Laramie sits on one of the, if not the largest island in the United States. I discovered this some years ago when reading James Galvin's *The Meadow*, wherein he tells that the waters of the Laramie River and the South Platte both begin in the same lake, high in Colorado's mountains, and meet again hundreds of miles downstream on Nebraska's plains. This unassuming island that is my current home —shared with more pronghorn antelope than people— encompasses many, many thousands of square miles of sagebrush

---

22   Just as I completed typing the words "quixotic quest for love," what did I spy upon gazing up from the screen, but a man leading a mule across the long footbridge that crosses the tracks here in Laramie. Despite the image some from big cities might have of Wyoming, this is far from a common sight these days. Ha, ha!! Hee, hee!! Synchronicity!! And a bit of a déjà vu too . . .

plains and pine and aspen covered mountains and alpine peaks, lakes, and creeks, and despite not looking very much like an island, definitely fits the technical parameters. I suppose my anxious return to this island hideaway on the high plains was to find certain harbor from the Ocean of Worldly existence and the uncertainties, the gamble of love and romance and the road.

    A while after completing this journey, I decided to trace the paths of my meanderings to the east coast and back on a map of North America, and upon gazing at the lines drawn realized that the dot-to-dot created by this most odd of journeys I've endeavored created a rough outline corresponding quite startlingly to the shape of the continental United States! What this doth mean, I cannot yet say with certainty, though more than a slight symbolism was obviously at work, and perhaps a mystical meaning far beyond the scope of a simple journey of a man from place to place to place . . .

    Disheartened and nigh broken after somewhere near three years mostly on the road, I boarded a bus to escape back to the Western U.S. and the high mountains. After a long ride through the south with a long layover in Dallas and on to Santa Fe, a hitchhiking trek to Taos and a much needed respite at some hot springs deep in the Gorge and next to the rushing waters of the Rio Grande, I continued up through Colorado and on to the closest place to any I have known as "home" over the span of this lifetime, the high plains and mountains of Wyoming, and to this great island between the South Platte and the Big Laramie Rivers' flows.

    Today I am sitting on the back patio of the very coffee house where I first encountered the woman who was the inspiration for this insane journey to Montreal and back, and for much of my searching and practice and devotions over the ten years preceding. Here I sit, wearily and warily typing an abbreviated conclusion to this epic adventure, with so many subtler implications and interpretations and long occulted secrets and esoteric fragments recently revealed spinning round my conscious and unconscious mind, mythemes and memes madly meandering my neurological and spiritual pathways. And with yet some slim hope of some reasonable conclusion or culmination of events and memories recent and ancient, with some semblance of trust in the certain transformations or the destruction of darknesses and confusions sown by some as yet undisclosed source, and with faith there is still some mode to manifest a healthy integration of information derived from historic and esoteric studies and dreams and odd experiences, all whilst yet maintaining the stubborn intention to do whatever I might in this world to help and heal, and to maintain proper devotions, divine and human and otherwise.

Despite the trialsome times and psychic assaults I increasingly experienced after parting company with Leslie, and the rather soured sensibilities I've been left to digest and injuries I've yet a need to heal from events and experiences mostly manifesting thereafter, I do not regret embarking on this quixotic quest to find the beautiful belly-dancing barista and yogini who had so entranced and inspired me years before. Indeed, I might well read the resistance and subtle and psychic treacheries faced as an indication that my absurd heroism and extremes of devotion have had some certain effect, if perhaps not to bear overt fruition for now or at least not in the precise manner I might have imagined.

I still think about Leslie, though we have not maintained communication, save perhaps at some subtle or psychic level. I hope she is happy and healthy and fulfilling her good potentials, delivered from whatever sorrows and suffering, dancing and doing yoga and continuing to be an inspiration to those who happen to cross her path. I doubt I shall ever fully abandon my visions of this beatific dancer as inspiration to my own personal growth and practices embraced since my first pilgrimage on the road, as envisioned object of whatever appropriate degree of devotion in practices of bhakti yoga, and at least remembered as a near approximation of an avatar of Devi, the Divine Feminine incarnate, the Beloved.

Collusion . . . er . . . Conclusion

I would like to conclude these true if difficult to believe tales, these mad short story accounts from my crazy wanderings around this land, with something of a denouement. I would like to, but it seems the story persists, the odd occurrences continue, the mysteries maintain their grasp on my day to day, and often of late less lighthearted or playful than during most of my journeyings. Though I certainly hope to experience other adventures and explorations of this wonderful and sometimes terrible world, for now I am at rather an impasse and the longed for conclusion continues to elude. One cycle, to some degree represented in these accounts (though with much of the subtler and esoteric insight left unrecorded), seems to have come to an incomplete or at least ambiguous close. What comes next, I do not know.

I have been living (if that's the proper term for one who has been murdered on multiple occasions) in Laramie for just about one year, and have been psychically and otherwise vying with what might be called "metaphysical" critics (though there is likely a more accurate Sanskrit word than said Greek term) of my adventures, and of my renderings thereof. It may well be I have "metaphysically" or otherwise stepped on someone's toes by seeking to uncover hidden truths or by pursuing a romantic dream with such fervor, else I have been facing the assaults of some mad muse improperly assigned to my service and intent upon prodding my mind with mischievous intent. Whatever the case, I have been languishing in Laramie, dealing with a milieu of mind and spirit (or spirits) that seems to be something not unlike a judgment of my critical response to the *lila*—"divine play," or facsimiles thereof—that I have lived through over the last ten to twelve years. I suppose whatever vicious critique this work might receive from whatever book reviews in whatever newspapers might deem it worthy of mention will seem trifling in comparison, so perhaps I shall try to transform these subtle-plane assaults by receiving them as "good practice."

Since I returned to this purported[23] place of my birth and for some months previous I have been forced into a rather confused retrospective, encompassing not only the mostly happy years of my travels, but also everything I have memory of from this life, and seemingly some other's (and perhaps a number of others') memories and twisted versions of *my* memories appended to my own remembrances, abject channeled confusion. This rather skewed review of my days and nights has been forced under the scrutiny of any number of lenses, from the purview of various dogmas and interpretations thereof, to perspectives at least represented as representing the points of view of various people I have known in this life in whatever capacity, to various portrayals of the purviews of various mythological constructs and mythical figures, deities and the likes. In addition, seems tricks and manipulations of illusion whether playful or mischievous in intent have found no cessation.

An old door frame on the side of Jeffrey's Bistro which should be ashed and trashed, back in place where ought to be a replacement, stands as but one example of the temporal anomalies and inconsistencies in the makeup of the reality I've observed upon returning to my "hometown." Regarding this mysteriously unburned door frame discussed in the last chapter, by the way, I have consulted others who were present here during the same span of time, and even one fellow employee who was there when this incident occurred, yet no one seems able to offer a reasonable explanation for how such a thing could be.

As another example of my uncharacteristic malaise and the unusual characters seem to idiosyncratically materialize as if actors on cue, on my way to a morning (er, mid-afternoon) cup of coffee the other day, I encountered a *Brahmachari* fully clad in ochre pants and *kurta* and scarf walking past Daylight Donuts in downtown Laramie. I was feeling a bit put off in general, and the unusual sight of a shaved-headed Hindu monk in Wyoming seemed

---

23   "purported," as I cannot recall the specifics of my entrance into this life, save that my first memory was of waking from a nightmare in a crib in my childhood home on Seventh Street, screaming from a terror of confined spaces after transiting from a buried sarcophagus and through the ground and into this body.

exemplary of the sort of bizarre manifestations I've been experiencing, regardless of affiliations or affinities, so I raised my open hand in the *mudra* for blessings and growled in a rather gruff voice, "Hara dharma! Haaarraaaa dhaaaarmaaaa!!" This rather startled renunciate raised his hand likewise in the *Abhaya mudra*, staring in disbelief as I then proceeded across Third Street.

    Indeed, mind and illusion manifest 'round me have grown more than a little insane, super-synchronistic and dreamlike, else at the least I've a manic and mean muse either prodding me to finish or to not finish writing and revising this text, and who also happens to have the ability to significantly alter the illusion of this reality. Needless to say, this has pushed me to the edge of my sanity, or at least to the margins of collectedness. Thus, if these last pages seem a little disheveled and a tad confused, this is because thus are my thoughts. I returned to this high plains valley expecting some good culmination or fruition, to begin some hard work for some semblance of tangible returns, and not to face further intrigues, deepening riddles and increasingly absurd *lila*.

    Indeed, were I to endeavor to record all of the intricate and complex strands of the absurdly interwoven interpersonal mesh (and sometimes mess) of relationships and synchronies and causalities I have perceived or been forced to consider related to these tales I've written herein, the work would necessarily be comparable in length to the Vedas, and would likely still miss certain salient factors amongst those my mind's meandered through like transiting some ethereal gauntlet. If I recorded every odd occurrence or curious coincidence that evinced the strange or paranormal, the resulting journal would be constantly writ from day to night, and then I'd need start again to pen these revelations as soon as I wake from dreams the next day.

    Were I to write a thorough account of the mystical visions and subtle constructions and deconstructions have passed through my mind and exterior field of view and hearing and perception generally in the past few years, this account would likewise require a compendium nigh the breadth of the Vedas to record and explicate and consider. These short accounts of a rather surface reading of a few true to life experiences from my bizarre and beautiful adventures are what I might easily relate to a wider audience. A more in-depth critical analysis of karma-dharma, causation and philosophical explanations of the inexplicable shit and wonders I have experienced would leave this work rather wanting as a fun read, as well.

    Whatever you might imagine of my sanity or honesty from what you've read herein, I do solemnly swear that what I have recounted in these passages is a true telling of my (mostly) quite lucid and self-critically considered and reconsidered perceptions of certain unusual life experiences and events. These tales are true, as much so as is the truth of my own existence . . . though perhaps I ought once again note, if anyone who reads these accounts has inside information, a clue or an informed alternative perspective on these evidences recorded herein, I'm always willing to revisit certain conclusions already considered, reconsidered and contemplated over-and-over in mind and in conversations with skeptics and believers alike. I'm not one to hold faith in well-debunked myths—not even my own, should they prove errant.

    What means these odd occurrences within the broader context of what "Western" thought has termed metaphysics, ontology and epistemology or from the perspectives of theology or sectuality, I cannot begin to express within the bounds of this work. Had I a mastery of Sanskrit, I might be able to approach a taxonomy of these phenomena. I am just a beginning student of that more precise language, however, and so shall be forced to leave you, dear readers, to consider these whimsical true tales with only the rather limited commentaries and sometimes imprecise subtle analyses I have provided. And myself, now left to sift through the preceding pages to perfect sentences and paragraphs and simultaneously to exist outside text and past times in spite of questions begging and other coherent and contending plots pressing some point or theme or other upon my mind.

    Dark and light reflections of varying hues in far faster than sound bite progression proceed before my visions outside and in self and story. Important themes I've in mind even sometimes simultaneously appear as surreally acted-out skits performed by seemingly random characters observed in my day-to-day, at the coffee house or library or marketplace. Else I might see someone's doppel walk by whilst I am revising a sentence about him or her, experience the synchronous manifestation of a word typed and simultaneously sung over satellite radio and through the coffeehouse's PA, etc. Such things are more constant these days than I've ever known before, and not always the fun they once were.

Once again, I would make no claim of uniqueness by these experiences, nor make presumptions of being "chosen," holy or inimitably gifted. Rather, I would proclaim that these sorts of experiences ought bravely be recognized for what they are by any who might experience similar anomalies, accepted as containing potential and significant meaning and not merely reflecting psychiatric symptoms, despite the comfortable categorizations psychology might try to impose to suppress any "supernatural" content within any given life story.

Though the twisted intrigues portrayed and then deconstructed in this sometimes perverted retrospective forced upon me (only scarcely eluded to in the latter parts of the preceding narrative) would indeed drive most to madness, and far beyond whatever degree of crazy it is I've been driven, I'd still encourage others to challenge the lies of politicians and preachers, professors and pundits and other perceived authorities. Plays of words and memes and mythemes, memories and misrepresentations and machinations have been forced upon me like a flood or firestorm or volley of bullets (figurative or otherwise) as I have endeavored to make presentable sense of these bizarre happenings on my pilgrimages and other trippy pathways trodden, and as I seek to comprehend encounters and conflicts and communions with so many others, with past and present and future (if not necessarily in such a succinct sequence), with life and death, the in-between and outside-of, karma and dharma, all considered. Still, I believe it is well worth it to live life as a heroic quest for what is true and beautiful and good, and would encourage others to unabashedly seek and question the status quo in favor of freedom, purity, justice and honesty—if not without a cautionary note. Revolutionaries end up dead at least as often as not, after all.

I have plans to build an amphibious-psychedelic-peace-presenting-pleasure-cruising-wind-and-biodiesel-powered-dharma-conveying-fun-mobile, something I have contingently dubbed "the sailbus." I have a want to purchase some land to create a haven, a sanctuary space for myself and other weary pilgrims, something not unlike an ashram, but by no means of the traditional sort, nor precisely a commune, etc. I have a wish to find my true beloved, my eternal consort, a woman divine and human, gracious and beautiful and kind, fierce yet compassionate, fun and wise and properly matched to me.

In the meantime, supposing my dharma permits and assuming I do not experience some breakthrough in the milieu in which I am currently mired, I may soon wander into the wilderness, only carrying whatever tools I'll likely need as I part ways with the contemplative overload of recent times, and taking whatever time I've need to practice and meditate away from the confusions of so many other minds and the so often senseless chatter of society's various neuroses. Nature is nigh always the best healing.

Supposing this book is published and proves popular, I suppose I'll find the means to accomplish the aforementioned material goals, though I intend to carefully weigh whatever consequences might exist, to cautiously contemplate whatever dharma might accompany said karma before I proceed. With much (er . . . whatever degree of) understanding comes much responsibility, and I have no intentions of foregoing due consideration of what consequences might accompany even those humble wants. To make the transition from even *dilettante* ascetic to even *dilettante* householder is no small step.

There is indeed much more to life than material possessions and comfort, though given the choice, all things considered, some humble share of home and hearth and happiness seems not at all a bad thing. Whether those things are indeed forthcoming or whether instead I shall embark on other mad meanderings "off-the-cuff"—or perhaps a bit of both—remains to be seen. Until accounts of those (mis-) adventures find their way into printed accounts or other medium, I hope you have enjoyed what you have read (or shall, if you skipped to end before reading the beginning and middle) in these mad meandering whimsical pages, these difficult to believe but true accounts, these memories and musings of a post-postmodern nomadic mystic madman.

नमस्ते—Namasté

www.ingramcontent.com/pod-product-compliance
Lightning Source LLC
Chambersburg PA
CBHW020611300426
44113CB00007B/601